The  MANual:

Less Drama, More Love

A SINGLE WOMAN'S GUIDE TO

Choosing Mr. Right

Dr. Shane Perrault

The BLACK MANual:
Less Drama, More Love
A Single Woman's Guide to Choosing Mr. Right
Dr. Shane Perrault

Copyright © 2015
ISBN: 978-0692518663
Press Company:
"40 Acres and A Man"
6301 Ivy Lane, Suite 700
Greenbelt, MD 20770

This book is presented solely for educational and entertainment purposes. The author and publisher are not offering it as therapy, psychotherapy, or other professional relationship counseling services or advice. While best efforts have been used in preparing this book, the author and publisher make no representations or warranties of any kind and assume no liabilities of any kind with respect to the accuracy or completeness of the contents and specifically disclaim any implied warranties of merchantability or fitness of use for a particular purpose. The information in this book is meant to supplement, not replace, psychotherapy with a trained licensed professional. Neither the author nor the publisher shall be held liable or responsible to any person or entity with respect to any loss or incidental or consequential damages caused, or alleged to have been caused, directly or indirectly, by the information or programs contained herein. Every individual is different and the advice and strategies contained herein may not be suitable for your situation. You should seek the services of a competent and licensed professional before beginning any of the programs and activities described in this book. Finally, if any of the characters in the book resemble you or your situation, note it is merely a coincidence as the case studies used herein represent a compilation of experiences Dr. Perrault has had with numerous couples over the years. All names, towns, professions, and other facts related to various scenarios are fictitious, and do not represent any former client Dr. Perrault worked with in therapy.

Printed in the United States of America

ABOUT THE AUTHOR

Dr. Shane K. Perrault
Psychologist, Author, and Speaker

Whether single, divorced, or widowed — the rules are different for African-American women looking for Mr. Right! They face a starkly disparate reality from their non-black counterparts. Nevertheless, Shane Perrault, Ph.D. (Dr. Shane), has learned: "It is never too late to live happily ever after."

In 2004, he founded African American Marriage Counseling. He partners with 15 to 25 couples a week to help them begin to develop the skills to hear (and be heard by) each other so they can make peace with the past and move past the pain, strengthen their families, and learn to turn toward each other instead of on each other in overcoming life's challenges. Throughout his work, he has found one of the key factors in relationship success is choosing the right partner.

So to help women make the best choice possible, he penned *The Black MAN-ual*, where he shares years of insight from counseling hundreds of couples to provide bold strategies about how men and women approach relationships, intimacy, and commitment. He also acknowledges and explores how women can overcome cultural and historical hurdles to take advantage of the unique experiences of being a black woman—emotionally, financially, and romantically.

Dr. Shane received his doctorate in clinical psychology from the Ohio State University and completed his undergraduate studies at Southern University—Baton Rouge. He has also completed Level I, II, and III training in the world-renowned Gottman Marital Therapy Training Institute.

He is regularly invited to speak at church retreats, has spoken at the Congressional Black Caucus, blogs for *Psychology Today*, and is a media favorite who has been featured in *Ebony* and *Essence* magazines, the *Washington Post* and *Washington Times*, and on XM Radio, BET, and TV One. Dr. Shane has also appeared as a guest expert in movies, including "You Saved Me," a documentary about marriage in the Black community.

In *The Black MAN-ual*, he offers the ultimate guide to help empower you to repel Mr. Wrong and to choose—and keep!— the relationship you want with Mr. Right.

ACKNOWLEDGEMENTS

To my mother, Gaylene Ann Perrault, Ph.D., and to my step-mother, Mrs. Rosa Herring-Smith. I've learned so much about life, women, relationships, marriage and divorce, and blended families from both of these exceptional women who were as different as two women could be. While they both chose my father as their Mr. Right, they proceeded to have very different relationships with him.

These two mothers taught me that timing, disposition and natural compatibility, and the ability to resolve conflicts in a win/win fashion are critical—and that every hand is a winner or a loser. I am eternally grateful for their examples.

Next, I'd like to thank the countless women, men, and couples who shared their life stories, relationships, and marriages with me. It was also extremely beneficial to have several women to serve as my beta-testers. While they are too many to list, I am humbled by their willingness to read and reread every chapter, and share with me how the content of this book mirrored their personal experiences and addressed their needs.

Finally, I'd like to thank my unofficial co-author, Ms. Gena Morris. She invested hundreds of hours poring over various details related to this book's cover, content, and marketing. It was definitely my good fortune to be able to draw upon her instincts, superior intellect, and keen insights as a woman. Her input, support, and passion were invaluable: This book would not be the same in many respects without her.

TABLE OF CONTENTS

INTRODUCTION

"Slavery isn't our history;
it's the interruption of our history."
– Dr. Shane Perrault

Marriage was the cornerstone of African society, which gave us perhaps the most highly advanced and stable civilization planet earth has known. These architects of the pyramids recognized the importance of both the feminine and masculine on the development of a healthy culture, and established vastly evolved spiritual systems. They also left us the "mystery systems" that fathered mathematics, physics, and astronomy;

and created unparalleled advances in art, architecture, medicine such as cataract surgery, and electricity such as the "Baghdad battery."

Recent DNA analysis of ancient Egyptian mummies reveals Rameses III, his son, and King "Tut" Tutankhamun (the son of Egyptian queen Nefertiti and her husband, Pharaoh Akhenaten) were of Sub-Saharan African descent. Also, DNA evidence secured from the ancient bust of Queen Tiye of ancient Egypt unveils she was a Black African whose DNA maps to the people of Uganda. In addition to DNA, these artifacts confirm their African ancestry and the importance they placed on marriage.

Yet, African Americans today find themselves asking questions, like, "Is Marriage for White People?" as discussed in Ralph Banks' book, where this rhetorical question serves as the title. Banks' book highlights marital statistics indicating that during the past half-century, African Americans have become the most unmarried people in our nation. This racial gap in marriage extends beyond the poor, as affluent and college-educated African Americans are also less likely to marry or stay married than their White counterparts, hampering Black children's chances of growing up in a stable home and to have healthy relationships with both parents. Banks suggests the demise of our family systems is imperiling the growth and stability of the Black middle class, which is essential for the African American community to thrive. Taken at face value, this cultural phenomenon suggests African Americans don't value or desire marriage. If we accept this cultural aberration as the new norm, we will likely remain in our current position in society. In contrast, if we recognize our pre-slavery cultural practice of strong marriages as the norm, we stand a much better chance of resuming our historical and rightful place in society.

Countering this relatively recent trend will require us to recognize that slavery isn't our history; it's the interruption of our history and merely represents a momentary cultural snapshot of time.

As the founder of AfricanAmerianMarriageCounseling.com, I've come to realize Black folk truly value and are willing to fight for love, marriage, and their families — and want to "live happily ever after," too. These couples don't appear on the daily news, however, working with them on a daily basis has shown me they are news worthy. Witnessing those couples go to great lengths to stay together — putting family above personal needs and even personal happiness — makes me optimistic about our future.

WHY THE PARTNER YOU CHOOSE IS SO CRITICAL

In order for African Americans to overcome the relatively recent cultural and historical ills undermining our family structures, we should revisit what we are teaching our young people about selecting a partner. Lack of commitment or desire to be in a healthy relationship isn't nearly the threat to African American marriages as much as dysfunctional relationship patterns that are interfering with "choosing" a good mate are.

Although I see many strong couples who truly belong together and put in the work to ensure their families stay together, far too often I'm struck by the reality that the two people sitting on my black, tufted couch shouldn't have ever ended up together. Some of them say, "It's like we aren't even friends (though initially attracted to each other) and we never have been, but we've got kids and have to work it out." I truly admire these couples' commitment to their families and desire to stay together in spite of feeling they chose the wrong partner or spouse. Nevertheless, my heart goes out to their children because their path will almost always be a meandering, uphill, and traumatizing one within the family itself — and frequently in their future romantic relationships.

The goal of this book, however, is not to let this become your reality. When you and your partner decide to sit on my couch (or any of my colleagues' couches), I hope it's because you choose wisely and want to make a good relationship even better! To that end, if this book helps one woman make a better choice, I will consider it a huge success.

Your relationship's success or failure will be determined by the Five Cs: Choice, Commitment, Communication, Conflict Resolution Skills, and Coach-ability. While a therapist can generally work around and even up the last four Cs, the first C, "choice," is a fixed variable. We simply can't change who you chose to sit down with on our couch. You either chose wisely or you didn't. Yes, we can help a good partnership become great or stop a bad pairing from becoming catastrophic, but we can't transform a bad match into a good fit. Other than the decision to follow God (or not to follow God), the man you choose as a mate will singlehandedly have a more dramatic impact on your life trajectory than any other decision you will ever make.

That's why this book's primary objective is to empower you to make the best choice.

WHY A MALE PERSPECTIVE?

Perhaps you're wondering what gives me, a male, the right to write a book for women looking to choose a soulmate, and why I might have something particularly illuminating (without the typical judgments you've already heard) to offer women about themselves and their relationships with Black men — or *any* men, for that matter.

My decision to write *The Black MANual* stems from the reality that there simply aren't many African American psychologists who write about relationship issues. While I truly admire the ability of Steve Harvey and Hill Harper to get "the conversation" started in our community on a large scale, I felt the need to add to the conversation some proven research-based relationship interventions gained from my training as a psychologist and insights working directly with African American couples. While most books for African American women have been written by women, in my private practice, I find 90 percent of the counseling calls I field come from women who want to hear my perspective and not just because I'm a psychologist, but because I am a man — and more importantly a *Black* man. They want to know from a credible insider how Black men think, feel, communicate, make relationship decisions, and love.

It is my sincere hope that my insider-tips and the resources included in this book will help you better understand how we are hardwired and how we approach relationships, as well as help you to see Black men in a more balanced way.

Yes, I am painfully aware of the tensions between Black women and Black men.

Our mutual distrust for each other has been built over the years—stemming, in part, from slavery, where we were separated and pitted against each other, surviving Reconstruction, "Black Codes," Jim Crow, welfare, and marriage (as the movie "Claudine"* highlights), to the feminist movement, integration, affirmative action, a cultural war against Black women that celebrates misogynistic rap videos produced by Black male rappers, and our ascension up the rungs of the corporate ladder. No doubt our womanizing, manipulating, and otherwise disrespecting and deceiving Black women has played a significant role in this distrust, as well.

(*Note: "Claudine" is a landmark 1974 film that tells the story of a single Black Harlem mother, Claudine, played by Diahann Carroll, living on welfare with six children, who finds love with a garbage collector, Rupert, played by James Earl Jones. The couple's desire to marry is complicated by the fact that they cannot support her six kids without welfare.)

In spite of this historically induced divide and deeply embedded distrust, I know firsthand there are a lot of good, giving, caring, and, yes, mature Black men—or other men—out there for you who also want a committed, lasting, exclusive soulmate love or marriage.

This book is specifically designed to help Black women make better choices for four reasons. First, as the old saying goes, "women do the picking and choosing, while men do the hiring and firing." Second, unlike White women, who have more options and are more likely to get bailed out of a bad decision and therefore can afford to make a lot more mistakes, Black women have to be shrewder, as the cavalry likely isn't coming to rescue you. (If you hate the way this sounds, know I do, too.) Third, as Ralph Banks discusses in *Is Marriage for White Folks?*, more than two out of every three Black women are unmarried, and they are more than twice as likely as White women never to marry. Fourth, while women aren't the cause of African American marriage problems, they represent the most promising solution. As the African Proverb says, "If you educate a woman, you educate a nation."

THIS BOOK is WRITTEN FOR ... the woman looking at the men on the book cover trying to decide which type of man is Mr. Right for her.

Rather than superficially and disingenuously attempting to explain the various types of Black men and lumping them into a few one-size-fits-all categories, this book attempts to empower you to overcome any emotional blind spots that may cloud your ability to make the best choice in men for you, and to help you make better choices once in the relationship so you keep your soulmate love or marriage alive.

Who is the woman seeking soulmate love? She is a smart, career-oriented woman trying to balance work demands with a healthy relationship. She is open to personal development, even when it is uncomfortable. She may be single and looking to get into a relationship or in a relationship and trying to decide to take it to the next level; alternatively, she may be married, divorced, or widowed. The woman reading this book has likely accepted personal responsibility for the direction of her life, and is open to the reality that we all play a critical role in the success or failure of our relationships. Ultimately, she is interested in and committed to being/becoming Ms. Right, too.

While there are some aspects of this book that are unique to the African American experience, this book could benefit women and men of any race looking for soulmate love or trying to improve their current relationship or marriage. It is also beneficial for those who are dating with children and trying to blend their families.

Many female readers will thankfully have enjoyed positive relationships with the men with whom they have love relationships and a healthy relationship with their first love — their father. At the same time, despite having accepted personal responsibility for the role they play in their relationships, some women who read this book have had at least one love relationship in particular, or pattern of relationships, that may have been painful, frustrating, or confusing. This pain may also be a familiar one they experienced with what should have been their first love — their father.

SOME OF THE CONCERNS THAT KEEP WOMEN UP AT NIGHT INCLUDE:

1. Should I leave or stay in my current relationship or go? How do I fix it if I stay?

2. How do I find a good man with such slim pickings?

3. How do I determine who is a bad boy, a nice guy, or a keeper? And, why is this choice between them so difficult?

4. How do I know if he is Mr. Right or Mr. Right Now?

5. How do I deal with being the breadwinner?

6. What are some game changers or deal breakers that will positively or negatively impact my life with this man?

7. He or I cheated: Should I stay or go? If he cheated, how do I forgive? If I cheated, why ?

8. How do I learn to FLY (First Love Myself)?

9. What views about men, myself, love, and relationships do I need to re-evaluate?

10. How do I deal with his children's mother and create a successful blended family?

11. I am single, divorced, or widowed and want to know how do I find my next Mr. Right or first Mr. Right?

This book addresses all of these concerns and more.

Finally, this book may also be a great resource for mental health professionals and pastoral counselors who provide services to women or men in general dealing with relationship or family challenges, or specifically to African American women interested in personal growth or dealing with these challenges.

WHAT YOU CAN EXPECT FROM THIS BOOK

This book will provide unique insights about experiences and cultural phenomena unique to the African American experience that might be contributing to your finding or undermining your ability to find Mr. Right and maintain soulmate love or make it down the marital isle.

It introduces various psychological theories in an attempt to illuminate why and how various messages and events consciously and unconsciously impact your choice in partners and your subsequent decision making and behaviors once you are in a relationship. To this end, this author draws upon the works of psychodynamic, transactional, and self-psychology theories and the work of world-renowned marital therapists such as John Gottman, Ph.D., who uses a research-based approach to help predict which couples become what he describes as "marriage disasters" or "marriage masters." Of particular note is the work of Dr. Gottman, who has successfully predicted what couples will be together in five years, with a 91 percent success rate. I'm a Gottman Level 3 trained marital therapist, and his research has had a profound impact on my understanding of relationship therapy.

After you finish this book, I suspect you will be further along in developing the skills and insights needed to become more adept at identifying, attracting, and retaining men who are truly capable of being your Mr. Right—and quicker about repelling those who are not. I also suspect you will be further along in developing the conflict resolution skills needed to work through long-term relationship or marital problems, avoid costly family feuds, and minimize challenges that threaten your ability to meld your blended family. In either case, hopefully this book will at least empower you to recognize the gravity of these threats to your relationship and better inform you when it might be time to seek professional help, or leave.

To get the most out of this, I ask that you stay open and explore and embrace things you like (and perhaps dislike) about yourself. For example, in some cases the cultural experience of being an African American woman doubtlessly made you more resilient, insightful, and independent, while in other cases this experience may have potentially played a role in you having blind spots around potentially self-destructive relationship patterns and possibly unrealistic expectations of the men (or a lack of healthy expectations of the men) in your relationships.

To those of you who are open to looking at relationships in non-defensive ways, I suggest you utilize the resources, exercises, and tests referred to herein, and in the workbooks. You can also find additional resources at theBlackMAN-ual.com. These workbooks and other resources were specifically designed to help you convert your thoughts into actions.

FIVE THINGS THIS BOOK DOESN'T DO

1. I don't make sweeping generalizations about men or women — or whether the man you are in a relationship with is Mr. Right, Mr. Right Now, or Mr. Wrong. What may be a great choice for one woman may be a horrible choice for another. I have, however, found there are some common denominators in relationship choices that lead to success and failure. I will provide insights, tips, resources, statistics, and theories that could help you make your best choice or get the most out of the choice you have already made.

2. I don't attempt to provide individual or relationship psychotherapy in this book or the workbooks, nor should it be misconstrued as such. If some of the terms, concepts, facts, or approaches I discuss strike a nerve, or raise some deeper questions that you suspect need to be addressed, then I recommend you consider employing the services of a trained professional in your area. Here are three great referral sources: the Association of Black Psychologists, abpsi.org; *Psychology Today* magazine; and the Gottman

Institute, Gottman.com. All three have listings of qualified, licensed practitioners.

3. I don't attempt to provide a comprehensive archetypal profile of the male psyche. Black men, and women for that matter, are very complex. For these reasons, I believe a one-size-fits-all approach to understanding them would be naïve at best, and disingenuous at worse. I do, however, attempt to help you understand that while many men may be attracted to you, you alone are ultimately responsible for the ones you chose — or don't chose. My hope is to empower you to better understand yourself so you can understand what conscious and unconscious factors are impacting your choices, and how to make better choices in men once you decide to choose one — and, consequently, how to make better choices in relationships and marriages with men once you have committed to one.

4. I don't attempt to give any suggestions for women with partners who are physically, sexually, or emotionally abusive; partners with sexual or pornography, gambling, or substance addictions; or partners with other psychiatric disorders. Although it's been my experience that choosing a partner with any of these complex challenges will result in limited and unsustainable success, helping women with partners who present these particular challenges goes beyond the scope of this book.

5. I don't discuss the challenge presented by the "ratio of women to men" in great detail in this book. While this shortage of Black men in the dating pool is an epidemic problem in our community, it has been discussed at length in multiple sources, including Banks' *Is Marriage for White People?*, which brilliantly outlines this cultural phenomenon. The decision not to discuss this problem was a challenging one, but ultimately, I decided doing so would change the focus and length of this book in a profound way. For the sake of effectiveness and brevity, I opted to limit the content to areas where I could make a unique and significant contribution.

HOW THIS BOOK IS ORGANIZED

This book is divided into two parts. Part One: "Choosing Mr. Right" discusses selection strategies designed to empower you to make better choices. Part Two: "Being/Becoming Ms. Right" discusses ground rules and strategies for maintaining fulfilling soulmate love — with yourself, your partner, and your blended family, should you find yourself in that situation.

Throughout the book and in the accompanying workbook you can find at theBlackMAN-ual.com, you will find assessments, assignment, and referral sources to empower you to begin the process of finding Mr. Right and becoming Ms. Right — and to strengthen your relationship or marriage once you decide to commit or get married.

To Your Success,

Dr. Shane

PART I

Choosing "Mr. Right"

Part One: "Choosing Mr. Right" introduces theories and strategies designed to empower you to develop the skills to listen to yourself and your man to make the very best choice, given your options—even if it involves rediscovering the soulmate sleeping in the bed beside you.

I'm sure when you picked up this book, you wanted to know which of these men would be the better choice for your Mr. Right. This "lineup" pictured here also highlights the inherent distrust Black women frequently feel about Black men discussed in this section. While it would be nice if men could be neatly typecast into categories and you could predictably forecast your future with him based on the type of man you selected, the truth is any of the men in this lineup could be the right woman's Bad Boy, Nice Guy, or Mr. Right. This section provides insights on whether or not he is Mr. Right—or Mr. Right Now or Mr. Wrong—for you.

CHAPTER 1

How to Find Mr. Right
If You've Been Taught Not to
Depend on a Man

"Don't be afraid to feel as angry or loving
as you can. Because when you feel nothing,
it's just death."
—Lena Horne, Legendary Actress

> "If you don't like something, change it;
> If you can't change it, change your attitude."
> —Maya Angelou, Author, Poet, and Icon
> **"How you gone win, if you ain't right within.
> Uh-uh. Come again!"**
> —Lauryn Hill, Singer-songwriter and Producer

Ladies, when you were growing up, or even now as an adult,

I am sure you heard your mother, aunt, grandmother, or some other influential woman in your life, or perhaps even your father, say to you, "Whatever you do, don't depend on a Black man. Sweetie, you've gotta learn how to do for yourself." I do agree this advice is invaluable, if not critical, to prepare little Black girls for the fact that their reality frequently will be much harsher than that of their White counterparts. They must master basic survival skills to prepare them for the reality that the cavalry isn't likely coming to rescue them—and that they will be misperceived as angry for learning to fend for themselves. I don't agree, however, that these messages, which are designed to protect and prepare Black girls for an unforgiving world, should be adopted at the expense of undermining their ability to trust, depend on, or otherwise ask and allow Black men—or other men—to be providers and protectors. Rather, little Black girls might be better prepared to raise a family as a wife-and-husband team one day by a more balanced message, which encourages independence coupled with interdependence.

Failing to send little Black girls a more balanced message may ill prepare them for a healthy, mutually fulfilling, and trusting relationship with a man. So, why are generation after generation of Black girls being trained not to trust Black men? The answer may stem from a historical necessity. During slavery, Black codes, Jim Crow, and the mass incarceration and cultural exclusion of Black men from economic opportunities, our society systematically robbed them of the usual range and abundant supply of men and healthy male role models typically enjoyed by women who belong to a non-occupied people. Accordingly, previous generations of Black women emphasized the importance of being self-sufficient to prepare their daughters and nieces for a life of financial stability, should they have to go at it alone. Their message was tough, but fair. However, these mentors did not foresee the subsequent trust issues or inability to coexist peacefully with the male ego this approach would force on the next generation of Black women and Black marriages. (Again, I am not suggesting or otherwise implying that the Black male is blameless. We are culpable, too.)

Even the most cynical among us would resist the temptation to find Black mothers guilty of trying to poison Black girls against Black men. These decisions weren't made out of anger (although they had plenty of reason to be angry); they were made because Black mothers were placed in a difficult, if not impossible, situation and reacted in the only way they could, which was to prepare their daughters to survive. This practice was born out of necessity because Black men frequently weren't in a position to protect, provide for, or rescue them; or in some cases they were too self-focused, busy womanizing, or otherwise immature and elected not to provide for or protect them.

So how does this grown-up little girl adjust to being an adult in relationships or interact with men in a mutually fulfilling way that positions her to live happily ever after? Or better yet, how does the next generation of mothers, aunts, mentors, and fathers of Black girls ensure the next generation has a more balanced and healthy perspective on Black men? Perhaps our biggest challenge is instilling in the next generation of little Black girls the skills and temperament needed to prepare them for the reality that the cavalry may not be coming to rescue them, while simultaneously preparing them to embrace him and all of his chivalry should he arrive.

This would be akin to preparing little Black girls to seek and accept soulmate love, and herein may conceivably lie one of the most seismic opportunities of our generation—if we are to seriously attempt to bolster African American marriage rates.

So what is soulmate love? And how do I find it and keep it? In *The One: Finding Soulmate Love and Making It Last*, Kathy Freston describes our expectations about soulmate love. "The One. The love of our life, the fulfillment of our dreams. That glorious person who will set our soul on fire and stoke our passion for life. We get up in the morning to the song of this promise on the radio and lull ourselves to sleep at night with novels and films about two disenchanted people who finally find each other ... and the world is better off. We hope against hope that one day this will be our story. We long for this connection we've heard about, with all its magic and mystery and mojo; we want to be lit up and transformed simply by being in the presence of that heaven-sent 'one and only.'"

Ah, "soulmate love."

While this idealized, if not majestic, expectation of soulmate love represents a commonly shared view, it is in stark contrast to what generations of Black girls have been taught about relationships with men. And it frequently leads them to dismiss these daydreams about finding soulmate love as pipe dreams. This definition of soulmate love reflects the myth that it is entirely defined by the idealized state of romantic love, and is somehow mutually exclusive from mature love. In practice, romantic love is an earlier stage of soulmate love, albeit a critical component in the evolution of soulmate love. For romantic love to mature into soulmate love, the couple must learn to turn toward each other instead of turning on each other when faced with life's trials and tribulations.

Instead of teaching Black girls to wait for an idealized partner who may not be coming (or who may fail to live up to the hype should he arrive), or not to take a more pragmatic "just get a good man" approach, perhaps we should prepare them to look for a romantic love connection and know that if they stand the test of time, only then do they have a soulmate love worthy of their commitment. This more balanced approach of *growing* in love vs *falling* in love will avoid setting their relationships up for being another casualty in the soulmate love graveyard.

I am not trying to demystify soulmate love.

I am here to say Mr. Right is likely out there waiting for you (ratio of women to men aside), and it may partially be a matter of addressing your blind spots so you don't keep walking past him or not know what to do once you discover him. Alternatively, you may already be dating or married to Mr. Right and could benefit from a candid evaluation of some of your expectations of love and ingrained relationship patterns to make healthier decisions in your current relationship. In either case, you must become the very love you are seeking, even when that involves coming face to face with your intrapersonal demons, inhibitions, and fears so that in addition to finding Mr. Right, you become Ms. Right.

Becoming Ms. Right and being clear that you need to wait for a soulmate love partner will help you avoid some of the common romantic pitfalls I've seen smart women make when choosing a partner. Emotional blind spots prevented them from clearly seeing that the men with whom they were entering into long-term relationships were bad choices. Even though they were drawn to them like a moth to a flame, these men negatively impacted — or in some cases even ruined — their lives.

MEET SMART WOMEN WHO CLEARLY
CHOSE MR. WRONG TO BE MR. RIGHT

While the phenomenon of smart women being irresistibly drawn to men who were bad for them may be timeless, Dr. Connell Cowan and Dr. Melvyn Kinder were some of the first researchers to try and document these women's experiences in their groundbreaking book, *Smart Women, Foolish Choices*. These psychologists found that the smart and successful predominantly White females in their private practices were almost magnetically drawn to the wrong men and ended up frustrated and disappointed in love because of their unrealistic expectations about relationships, conflicts over needs for independence, the desire to be taken care of by a man, and a lack of understanding of the male psyche — to name a few reasons.

While many ways African American women's experiences with men who are bad for them are similar to these authors' clients, below are three types of dysfunctional relationship patterns I most frequently encounter in therapy, where surprisingly otherwise accomplished, educated, business, and street-smart African American women have made bad choices in men.

(Note: The names, professions, and other descriptive facts used in this book to describe clients have been changed in order to maintain confidentiality. Any resemblance to any former or current client's life is strictly coincidental.)

1. **I'm Too Busy for a Man.**

    Meet Brenda. Brenda is a 42-year-old IT specialist. She is unhappily married to a military man, Charles, who has a history of womanizing. Brenda is understandably upset because he seldom comes home at night before 2 a.m., never explains his actions or disappearances, and doesn't return her incessant calls. His response to her questions about his whereabouts is, "Why did you blow my phone up all night? That was rude. You embarrassed me in front of the friend I was with. Don't do that again." Having been approached by several of his mistresses over the years, she was fully aware he has had numerous extramarital affairs. She reports having remained faithful.

    When asked if Charles always behaved this way, and, if so, what made her pick him? She indicated, *"he was fun and didn't ask for a commitment, demand much of my time, and wasn't jealous. That was huge for me. Other men felt needy and insecure, wanting way too much of my time and were jealous when they didn't get it. I didn't understand their needs, restrictions, and demands on my freedom or for my time. I was working my way through school, starting my own business, and raising my son. Other than to 'hook up' every now and then, I didn't really need a man at the time, so our situation worked. I didn't care what he did when we weren't together. Besides, neither my mother nor my aunts were married or in serious monogamous relationships, so a man not being around wasn't that odd to me. I was taught don't depend on a man for anything.*

Charles fit the bill.

That was 15 years ago, but my son is gone off to college now, my business is thriving, and my needs have changed. I'm lonely in this marriage, and want a real relationship – a soulmate, like you see in the movies or read about in novels."

Charles came into therapy during our third session. However, he stormed out when she said they needed to re-establish trust. He felt she needed to let go of the past, and refused to return. The focus of our work shifted from her saving her marriage to her personal development, with the attention gradually shifting from him treating her like an option to her making herself a priority. She stopped worrying and started living, which included hanging out with the girls again, taking dance classes, eating better, drinking less alcohol, and enjoying her down time. He soon noticed her new-found swag and sense of independence. Ironically, he committed an about face and suddenly became available, especially once she put a hold on the credit cards (for which she was paying). Everything came to a head when he returned home at 5 a.m. one morning to find she had not only not called him that night, but wasn't home waiting for him to return.

His subsequent attempts to reconnect were too little, too late.

Brenda's personal growth spelled change. She has since filed for a divorce. When asked why, she stated, "I'm worthy of a real relationship, and want a committed, available, exclusive, and loving partner. He doesn't – and can't – meet those needs."

(Note: I do not promote, encourage, or otherwise recommend divorce unless one of the spouses is a characterological abuser. I typically find many couples' problems can be addressed with therapy. Alternatively, spouses seldom upgrade and don't necessarily live happily ever after the second time around, in part because of the challenges associated with blending families with new spouses. Blended families have very high divorce rates, unless family counseling is obtained. See Chapter 11, Dating With Kids: Strategies for Beating the Odds.)

2. **I Don't Require a Man Who Has It Together: I'll Take a Fixer-Upper.**

Meet Shannon. Shannon is a 25-year-old pharmaceutical sales rep who has a newborn son and is three months pregnant. Hardworking, controlling, highly motivated, and an adept social climber, this University of Virginia alum desperately wants Jamal to marry her. He's the father of her newborn son, and they live together, but Jamal is more interested in smoking weed and playing Xbox with his ever-present, equally underachieving friends. Other than talking about getting ready for the pre-NFL draft combines, he doesn't have any career-related ambitions. At best, the NFL is a pipe dream. Yes, coming out of high school at 6'3" with 4.3 speed, with every big college in the country recruiting him at wide-receiver — the NFL seemed inevitable. However, due to his poor grades, the big-name programs passed on him. He went to an unknown small school and broke a few records, but flunked during the first year, never following up on opportunities to apply for readmission to a junior college.

Today, their relationship has more in common with a mother-son dynamic than a healthy romantic partnership.

When asked what attracted them to each other:

Jamal: "She was a good girl, kind of sheltered, an 'A' student, responsible, and took charge of things. I admired her strength and vision. She's a winner."

Shannon: "He was the 'man' and supremely confident, at least on the football field. I knew his teachers were passing him along, but figured he was smart and would get it together in college. Who lets grades keep them out of the NFL? Besides, he had a ton of women, and I felt special that he chose me. He could have had any girl, so I thought I had won."

<u>Here's how they typically interact with each other:</u>

Jamal: "She always nags me about getting a job or a better paying job."

Shannon: "Yes, you need to man up. Your mother did everything for you. But, you are a father now. Time to quit getting high every day and start taking care of your family. I'm tired of wearing the pants around here."

(Ouuchhh!)

<u>Asked what she wanted from therapy, she responded, "Can you fix him?":</u>

Shannon: "Dr. Perrault, you need to motivate him. Last December, I had him set up for an interview with the park police. Despite his reservations, my uncle pulled some strings to set up that interview. Jamal told me the interviewers became negative when they recognized his name and realized he was the same Jamal who led his team to victory over their rival high school. When I called my uncle to check on why the interviewers discriminated against him, my uncle informed me that Jamal was a 'no show.' Come to find out he went out drinking the night before and didn't show up. I was so humiliated and felt completely betrayed."

3. **She Doesn't Make Her Man Feel Like a Man; Yet, She Needs Him to Makes Her Feel Like a Woman.**

Meet Deidra. Deidra is a 39-year-old, married mother of a 4-year-old-son, George Jr. She and George Sr. broke up during her pregnancy after a seemingly small disagreement and have not spoken since. They never talked to a professional to address their relationship problems. She works at the Patent Office as a patent examiner. She started there as a clerk and went to college in the evenings and completed her mechanical engineering degree. Self-made, critical, and confrontational at times, she is one tough cookie. Her husband, Theodore III, is a mild-mannered interior designer. Unhappy in her marriage, she feels he isn't a man's man, he doesn't understand her struggle, and she feels rejected because he no longer initiates sex. His family is a bit bourgeois for her taste, and she feels they look down on her because she comes from the other side of the tracks (e.g., she's from Barry Farms, a public housing project in SE Washington, D.C.). Comparatively speaking, she feels Theodore III was born with a silver spoon in his mouth because his family is from an upscale neighborhood in Prince George's County (the wealthiest African American county in the U.S.). She avoids family events as much as possible.

In spite of her tough exterior, Deidra has a really tender side and always reaches back to help others, including setting up a tutoring and etiquette program for young ladies who live in her old inner-city neighborhood. She also mentors several young female engineers at the Patent Office, and she is a favorite of the office support staff whom she encourages. Her staff and superiors love her. Unlike the co-workers and mentees she oversees, however, Theodore III's experience with her is a tale of two cities. He feels castrated by what he described as her hard driving, hypercritical, and controlling personality. Feeling angry, betrayed, and resentful, he has rebelled. For example, he has become distant and no longer brings her around his family, no longer approaches her sexually, and has begun to show interest in another woman.

WHAT DO THESE WOMEN HAVE IN COMMON?

While all of these women's stories are different, they are, in some uncanny way, strikingly similar. Brenda, Shannon, and Deidra are all highly intelligent, educated, sophisticated, confident, independent, resilient, desirable, and family oriented. They are all yearning for a fulfilling relationship, but making self-defeating choices in men and in their relationships with these men.

(We will discuss all of these women further later.) Without intervention, all three of these smart women likely become marriage disasters.

But why?

In *Smart Women, Foolish Choices*, Dr. Connell Cowan and Dr. Melvyn Kinder discuss why the smart women who come into their private practice end up with the wrong men, and how they can change their love-defeating attitudes to open up new opportunities for romantic relationships or marriages. While I agree there are many universal similarities between successful White and Black women who find themselves magnetically drawn to the wrong men, I've observed over time that the Black women in my practice didn't just find themselves in dysfunctional relationships. Rather, their involvement in these dysfunctional relationships was somehow linked to early childhood experiences. Some of their experiences with men were traumatic and made them feel eerily "familiar and safe" in unhealthy relationships with their particular man—be it with an unavailable man, a man who needs "fixing," or a man they dominate.

As our work together progressed, we found the unconscious draw of these familiar emotional patterns typically filled a need that was much stronger than even their physical attraction to these men. They all agreed they either witnessed firsthand a similar relationship dynamic, or there were similar patterns in their previous relationships. During our work together, these women had the epiphany that these choices were neither accidental, nor were they chance encounters.

As a marital psychologist, I strive to help empower women to better identify, understand, and illuminate the blind spots that may have been created in part by their personal histories, and to change those relationship patterns should they find themselves irresistibly drawn to men who aren't good for them. Equally important, I'm trying to help them recognize that the solution to healthy relationships doesn't just lie within the man. Simply changing men is the equivalent of them switching seats on the

Titanic instead of abandoning the ship. In treatment, I try to get rid of "the middle man" and go directly to the source of the problem, which generally has little to do with a woman's actual man. He's frequently just a means to helping her meet a misunderstood need.

To help illuminate the blind spots that may be playing a role in these three smart women making foolish choices, I will refer to the three schools of psychology: Psychodynamic, Transactional Analysis, and Self-Psychology.

THREE THEORIES THAT SHED LIGHT ON WHY MR. WRONG CAN FEEL SO RIGHT— AND HOW TO AVOID CHOOSING HIM

<u>Relationship Pattern #One</u> – The Psychodynamic Re-Occurrence: When Troubled Childhoods Lead to Troubled Adulthoods

> *"Just because you are done with the past doesn't mean the past is done with you."*
> — *"Steel Magnolias"*

To better explain how troubled childhoods sometimes lead to troubled relationships in adulthood, here is psychiatrist Dr. Sigmund Freud's "Repetitive Compulsion." According to Freud, a person repeats a traumatic event, or re-enacts the event by putting herself in situations where the event is likely to re-occur again. The *"repetition compulsion" is the emotional equivalent of the victim* returning to the scene of the crime, hoping to rewrite history or change the outcome this time. These re-enactments are driven by a subconscious defense mechanism that finds comfort in the familiar, whereby people endlessly repeat patterns of behavior which were difficult or distressing in earlier life. They typically revisit a troubled relationship with their parents, usually the opposite-sex parent.

When the early parental relationship is fraught with frustration, disappointment, rejection, abandonment, neglect, or abuse, the child finds herself in a delicate and confusing psychological predicament. In order to reconcile the painful reality that daddy isn't there to love, protect, and provide for her along with her intuitive need to be loved and protected, she attempts to resolve this conflict, but remains confused by her mixed emotions. Feelings of intense anger, depression, and despair are contrasted with the childish hope that "if only I can be good, perfect, smart, quiet, funny, or pretty enough, I can win his love this time around." Because she can't rationalize dad not being present to love and protect her, and it doesn't intuitively make sense to her, the young girl frequently and mistakenly believes she is the problem, and, therefore, erroneously assumes responsibility for fixing it. Many speculate the unwitting victim unconsciously finds herself irresistibly drawn to men who recreate this dysfunctional relationship pattern despite the presence of healthier and better options available.

Re-enacting these dysfunctional relationship patterns may include dating or marrying men who might be emotionally unavailable or abusive. These women develop an uncanny attraction or unconscious radar for men who resemble—psychologically if not physically—the father with whom she had difficulties. This is the nature of compulsive repetitions. For example, Brenda's decision to marry the emotionally unavailable Charles, despite having several available suitors. Our work together revealed her decision to choose Charles was related to unresolved emotional conflicts she experienced during her childhood. The combination of having an absentee father and internalizing the message "don't depend on a man" played a role in her concluding, "I don't really need a man, so why put myself in a vulnerable position by depending on one?" Her emotional resilience and self-reliance may have had great self-preservation value for her as a young girl, when she had to survive what she described as a difficult childhood. Years later, however, when she blossomed into an attractive young woman and started to date men, that blind spot came back to bite her when she settled for Charles, who remained emotionally unavailable. Of the several suitors she had, she opted to marry the man who made her feel most comfortable because he was scarcely around and demanded very little of her. Although her life was initially too busy for her to notice he didn't connect with her emotionally, after marrying him, she subsequently discovered he was so carefree because he was a womanizer who never really desired a close connection to her. Once her son went off to college, she felt a profound need to bond with and feel close to and nurtured by Charles, regardless of her being a very capable and strong woman.

For Brenda the solution wasn't to change or deny the past, but to confront it consciously (versus unconsciously recreating it), to own it, and make peace with it to release its powerful grip over her present relationship choices. Upon recognizing this pattern, her desire for Charles seemed to completely disappear over time. Accepting that he couldn't meet, nor had he ever met, her needs (which was precisely why he was chosen), she filed for divorce.

When confronting these troublesome compulsive repetitions, understand that simply recognizing why this pattern of behaviors has emerged won't instantaneously eradicate them, nor the associated ingrained behaviors or blind spots. To begin the healing process when it comes to your past, you have to find a way to make peace with it, and quit trying to deny, ignore, or just get over it. Like it or not, this defense mechanism helped you survive a traumatic experience, so it has a real "survival value" and it has empowered you to feel safe in an otherwise dangerous world. You didn't call upon this defense mechanism because you were weak or emotionally fragile; in contrast, you were emotionally resilient, otherwise you would not have survived. You have to authentically identify the good and bad underlying your defense mechanism(s) and embrace the beauty in them.

I encourage you to begin the process of forgiving yourself and making peace with yourself so you can begin to feel better, and not bitter — and make better choices in the future.

Relationship Pattern #Two – Transactional Analysis Conflict: When Adept Black Women Commit to Inept Men — "I'm OK. You're not OK, but I can fix you!"

A second group of women I frequently encounter in therapy seeking to make peace with their past and become better, and not bitter. To help them, we look at the internal messages and self-talk dialogue or "scripts" that frequently were developed during early childhood experiences. Namely, women who repeatedly found themselves in dysfunctional relationships were taught "I'm not OK. You are OK" or "I'm OK. You aren't OK, but I can fix you" during their childhood. The latter life position is frequently adopted by African American women. It seldom, if ever, works. Rather, it typically results in resentment, frustration, and infidelity (on his part).

In his best-selling classic book *Games People Play: The Psychology of Human Relationships*, Dr. Eric Berne introduces "transactional analysis" as a way of describing func-tional and dysfunc-tional relationships. Dr. Berne talks about four life positions that a person can hold, and how these positions can have profound implica-tions for how a person experiences relationships. The four positions are: 1)

PARENT EGO STATE
Behaviours, thoughts and feelings copied from parents or parent figures

INTEGRATING ADULT EGO STATE
Behaviours, thoughts and feelings which are direct responses to the here and now

CHILD EGO STATE
Behaviours, thoughts and feelings replayed from childhood

"I'm OK and you are OK," which is the healthiest position one can take (meaning you feel good about yourself and others), 2) "I'm OK. You are not OK," which is a position where you feel good about yourself, but see others as damaged or somehow flawed, 3) "I'm not OK, and you are OK," which is a position where you feel you are the weak partner in relationships, and your partner is definitely stronger than you, and 4) "I'm not OK, and you are not OK," which is the worst position because it ultimately means you believe you are in a bad place, and your partner is, too.

Based on these four positions, Transactional Analysis (TA) distinguishes three active ego states in each person's make up: the parent ("I'm OK. You aren't OK"), the adult ("I'm OK. You are OK") and the child ("I'm not OK. You are OK"). TA describes the ego-state (parent-adult-child, P-A-C) model. This model helps explain how people function and express their life positions in their relationships. Please recognize these life positions aren't fixed, and the behaviors, thoughts, and feelings associated with them are subject to change depending on the topic.

As Dr. Berne indicates (and my experience in therapy confirms), women who hold the "I'm not OK. You are OK" position unconsciously find themselves feeling entitled to less and magnetically drawn to abusive, dysfunctional, and non-mutually fulfilling relationships — no matter her intellect, level of success, beauty, or other strengths.

In my work with Black women, I find there is also a unique twist where they take on an "I'm OK. You aren't OK, but I can fix you" life position that results in them finding themselves in "mother-child" types of dysfunctional relationships with their partners. This theory explains how in our relationships we continue to re-play childhood strategies, even when this results in pain or defeat.

In the case of Shannon, my first goal was to help her recognize her life position "I'm OK. You're not OK, but I can fix you" with Jamal. Although this may seem obvious to you from reading about their relationship, it remains very difficult for her to recognize, much less accept. Shannon insists our work together should simply focus on my motivating Jamal to quit smoking weed and "man-up and get a good job." She also ignores comparisons to her father, who was around at times, but had addiction issues that interfered with his ability to be a consistent, positive, and healthy influence. She blames her mother for her parents' breakup, and insists Dad just needed some more support, treatment, and patience.

Despite recalling several examples of how she had run interference to save her father from himself, Shannon doesn't see herself as an enabler.

P-A-C Transactional Analysis

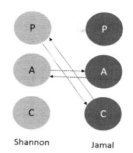

Shannon   Jamal

Solid Line: Current Parent/Child dysfunctional script.
Broken Line: Therapeutic Goal for an Adult/Adult functional relationship script.

Likewise, she can't recognize she is stuck in a similar pattern with Jamal. This denial is complicated by the fact that she has a newborn son and is three months pregnant, and may very well lose her pharmaceutical sales job once they discover her second pregnancy out of wedlock.

I wish I could report I had successfully changed Shannon's and Jamal's parent–child relationship dynamic, but I haven't. Currently, the discussion sounds something like this:

Shannon: "Jamal I need you to look for a more stable and higher paying job, and quit getting high and playing Xbox every day with your worthless friends in our basement."

Jamal: "There you go criticizing me again. My boys got my back. Why are you always so judgmental? I will soon be in the NFL, and you won't be saying this. Besides, you used to get high with me and my boys. Just because you stopped doesn't mean we should. That was your choice. Don't judge us."

In spite of the obvious challenges their interactions present, she remains in denial and insists that once they get married, all of their problems will magically go away. Further, should she be wrong about Jamal, the reality of her fatally flawed choice and the consequences that may follow could, in fact, be too painful for her to confront at this point. She is deeply committed to making her family work, and I am not willing to push an approach that could potentially undermine that prospect. She says, "Jamal is a loving father in spite of his flaws." However, if he won't get a job and gets high with his buddies most days, is he really being a good father? Good fathers, by definition, contribute what they can to provide for their families.

Ultimately the goal of Transactional Analysis is to move Shannon and Jamal toward an overall adult-adult relationship dynamic, reflecting a healthy "I'm OK. You're OK" interaction.

Relationship Pattern #Three The Self Psychology Syndrome: When Little Black Girls Are Forced to Develop Big Girl Alter Egos to Survive

The "Repetition Compulsion" and Transactional Analysis" theories stem from traditional European models of psychology, and tend to be universally applicable. I, however, have noticed there are unique phenomenon that require an Afrocentric approach to better explain some of the strategies Black women consciously or unconsciously employ to get their psychological and emotional needs met in life and in their relationships.

To address one unique reality of Black women in relationships, I postulate "The Kitty-Cat and the Myth of the Black Tigress" theory. This theory is born out of self-psychology, which employs the development of an alter-ego system to resolve emotional conflict. This psychoanalytic theory and therapy was originally created by Heinz Kohut, whose work suggests Superman is mild-mannered reporter Clark Kent's famous alter ego. Similarly, I've found that because early in life, Black women are frequently forced to deal with the reality that the cavalry isn't coming for them, they are forced to make some difficult decisions, including developing a tough exterior. Although naturally feminine, sensuous, and possessing a kitty-cat interior (like other women who purr to signal her mate to caress her), Black women develop an alter ego that is more akin to a "tigress" that growls and claws to protect herself.

The development of the tigress alter-ego is based on both historical facts and modern-day realities. First, I suspect that during slavery the harsh reality of her (and her man's) powerlessness impacted her in a unique fashion, as at any moment either she, her child, or her man could be sold to another plantation with no regard for her family values. This forced her to confront the precariousness of her situation and become painfully aware just how unsafe, unpredictable, and harsh her world could be. Having to accept that there was no cavalry to call to rescue her, she was forced to learn to do for herself and not depend on a man — or anyone else, for that matter. Second, while slavery was abolished in 1864, post-slavery reality was every bit as harsh. Whether it be the "Black codes," which was "slavery by another name" because a Black man could be arrested for being unemployed, homeless or having too nice a home, or no reason at all and put onto chain-gangs; "Jim Crow," which meant educational and employment opportunities were always separate but never equal; or a criminal justice system that was anything but blind when it came to incarcerating her husband, sons, or father, the Black woman had to accept that her pool of eligible men was severely limited and vulnerable. She passed the reality she learned from her mother down to her daughters, whether she came from a one- or two-parent, low- or high-SES (socio-economic status) household.

For these and other reasons, I find many of the Black women in my private practice have developed the tigress alter-ego. Herein lies a catch-22 for many Black women when it comes to getting their emotional needs met in their relationships. How does a man, who has just been clawed and is bleeding profusely from being gouged by this ferocious feline, recognize she is, in reality, a mere kitten trying to protect herself — and that the roar he just heard was actually a disguised purr beckoning him to tenderly stroke, nurture, protect, and love her? At best, her protective alter-ego leads to mis-communication, unmet needs, and confusion; at worst, it leads to hostility, resentment, isolation, break-ups, divorce, or infidelity.

In the case of Deidra, Theodore III is confronted with her tough exterior and alter ego, and no longer sees her as needing him to meet her emotional needs, much less be her protector. This same tigress alter-ego empowered her to become a self-made, first-generation college graduate female engineer and work her way up the ladder. At work, her fierce work ethic, stoicism, and hard-driving interpersonal and critical management style drive results and have solidified her as a bonafide team member. At home, that same personality style has left Theodore III confused about where he fits in her life and how he should love her — if she needs him to love her at all.

As we discussed their plight, he quickly got the tigress persona, but struggled to recognize anything remotely resembling a kitty-cat. He recalled the way her claws gouged his ego, pride, and manhood and asked what type of kitten could inflict this kind of damage.

Theodore III admitted in session that over the years he had come to resent being disrespected by her Deidra in front of his step-son (whom he clearly loves as his own) and his family during the holidays. For these reasons, he admitted no longer desiring her sexually. She recently discovered he was having an affair with another woman, Nicole. Nicole doesn't have a college education and works as an artist at a local tattoo shop. Deidra had been too busy to notice the smile that recently emerged on Theodore's face or his new tattoo. When confronted about some emails she found on the family computer, he unapologetically responded, "She actually likes me, laughs at my jokes, respects me, and makes me feel like a man. It's nice to feel like a man again." Much to his surprise, Deidra burst into tears when he discussed his affair with Nicole and was clearly devastated, unveiling a love for and commitment to him he could scarcely have imagined. Despite his thinking she didn't care, it became clear she loved him deeply and wanted to fight for her marriage.

After months of couples therapy and removing protective layer after layer, he started to hear (and be heard by) her and to forgive (and be forgiven by) Deidra, and accepted that she needed his validation, affection, love making and love. Finally, he opened up about feeling emasculated and resenting her for embarrassing him in front of their son and his family, which lead to him shutting down on her sexually. He had made a pact as a child to manage his behavior better than his volatile father had. However, that didn't include being "punked." She began to recognize while she felt validated for taking on some of the masculine, she needed to stop invalidating him for taking on some of the feminine to balance them out. Gradually they began to trust each other again, and closeness replaced distance as he began to see her through more balanced lenses. He started to recognize the woman he fell in love with: tough, determined, and ambitious; yet, sensitive, caring, and committed to their family and him. He reconciled that Deidra was both tigress and a kitten who really did love and respect him, and was completely committed to their family. He agreed to end his affair with Nicole and recommit himself to rebuilding their life together.

BUT, WILL WOMEN WHO GOT IT SO WRONG EVER END UP WITH MR. RIGHT?

No matter what you may have concluded about Brenda, Shannon, Deidra, or any other women you might know in a similar situation (or yourself, should these women's stories seem all too familiar), you would be sadly mistaken to pathologize or think of them or yourself as weak, self-destructive, fatally flawed, or incapable of forming a trusting, healthy, and loving relationship. All of these women possess numerous qualities that will likely ultimately make them successful in relationships—namely, they are emotionally resilient, salt-of-the-earth, and selfless; open to taking a hard and non-defensive look at themselves; and deeply committed to family.

That said, given their negative experiences with men, I was struck by their commitment to their families and belief in men, particularly their trust in me as an African American male therapist. (I found that trust particularly humbling.) I've come to better understand and appreciate the strengths and apprehensions of these Black women who are typically misunderstood and mislabeled as angry Black women. In actuality they were survivors protecting themselves from childhood psychological wounds and historical factors outside of their control, which have left them to deal with a hostile world as best they could. They all wanted a Mr. Right and a healthy relationship with him. Yes, they were human and had their blind spots, but their partner or spouse (or the next man) is truly lucky to be with them once they make peace with their past and become better instead of bitter. They are just traveling their journey, and undoubtedly will one day get it right when their Mr. Right appears.

Note: Should either of these three situations remind you of your own, it may be a good idea to talk to with a professional. Not because it is a sign you can't be in a mutually fulfilling relationship, but because you can and will likely make an awesome partner or spouse. However, these are difficult, complex, and deeply entrenched emotional dynamics and will likely require the help of a trained professional.

CHAPTER 2

Bad Boys, Nice Guys, and Keepers: What Type of Man Is Right for You?

Whaat type of man should you choose? I'm sure when you picked up this book you wanted to know which of these men would be the better choice for a relationship or marriage. While it would be nice if men could be typecast neatly into categories and you could predictably forecast your future with him based on the type of man you selected, truth be told, although from various walks of life, any of the men in this line-up could be the right woman's bad boy, nice guy, or Mr. Right.

(Like in the crime thriller starring Kevin Spacey, you have to look beyond "The Usual Suspects" in this lineup because none of these men hold the answer to this riddle. You do!) The question is, is he Mr. Right for you? Choosing "The One" is more about finding the right fit than cherry-picking from a one-size-fits-all grouping. Another reason generalities don't work is because all bad boys aren't just bad, and all nice guys aren't, well, nice. Some bad boys are good catches; some nice guys are bad catches. To muddy the waters further, all bad boys and nice guys aren't created equally. Some bad boys are great prospects, while others are projects or predatory; similarly, some nice guys are great prospects, while others are projects or perpetrators. These within-group differences are precisely the reason why deciding between a bad boy and a nice guy can be so puzzling.

Simply put, choosing the right man can be complex.

Possibly the most problematic and baffling piece of the puzzle centers around authenticity. You expect bad boys to be inauthentic and nice guys to be authentic, but, when your expectations meet reality, you discover these stereotypes frequently don't exactly hold true. In fact, bad boys frequently place a premium on being real and true to themselves, exhibiting a devil may care attitude; while some nice guys place more importance on being perceived as nice than on being real or true to themselves, displaying a willingness at times to make a deal with the devil to be liked.

Many women tell me authenticity and having a trusting relationship is key, even if it involves a man telling her he isn't ready to commit or be monogamous just yet. Women tell me all the time, "At least the bad boy told me the truth, so I knew what I was getting. He gave me the choice." Although it seems like a simple trait, given all of the important qualities you consider when selecting a man, authenticity is a powerful thing and frequently can be a deal breaker. In contrast, the thought of entering into a serious relationship with an inauthentic partner is both frightening and unsettling. Because most people wear masks and put their best foot forward, it is refreshing and can be a real turn on not to have to second guess where he is coming from. Consequently, you drop your defenses and feel relaxed and genuinely start to enjoy his presence. This sense of authenticity results in bad boys sometimes having a positive vibe or aura about them. Herein lies the mystifying contradiction: Nice guys and not-bad boys are supposed to have a positive energy around them. However, if that nice guy isn't willing to take a risk being real enough to forge an authentic connection with you, then you are likely to feel uneasy because it is hard to trust men you experience as having a "negative vibe." As a woman, you are frequently naturally intuitive and are particularly adept at picking up on these vibrations, saying, "I just didn't get a good feel about him, so I moved on."

So, how do you choose between a bad boy, from whom you're getting a positive vibe, and a nice guy, from whom you're getting a negative vibe? Perhaps this dilemma is what Beyoncé is singing about in the Jay-Z song "She fell in love with the bad guy." Beyoncé sings about not having a need for a perfect love story, but falling for the bad guy her gut instinct tells her will go good. Perhaps their love is misunderstood. Jay Z responds only she believed and saw that goodness in him, and he embraces the prospect that it might be them against the world.

Nice guys place you atop a lofty but uncomfortable pedestal, while bad boys take you off your pedestal and let you come down to earth where you feel most comfortable. Nice guys make sure you never have to guess about how much they value you, while bad boys keep you second guessing yourself, which ensures you value them. Some nice guys expend vast amounts of energy telling you that you are a queen, while a bad boy will let you expend energy treating him like a king. Bad boys will leave you hanging, while nice guys seemingly will hang in there forever, holding on no matter what. Bad boys are aggressive, whereas nice guys sometimes are passive-aggressive. Some nice guys try to convince you they are perfect and above other male beings, while bad boys appear comfortable with their imperfections—and, make you feel comfortable with your imperfections, too! Nice guys can be needy and pushovers, while bad boys know what buttons need pushing.

As the all-female chorus sang in Mase's hit song "Feel So Good," "Bad, bad, bad, bad boy you make me feel so good ... I wouldn't change you if I could."

Undoubtedly for some of these reasons, dating bad boys has been an ongoing struggle for girls everywhere. Your girlfriends complain about it, you complain about it, and God knows you hear the nice guys complaining about it. Yet, women date them anyway. You know going into it that he's probably an asshole, but you do it anyway, each and every time convincing yourself it will end differently this time. But why? No woman actually wants to date a bad boy, she just wants to be the woman who changes the bad boy. She wants to be like Beyoncé and inspire the player to quit the game.

Believe it or not, though you are unlikely to convert a bad boy into a nice guy, your instincts to find a partner who respects, asserts, and trusts himself are on point. The challenge is finding an authentic man who provides the sense of excitement, confidence, and optimism you desire from bad boys, yet who can meet your long-term needs, too. He must represent a balance with the sense of security, validation, and commitment you get from nice guys, coupled with him possibly being ready to and capable of committing to you. For these reasons, I will provide you more information about a third group of men: great guys. (To help you better understand these three types of men, I will rely on a body of literature that prototypically classifies and describes these men as bad boys or alpha males, nice guys or beta males, and great guys or gamma men.)

Great guys — aka gamma men. Not often talked about, the more ideal gamma male is a blend of traits shared by both the alpha and beta males. This man has principles, really understands and respects himself and you, makes you feel secure and protected, provides enough excitement to keep a smile on your face, and is able to hear you (and have you feel heard by him). Former Chairman of the Joint Chiefs of Staff and four-star general Colin

Powell, who married his wife Alma in 1962 (and they report living happily ever after), would be an example of a pure gamma man. Ladies, if you are looking for your Mr. Right, this may very well be your man. The gamma man may also be the bad boy (alpha male) who grew up and toned down his womanizing ways, risky lifestyle, and the associated drama, and is finally ready to be a partner. Alternatively, he may be the nice guy (beta male) who found his true voice, grew a pair and started taking risks, and decided to stop seeking the approval of others.

To help you gain further insights into these three types of men, I will provide key distinctions between bad boys (alpha males), nice guys (beta men) and great guys (gamma men), and provide some valuable distinctions of the three subtypes within the alpha and beta men.

(Note: The theories presented in this chapter recognize some widely held rules of thumb about male-female relationships, attempts to share certain insights about specific types of men — and how women typically respond to them. I do not want to suggest or otherwise imply that all nice guys are duplicitous or weak, or that all bad boys will get you and meet your needs, or that they are all strong. While I recognize there simply isn't a viable one-size-fits-all approach to classifying men, I found the use of some generalizations to be unavoidable; nevertheless, the groups of men described herein are best viewed on a continuum. Many traits associated with alpha and beta males present a limitation in one situation and a strength in others. When deciding on a partner, you need to decide which combination of traits represents a better fit for you over a lifetime. Finally, I identify several popular television characters, celebrities, and politicians in this chapter whose widely reported behaviors are consistent with the group of men I am profiling; however, all accounts of their behaviors are taken from popular media sources and I am in no way implicitly or explicitly suggesting that I have interviewed them for this book to confirm they are indeed a member of the group of men I describe. I am simply utilizing the way they are perceived or misperceived in the media for illustrative purposes.)

INSIGHTS INTO MEN THAT CAN HELP YOU GET THE BEST OF BOTH WORLDS: A BAD BOY WHO IS NICE; OR A NICE GUY WHO IS FUN

Many unhappy women come into my office with partners who represent the extreme: bad boys who are unfaithful or irresponsible, but fun and the love of their life; or nice guys who are faithful and responsible, but they complain their marriage is loveless and on life support. Perhaps, the key is better understanding men, and picking one who represents a balance of both worlds.

So, who are these alpha and beta males, and how do you decide which one will make a better partner for you? Alpha males certainly do get more than their fair share of women. Exciting, unapologetically male, unpredictable and mysterious, great in bed, physically fit, and attractive with a flair for style are just a few of the reasons you dated him, despite suspecting from the first kiss that it may not last long or end well. You were magnetically drawn to him anyway. Nevertheless, these relationships typically are short lived or one sided should they become long term, with the woman eventually becoming uncomfortable with the lack of mutual emotional support, commitment, and fidelity. Yet, when compared to his seemingly less remarkable, careful, unaggressive, risk avoidant, non-charismatic, and unconfident beta male brethren — who frequently lack the alpha male's physical presence — women roll the dice and double down on the bad boy anyway. While alpha male traits are associated with masculinity itself and signal strength to women, many beta male characteristics are disassociated from masculinity and can turn women off because they signal weakness.

Mary J Blige, unwittingly sings about how alpha and beta males make her feel in her hit "Mr. Wrong": "Bad boys ain't no good. Good boys ain't no fun. Lord knows I should run off with the right one ... Me and Mr. Wrong get along so good (so good) Even though he breaks my heart so bad (so bad)...."

When trying to understand what sounds like a maladaptive approach to selecting a partner, perhaps Darwin's survival of the fittest theory provides insight into women's tendency toward selecting alpha males in spite of the inherent risks. In addition to being confusing, this leaning toward risky men appears like hypocrisy when it comes to women's choices in men: They say they want a nice guy, but when push comes to shove, that's not who they go home with at the end of the night. Although seemingly maladaptive by today's standards, this potent mix of excitement, mystery, untamed masculinity, confidence, and independence associated with warriors, gladiators, and soldiers has remained an aphrodisiac for women since our hunter-gatherer days, making them feel protected, likely to be provided for and comfortably on edge. However, as women mature and recognize other traits and stability are necessary to sustain a long-term relationship, marriage, and family, this fascination and inclination appears to be a passing phase — at least, for some women.

The behaviors and actions listed below — albeit, admittedly written to highlight the extremes — will further clarify the differences between alpha and beta men (and why you react so differently to them):

Although the alpha male is frequently the more popular pick over his beta brethren, he may not necessarily be the best pick for you in the long run. The transitory nature of relationships with bad boys undoubtedly contributes to women ping-ponging between bad boys and nice guys. Bad boys are a good time, meet her sexual needs, and offer the hope of a fulfilling or even exhilarating long-term relationship, while the nice-guy provides a sense of security, is a steady source of admiration and validation, and, if all else fails, a long-term partner. This pattern repeats itself over and over until the music stops around age 35, and it's time to get serious about life, or grow up, as they say.

In choosing Mr. Right, it is not imperative that you select either an adventurous man or settle for a safe one; rather, it is important to select the right man for you. For example, alpha females are ambitious and high achievers whose relationships tend to revolve around their careers, and sometimes the biggest mistake an alpha female can make is to marry an alpha male. Attracted to a man who takes charge, exudes confidence, and is just as accomplished as they are, these women find themselves naturally drawn to alpha males. While these pairings make for an incredible courtship, over time these partners will frequently end up locking horns. Because alpha females tend to have a hard time separating their leadership persona from their romantic persona in their relationship with an alpha male, these partners tend to experience a mental tug-of-war. Taking charge and being in control serves her well professionally, but can create problems in her personal life should she find herself in a relationship with a man hard wired to take control himself. If you are thinking about choosing an alpha male for a soulmate, you must understand that chances are he would rather be respected than loved because when respected, he feels loved.

Frustrated alpha males, who desire to lead but aren't allowed to do so, tend to feel disrespected and unloved, and subsequently may gravitate toward beta females. Beta females are usually less aggressive, more submissive, and less confrontational than their alpha female sisters. While it may be the case that he can't deal with your success, it may also be the case that he may need to feel like the leader in order to feel successful. In either event, the naturally nurturing beta female is keenly in touch with her feminine wiles and unafraid to display her emotional side, and her sense of emotional success comes in part from her man taking control and leading. Alpha males are also drawn to them because these men are genetically programmed to be rescuers, and beta females' disposition intuitively caters to his male ego in a fashion frequently lost on the alpha female. Countless studies have concluded that beta females make the most amicable partners for alpha males, and there is less tension in these relationships. However, I would be remiss if I left you thinking beta women are more feminine or womanly or otherwise represent a better match for alpha males than alpha females; rather, they frequently just are wired in a fashion that makes the alpha male ego feel most comfortable. This trade off in tension, however, may be made at the expense of the alpha male's personal and professional development, as the alpha female may be more likely to demand the growth and change needed to blossom into a gamma male.

It is a rare woman indeed who can measure up to the alpha female, for she could be like Nzinga of the Congo in West Africa or Egypt's queen Nefertiti. These two queens represent a stark contrast in alpha women and their relationships with men.

Nzinga, the 17th century queen, was referred to as "a king." According to legend, spurred by Marquis de Sade's *Philosophy in the Boudoir*, Nzinga immolated her lovers. This legend claims she kept a harem of men who fought diligently in war for the honor of making love with her. After a single night of pleasure they were put to death.

A brilliant military strategist, at the height of her reign she formed an alliance with the Dutch and defeated the Portuguese in 1644. Although the Portuguese would defeat her in 1646, she routed a Portuguese army in 1647 and would lay siege to the Portuguese capital of Masangano. Personally leading troops into battle, she resisted the Portuguese well into her sixties. In 1657, she negotiated a peace treaty with the Portuguese. Despite numerous efforts to dethrone her, Nzinga died a peaceful death at age 80 without an heir. Her death and failure to leave a successor to assume leadership fueled the Portuguese conquest of the interior of West Africa and the expansion of the Portuguese slave trade. A statute of Nzinga stands in her honor today in Angola.

In contrast, Nefertiti, perhaps the most powerful and mysterious woman to ever rule, commanded ancient Egypt during the mid-1300s B.C. alongside her husband, Pharaoh Akhenaten. They were parents of Tutankhamun, famously known as "King Tut." Akhenaten went to great lengths to assure the king and queen were depicted as equals. She appears almost twice as often as her husband in ancient Egyptian artwork. In addition to appearing behind her husband in offering scenes in the role of the queen supporting the pharaoh, she is illustrated in postures that would normally be reserved for a king in Egyptian depictions. For example, in scenes carved in the talatat (stone blocks used to build the temples), she is frequently portrayed wearing a crown, smiting her enemies, and riding in chariots with her husband. A bust of Nefertiti is one of the most famous symbols of Egypt and has become a global icon of feminine beauty and power.

It is also speculated that in an unprecedented move, she ruled outright after her husband's death, under the name Neferneferuaten.

These two powerful queens represent divergent approaches to partnering with men, and if you are an alpha female, you will have to decide which style best suits you — be it with an alpha or beta man. I'd be remiss if I didn't mention that it is a widely held stereotype that alpha females normally build long-lasting relationship with beta males, because they are more than willing to comply. Although the lure of a more cooperative, and in some cases more passive, male makes the beta man more appealing for some alpha women in relationships, if you are an alpha female you must find the right beta or alpha male to be happy in the long run. Otherwise, you may find yourself frustrated and overwhelmed with always having to be the one in charge, perpetually bored and wanting more out of your man. Luckily, all men and women exhibit alpha or beta male traits in various combinations and to various degrees.

KEY WAYS ALPHA AND BETA MEN ARE DIFFERENT FROM EACH OTHER

A little more insight into these men, however, may make your decision easier. Below is a chart that offers one possible explanation of how all alpha and beta men aren't created equally. In fact, there are at least three types of alpha and beta males, and while some are predatory or perpetrators, others are projects or prospects.

Three Types of Alpha Males	Three Types of Beta Males
Alpha male–ish	Beta male–ish
Predatory. He may be misogynistic and very capable of destroying or abusing you. Selfish, with almost a pathological disregard for others. Un-empathic. Challenging, but challenged. Not a true alpha male, he just possess some similar traits without the requisite solid character. He studies women much like a hunter studies the habits of a prized buck. He knows your fears, inhibitions, and secret desires, and he preys on them. Despite your virtues, he may not cherish you as a partner—or not even as a person for that matter—but as a challenge. The chase is much more important than the catch. May be charismatic, but superficial. This bad boy is just bad news. Avoid at all costs.	**Perpetrator**. He isn't misogynistic, but may secretly resent women because he doesn't understand them and gets rejected a lot and for seemingly superficial reasons. Other than neglecting you to death, emotionally speaking, he's some-what harmless. May destroy your desire to remain in the relationship or marriage, however. Self-focused with a disregard for what women and others tell him. He is tone-deaf and doesn't get it. Tends to be fake-nice, and at first glance appears to be a great guy. Yet, although agreeable and available, he strikes you as inauthentic, aloof, and rigid. You don't feel comfortable, but can't put your finger on why. If his counterpart is a marksman, he takes a shot-gun approach to identifying your needs, rambling on in his monologue, hoping he lucks up and says the right thing or somehow pushes a hot button. This nice guy isn't nice.

Alpha males	Beta males
Projects. These men have a real upside, and whether or not he is a keeper hinges on him having demonstrated sound character and his sincere desire to commit to you. Non-misogynistic, he genuinely loves himself and women. Two types of alpha male projects stand out here. Both possess high character. The first is the high-profile man who has arrived; the second is the man who is clearly going places and has the potential to be everything you want in a man. In either case, before investing too much time and energy with him, the key is to determine if he sees you as an option or a priority. Accept that he has many options, and if he hasn't classified you as a priority, he has deliberated his decision—and, frankly, given his strict code and trust of his gut instinct, chances are he isn't going to upgrade your classification. You likely will never be a priority. Move on and spare yourself the heartache.	**Projects**. These men have a real upside, and whether or not he is a keeper hinges on him demonstrating a willingness to accept your influence, focus on your emotional needs, and more adeptly attend to cues. Non-misogynistic, he genuinely loves himself and women. He may be a diamond in the rough —socially or aesthetically speaking —and the key here is determining if he is or isn't tone-deaf and fluid, which will define if he is indeed coachable. To make this decision, consider his habits, hobbies, associates, and career path, and determine how they might impact his trajectory. For example, a career in sales or a membership in Toastmasters or Aikido could develop needed listening and people skills. If he isn't socially graceful, consider how he responds to your gentle nudges suggesting improvements.
Alpha males who become gamma men	**Beta males who become gamma men**

Prospects. A reformed bad boy who is ready to get out of the game and commit, but will only do so with certain women.	Prospects. Nice guys who have come into their own, learned to listen, trust themselves, become self and people smart, and more fluid.
His integrity is unshakeable. He has a solid plan, a positive trajectory, and a proven history of professional success. He's a great catch!	He is willing to take appropriate risks, communicate directly, and handle conflict deftly. You feel an authentic connection with him, and he has developed a captivating presence. You truly enjoy his company. He's a great catch!

As this chart suggests, there are at least three distinct types of alpha and beta males. For these reasons, your first task is to determine if the man you are interested in is the alpha or beta male-ish man who may be a predatory or perpetrator type (who you should discard), the alpha or beta man with an upside who could be a project worth taking on, or the gamma man or great guy who was originally an alpha or beta male and is a prospect indeed — a real keeper, your Mr. Right.

Choosing among these various alpha and beta males can be confusing, as things aren't't always what they seem. For example, Huma Abedin, top aide to former Secretary of State Hillary Clinton, had a tough choice to make between what appeared to be an alpha male, actor George Clooney, and what appeared to be a gamma man, Congressman Anthony Weiner. She chose Weiner, who appeared to be the safer, nice guy. In reality, Weiner's behaviors and character, however, were more consistent with an alpha male-ish, predatory type who somewhat disingenuously presented himself as a gamma man. In sharp contrast, Clooney, who had been a confirmed bachelor and legendary ladies' man, was the better choice. His behaviors and character are consistent with an alpha male who had matured into a gamma male and was ready to leave the game. At age 53, Clooney would go on to marry Amal Alamuddin —

who looks strikingly similar to Abedin (and as of this printing date, there haven't been any reports of infidelity or other challenges of any sort).

Abedin got duped!

In what could only be described as a Greek tragedy, after a scandal involving him sexting pictures of his genitals to several women was uncovered and he initially vehemently and publicly denied sending them, Congressman Weiner would go on to leave office in public humiliation after it was revealed he indeed had sent them. For an encore, he would publicly humiliate Abedin again when he embarked upon a redemption bid for the New York City mayoral race, and was a leading contender in early polls. However, what could only be described as self-destructive behaviors and character flaws undermined this bid when a subsequent sexting scandal came to light. Weiner, using the alias "Carlos Danger," had unimaginably continued sexting three women after his resignation from Congress. Instead of resigning with dignity when news of the second sex scandal became public, he held a press conference with wife Abedin loyally by his side, where he said "other texts and photos were likely to come out." Despite calls by *New York Times* editorial board, amongst others, for him to leave the mayoral race, he defiantly remained in the campaign. He would go on to lose the primary with less than 5 percent of the vote.

While Weiner is more consistent with the predatory alpha male-ish man who erroneously appeared to be a gamma man, the beta male-ish man can be misleading, too.

Meet Mia and Justin. The pain felt by marrying a tone-deaf, self-focused man who perpetrates the image of being a great guy is well represented by Mia and Justin. Justin came into my office requesting marital therapy, while Mia felt they had irreconcilable differences and wanted to figure out how to co-parent their children after the divorce.

They met while in college at Prairie View University in Texas, where they both majored in architectural engineering. He was the geek who ended up with the "hot chick." Although she never felt chemistry or that thing with him, she thought he was a nice guy, and he was plenty smart, which meant a lot when they were studying together weekend nights and getting good grades. Ignoring reservations about her attraction and connection to him leading up to the marriage, coupled with her feeling she should marry the man to whom she had given her virginity, she figured why not marry him. She did, and they had twin girls. However, over the course of their marriage, he refused to court or spend quality time with her, and instead spent the majority of his free time on his computer and with his similarly introverted techy friends.

For the first few years of the marriage, she begged him to do marital therapy, and signed them up for several marriage bootcamps and webinars to strengthen their marriage. He refused to attend. Instead, he insisted she wasn't really unhappy, but was just frustrated with her lack of progression on her career since having the girls. Two years before they started therapy, she told him that a co-worker, Hank, was showering her with attention and she felt flattered. Admittedly arrogant, Justin told her to go out to lunch with him. She did and enjoyed it, which was followed by dinner, and ultimately breakfast—in bed. She then suggested to Justin that they try a separation, and he told her he'd help her find a place if she were so unhappy. She didn't move, but his dismissive and cavalier attitude hurt her deeply and irreparably. Meanwhile, the sparks kept flying between Mia and Hank, who was having his own marital problems.

When the couple came into my office, Justin remained tone-deaf to the reasons for her marital unhappiness and about how his aloofness made her feel alone, unloved, and abandoned in the marriage. He insisted they had a happy marriage, and she just had unrealistic expectations for a marriage because she came from a single-parent home. Instead, he blamed all of their marital problems on Mia's affair with Hank. He implored her to "quit being a whore" and work things out for the kids. Besides, he insisted, the detective he hired to snoop on Hank informed him that Hank was simply a womanizer who would never leave his wife, and that he lacked real substance and could never make her as happy as he could. After all, he was an architect and Hank was merely a sales representative. Why would she make such a downgrade? None of this changed her mind, and they separated. Mia was filing for divorce last we talked.

As Abedin and Mia discovered, alpha male-ish and beta male-ish men have some traits that lend to them behaving in a predatory or perpetrator-like fashion, respectively, that can make life miserable. These two types of men are to be avoided.

The next group of men discussed in this chart are alpha and beta males, men with an upside who might be projects worth taking on. Assuming he has solid moral character, is empathetic, and has a history of developing and executing his plan, he may be a worthwhile investment for your efforts. Whether he is the high-profile alpha male who has arrived, or the alpha male who is going places and has the potential to be everything you desire in a man, trust and believe, he has plenty of female options. Before pouring too much time and energy in him, it is imperative that you honestly assess whether or not you are just another one of his options (assuming you are OK with that) or a priority. Alpha males typically abide by a strict and unforgiving moral code, especially when it comes to women. As such, if he hasn't classified you as a priority, he has deliberated the matter and concluded you are merely an option (See Chapter 9, subtrACTION #2). Chances are you aren't going to be the one to inspire him to quit the game. Accept your fate, cut your losses with this man, and move on, sparing yourself the heartache.

Alternatively, if he is a beta male with an upside, it is imperative that you determine he isn't tone deaf and is indeed coachable—that is, you see changes and evolution in his growth based on the input he receives from you, other mentors, or significant influences. Should the alpha male with an upside make you feel you are indeed a long-term priority for him, or the beta male with an upside make you feel he can grow into the man you need (who can meet your needs), then you probably have a project worth taking on.

If you are interested in having the best of both worlds, you may have to look no further than the ideal gamma male — AKA great guys. Often ignored in popular magazines, gamma men come in three forms: 1) the pure gamma man who came into the universe that way, 2) the alpha male who grew up and toned down the antics slightly and started being socially conscious and more of a team player, or 3) the beta male who came into his own, found his voice, and started standing up to the rest of the world. All three types are keepers who will bring out your best. The reformed alpha males, like George Clooney; beta males, like Chris Rock, who came into his own despite being teased and ostracized as a kid; and the pure gamma men, like Colin Powell, are out there. Like Colin Powell, the gamma male uses diplomacy as his first line of defense, but when required, he will respond with adept force. He is aware of your needs and his own. He is fluid, sometimes being decisive and forceful, while sensitive and supportive at other times. Great guys treat people well and also stand up for their own principles. He isn't afraid to stand up to you just because he's attracted to you. He truly understands and respects himself.

Gamma men are catches!

There you have it: alpha, beta, and gamma men well defined. When deciding between these three types of men, it may be simpler to think of them like a traffic signal. That is, 1) if he is alpha or beta male-ish, then imagine a RED light and stop; 2) if he is an alpha or beta male, then imagine a YELLOW light and precede with caution until you get more information; or 3) if he is a gamma man, or has evolved into one, then imagine you have a GREEN light, so GO. You likely have a good catch.

That said, ultimately you have to trust your spiritual discernment when deciding which men meet this criteria and are worth the investment of your time and emotions. Please, accept that none of these group traits outweighs a man's character, level of empathy, propensity for self-focus, or spiritual development. Alpha or beta, a selfish or self-focused man is still that: a selfish man. At the same time, remember Malcolm X was originally known as "Detroit Red" — a sociopathic, predatory alpha male-ish felon. Yet a spiritual conversion embarked on during his incarceration transformed him from a criminal into one of the greatest civil rights leaders — and gamma men — of our time.

FIVE QUESTIONS EVERY WOMAN SHOULD ASK HERSELF BEFORE DECIDING WHICH MAN IS RIGHT FOR HER

Rather than weighing the pros and cons of these men, a better approach is to ask yourself which man best fits with who you are and what goals are most important for you to accomplish during your lifetime. Your man's personality traits and disposition — even worthy ones — are only beneficial if they are compatible with what you need from him to accomplish your long-term life goals.

1.   **"What do I desire most in a partner, and in life?"**

A typical approach to choosing between two lovers would be to start a list: "He is ..." or "He is not ..." Resist this temptation. Instead, begin with statements, like, "I want _____ out of my life." Sure, many of the items will describe desirable attributes you hope for in a partner, but by shifting the focus, you'll avoid defining the choice only in terms of him. You'll remember what you want out of life, and that you want a partner who helps you feel adventurous, helps you accomplish personal achievements, is authentic, provides a sense of security, or is a challenge. Then consider whether the alpha, beta, or gamma male in your life or that you desire is most likely to give you that lifestyle.

2.   **"What do I fear most — and least desire — in a man or relationship?"**

The polar opposite of desire is dread. If the question above is about discovering your personal "must haves," then this one is designed to remind you of your "must avoids." We all have fears based on life experiences and childhood wounds. Perhaps you dread the prospect of abandonment, feeling vulnerable by depending on a man, infidelity, living with an abusive man, or failing to meet your personal goals. Identifying your fears will help you see more clearly whether an alpha, beta, or gamma partner in your life (or that you desire) gives you the best chance of avoiding those fears.

3. **"Which man best compliments and maximizes my strengths?"**

If you were a super-heroine, what would your signature power be? And, if you were recruiting a sidekick, what traits would that man need to possess to best complement your own strengths? This question doesn't suggest your future relationship is all about you and playing to your strengths, as there will doubtlessly be times during the relationship when you will play Lois Lane to his Superman. When torn between two appealing options, you are always best served to understand your own strengths and to consider how the alpha, beta, and gamma male might enhance or diminish them.

4. **"Where and how do I need my man to make me a better woman?"**

To evaluate how your alpha, beta, or gamma man can impact or is impacting your life, assess both your and his weaknesses. Do you struggle with subordinates and co-workers at your company? Have trouble managing your finances? Give in to self-destructive eating habits? Engage in risky business investments or strive toward security to a fault? Are you overly engrossed in your career or company? Alpha, beta, and gamma men could buoy your personal and professional shortcomings differently, with all of them having the potential to make you a better or worse woman in the process. Understanding how your limitations and needs interact with these various males' dispositions is critical in choosing or making the most out of life with the partner you have chosen to positively impact your trajectory over a lifetime.

5. **"How will this relationship impact my life trajectory over the next 10, 20, or 30 years?"**

    There is no crystal ball that will predict the future, and any number of unforeseeable events can dramatically impact your life, rewrite your history, and alter the best-laid plans. Nevertheless, this shouldn't prohibit you from projecting the impact the alpha, beta, or gamma male you choose will have on your life over the coming decades. Namely, how will he or does he affect the pursuit of your life dreams and goals? Additionally, consider how you will impact his unique vision, and what type of common dreams you two will create together.

Summary: Whether you decide on an alpha, beta, or gamma man, no choice will be perfect. But when you must pick or have picked between these men, you have to consider which man gives you the best chance of realizing your short-term, intermediate, and long-term personal, professional, family, spiritual, financial, educational, self-development, and health goals.

CHAPTER 3

Is He Just a Good Date— or Is He My Soulmate?

You've met a new man, and it's going like you planned. Better yet, like you dreamed.

Wham! The chemistry jolted your body from the first kiss. He passes the all-important eye test, too. Plus, he's smart, funny, gets you, and is just the perfect height. You can complete each other's sentences. He's thinking about going back to college, and with your support he will. He just needs some polish, but you're sure with a little elbow grease he can be top brass. This one's definitely a keeper. Images of him in a tuxedo start to swirl around in your mind. He's got rhythm so that first dance will be a show stopper. Yeah, it's only been a few months, but you've never felt like this before.

At last, your chance at perfect love is finally here. You were on your very best behavior. You chased him, but let him catch you. You reeled in the big one. Finally, you get to declare your love and project all of your hopes and fantasies on to him.

You suspect he is your soulmate. As Whitney Houston sang, "How Will I Know?"

You say to yourself, "This love feels so right. Who could imagine a love so magical not lasting forever? Just watch us together: We have happily ever after written all over us. Right?"

Everyone hopes it works!

For a couple of months, all is well in paradise! Unexpectedly, something goes awry, and you two have your first fight. There was only one way to resolve it, and the choice was so obvious. Yet, he didn't get it. Initially, the disagreement seemed small. Surely, he will come to his senses and see it your way, but he doesn't. You notice a side of him you hadn't recognized before. Hearing your "objective" side of the story, your friends unanimously agree with you: You're selfless; he's selfish. Prince Charming has a wart — or two, maybe three.

How could he want to go to the CIAA basketball tournament (the Bayou Classic of college basketball) in Charlotte, North Carolina, with his boys? Doesn't he know men serious about the woman they love don't do stuff like that? All those blood-thirsty vixens down there will be on the prowl. In contrast, he is concerned that she wants him to stop hanging out with his road dogs. He knows they can be kind of wild, but they do this every year. Ugh! Why can't he/she see he/she is being so selfish?

Too bad your relationship manual didn't come with conflict resolution training, and you can't locate the secret formula on YouTube.

Your reaction is "how could you?" instead of what happened that "made you" feel so frustrated and hurt. Since this fight, conversations once light and easy become heavy and difficult. As Peabo Bryson sings in "This Masquerade": "We tried to talk it over, but the words got in the way."

The soulmate's graveyard is littered with couples who couldn't make the transition from romantic love to mature love. Instead, they faltered when their expectations and projections onto one another intersected with the reality of who they actually were, prematurely shoveling dirt on their graves. Because couples mistake romantic love for soulmate love, they expect every interaction to always be filled with magic. Nevertheless, the true magic of soulmate love is the couple's ability to mature by working through life's challenges together, turning toward instead of away from each other in times of conflict, and developing the skills needed to start approaching conflicts in an "I'm OK. You're OK" vs "I'm OK. You're not OK" fashion.

LOVE CAN BE AN ADDICTIVE DRUG: HOW TO AVOID GETTING STRUNG OUT

Soulmates appreciate that the magic lies in finding ways for both partners to get at least some of their needs met and their feelings heard during their conflicts, while partners in the romantic phase of love sometimes let the magical feelings of love blind them to their partner's needs. If they aren't careful, their shortsighted focus on getting their needs met at the expense of their partner's needs can result in their partner checking out of the relationship. This is the romantic equivalent of cutting off your nose to spite your face. Once their partner checks out, because love triggers chemical reactions within the body, the jilted partner may find herself literally going through withdrawal. "But, I felt such powerful chemistry," the spurned lover gripes. Her comment accurately reflects her physiological experience.

To help humans remain committed to one partner for the protection of offspring and the survival of the species, love triggers the release of a potent cocktail of neurotransmitters to help us bond—namely, Phenylethylamine (or PEA), norepinephrine, oxytocin, endorphins, and dopamine. PEA is a stimulant, much like the amphetamine-based chemical found in chocolate, responsible for that head-over-heels, elated feeling. Norepinephrine causes the palms to sweat and the heart to pound, and a growing body of research suggests the oxytocin released in high-trust relationships stimulates a woman's production of the cuddle hormone. Love also triggers the release of endorphins (a morphine-like substance originating within the body), which is an opiate associated with attachment and comfort. Finally, falling in love is associated with elevated levels of dopamine in the brain, which is linked to cravings and dependency and leads to extremely focused attention, causing partners to block out everything and everyone around them — and lock in on their partners. Together, the release of these neurotransmitters produces a powerful mix that can lead to addiction and withdrawal should one partner abruptly detach.

During conflicts, partners can become angry when they suddenly realize the high associated with their new love is a short-lived one. As they experience withdrawal, some partners allow the shortage of these neurotransmitters to lead them to resent their detached partner, and this love jones can prevent them from trying to uncover their partner's reason for retreating. ("What role did I play in them rejecting such a promising relationship?") Instead, the pain associated with their withdrawal leads them to become forceful, demanding to secure more of their new drug of choice. Feeling coerced and sensing their needs aren't important, the checked-out partner becomes even more distant. Unlike these romantic lovers, soulmate lovers systematically overcome the need to be emotionally forceful or needy, and focus on making their partner feel their needs are a top priority — and that they will try to fix the problem that caused them to shut down. This looks something, like, "Enjoy your weekend and I hope your team wins." Ironically, soulmate lovers' ability to focus on their partner's needs and minimize the effect of withdrawal pains live to get high another day.

Such is the nature of soulmate love.

Soulmate lovers who make it truly accept that their partner wouldn't be so hurt if they didn't have a valid point—whether they agree with that point or not. They make the decision to sacrifice the short-term feeling "they are right" for the longer-term practice of "being effective," by attempting to discover how in some regard they are both right. He needs to know their relationship will make space for his friends and respect his need for independence. She needs to feel their relationship will be secure and respected. In the long run, the process of making each other feel heard is more important than the point being articulated. The extent to which both partners' needs are addressed will determine the relationship's fate.

This is the reason that the person who's truly right for you may be cleverly disguised as the man you interact with every day. Yes, the unassuming and quiet confidant who you've peacefully interacted with in your close circle of friends for the last few years. He has seen you at your best and at your worst, and proved he can partner with and appreciate you on both occasions.

Perhaps, your Mr. Right isn't actually the man you have projected your fantasies on to.

I know that doesn't sound magical or even romantic. But soulmate love is a combination of both romantic and mature love if it is to stand the test of time.

KEYS FOR DETERMINING IF HE IS A CLASSMATE OR SOULMATE

To decide if he is your classmate or soulmate, take a closer look at how he interacts with you and makes you feel on a daily basis, and how he will likely impact your life trajectory over time. Instead of that intoxicating and fleeting feeling romantic love induces, let your answer to these questions inform you of the role he is meant to play in your life. The term "classmate" here represents someone with whom you share a definite soul-tie, but their purpose or role is to teach you (and learn from you) important life lessons—and maybe to help prepare you for your eventual soulmate. As Caroline Myss writes in *Sacred Contracts*, spirits travel in packs and often have prearranged agreements to meet up in this life at critical junctures to teach us important life lessons, or to prepare us for, or assist us with an important purpose. Although both classmates and soulmates may elicit strong emotional feelings and attachments, they are not one in the same.

Chances are he's a classmate if:

1.   He characteristically makes you feel anxious, insecure, unhappy, or miserable. All I can say here is that pain is unavoidable, staying around and suffering is optional. For example, if you are involved in a love triangle, that is not soulmate love, whether you are the other woman or the main woman looking the other way. Remember Dorothy in the *Wizard of Oz*: All you have to do is click your heels three times.

2.   It feels like it's too much work — and you are doing most of it. For example, it feels more like 80 percent you — 20 percent him, instead of feeling like it should feel, which is more like 100 percent you — 100 percent him.

     Note: While your relative financial contributions may differ, the commitment to the relationship's success, level of support, and love should feel the same. It shouldn't be a struggle, which isn't to say you won't have struggles. You won't have to drag a soulmate along; he will be by your side or take the lead.

3.   You two argue and fight over the same things all of the time, and things never get better. While all couples have growing pains and will have to learn to partner and resolve their problems, soulmate lovers strive to hear each other out so the source of their problems is identified, acknowledged, and fixed. By definition, they partner in a healthy way that empowers them to turn *toward* each other and not turn *on* each other in times of conflict. Soulmates ultimately take pride in how life's challenges and their differences have strengthened their partnership, enabled

them to grow closer, and developed the confidence and skills to know they can stand the test of time.

4. He brings out the worst in you. For example, soulmate love doesn't cause you to humiliate yourself by compulsively calling or pursuing someone who doesn't respect you enough to return your calls (and you don't keep disrespecting yourself by calling). If he isn't that into you, then wait until he is, or make room for a soulmate who really is into you. (Again, just click three times, Dorothy.)

5. The decision to be with him is fear-based, stemming from a scarcity of good men outlook. A soulmate is a man you want to be alone with, not a man who you are with because you are afraid of being alone.

6. The decision to be with him isn't practical—financially, educationally, or emotionally. Yes, opposites attract, but you two have to have enough in common and share enough common goals to be able to coexist peacefully in and navigate each others' worlds. He must have a vision and a plan; not one wing and a prayer. "I'm OK. You're not OK, but I can fix you" is maybe more about being classmates than soulmates. You must genuinely respect and admire some aspect about him. Soulmate lovers don't ask you to choose between your relationship and your family and friends.

7. Your relationship is steeped in hyper-critical, defensive, or contemptuous behaviors. Although your relationship should push you out of your comfort zone, Soulmate love doesn't make you feel uncomfortable—AKA, like "You aren't OK." The impact of not "being OK" over the course of your life will likely prove catastrophic in one form or another—emotionally, physically, and spiritually. Even worse, that catastrophic effect could leave a generational curse on your children and grandchildren.

Chances are he's a soulmate if:

1. He characteristically uplifts, strengthens, empowers, enhances, expands, and replenishes you. Soulmate love

complements who you naturally are and pushes you to realize your supernatural potential.

2.   It just feels right: when you are with him, with others, and alone. It doesn't have to feel perfect, but it should feel comfortable and unforced in any major way. You two aren't crowded by all the elephants in the room.

3.   It is honest. Both partners maintain their integrity, self-respect, and dignity. Soulmate lovers can let their hair down with each other, feel comfortable, and are willing to risk being vulnerable. They can look in the mirror and feel good about their relationship and themselves.

4.   It is based on love not fear. A soulmate is someone you would like your son to grow up to be like. You genuinely admire, respect, and like him. That doesn't mean he is perfect or you two don't have any challenges. Rather, it means despite those imperfections and challenges, if you had to ask for another partner, your soulmate lover is the type of man you would pray for him to be like.

5.   It makes practical sense—emotionally, intellectually, and financially. No matter who earns more, is more educated, or has the most dynamic personality, in the long run, soulmates complement and add value to each other's lives in a way where the benefits outweigh the perceived costs or financial bottom lines.

6.   It allows each partner to hear (and feel heard by) their partner. This is not to say there still won't be miscommunication sometimes, but soulmate lovers give each other the benefit of the doubt and trust their partner has another side of the story worth trying to understand.

7.   He loves you back. Soulmate love is mutually fulfilling. You two start and end your discussions about your differences with an "I'm OK. You're OK" assumption. Over the course of your life, the rewards for such a love are abundant emotionally, physically, and spiritually.

As you attempt to discern if he is your classmate or a soulmate, be still and accept what your spirit tells you. It always knows. If there is a lesson you need to learn from your classmate, learn it, embrace it, and get on with it. The soulmate love God is preparing you for may be around the corner.

WHAT SEAN PENN AND MADONNA CAN TEACH YOU ABOUT WHETHER YOUR MAN IS A SOULMATE OR CLASSMATE

They met in February 1985 on the set of her "Material Girl" video. The rough-edged Sean Penn, a rebel who starred in the movie "Bad Boy," was one of America's hottest serious young actors. She was, well, Madonna. Their budding friendship quickly gave way to a tumultuous romance. Attractive, famous, rich, and with an unimaginable upside, the young ultimate power couple seemed to have it all. Clearly smitten, Madonna dedicated her third studio album "True Blue" to Penn, and designated him "the coolest guy in the universe." They appeared to be the very picture of soulmate love. Right? It was a no-brainer. In September 1985, they got married. Judge John Merrick, who married them, said, "I felt they were as much in love as any couple I've married, and I've married hundreds of them." Neither of these lovebirds, nor anyone else, seemed to care much that they hadn't known each other for very long, nor noticed their personality differences or the conflicts they were beginning to cause. Before getting married, Madonna said, "We have so much in common that he's almost like my brother."

Yet just four years later, the material girl and her rebel-without-a-cause husband's high-octane marriage would sputter, ending in divorce. Was anyone surprised? By the time they divorced – no. The real mystery was what took so long. After watching in horror as he pulled out a gun and fired at a hovering helicopter that intruded on their wedding day to take pictures, it was clear this wouldn't be a storybook marriage. Madonna, by all accounts, was screaming at him to stop being so crazy. "What's the big deal, Sean?" she protested. Guests, including Andy Warhol and Cher, looked on in astonishment. Friends and insiders would come to refer to them as the "Poison Penns" — or S&M. (Jada Pinkett-Smith and Will Smith they were not.) They were opposites who had initially seemed cosmically attracted to each other. He detested the lime light; she seemed insatiably drawn to having one shine on her every move. He was a possessive, controlling, gun-toting, jealous recluse with anger management issues; she was a free-spirited, fun-loving, unruly non-conformist who never met a boundary she felt bound to accept. She kept lovers and ex-boyfriends around, openly courting the attention of the media, other men, and women.

The tension created by their differences took a turn for the worse when Madonna's friendship with the openly bisexual Sandra Bernhard evolved into something else. The pair was spotted around town and the world hugging, cradling, and kissing one another. Penn failed to see the humor in his wife's latest escapades. Nor could he accept the news that, without his knowledge, Madonna had secured the role of Breathless Mahoney in Warren Beatty's movie, "Dick Tracy." Violating her earlier commitment for the couple to have a baby in 1989, she told him they would have to postpone their plans for a family until another time. (Madonna would later date Beatty, and is rumored to have dated Bernhard.)

Fueled by distrust, rage, and jealously, Penn's infamous temper lead to a series of altercations with his wife, the press, her friends, and other Hollywood types. Many of Madonna's closest friends came to dislike him. As Penn's erratic and violent behavior grew increasingly out of control, the world would come to share their misgivings. Growing increasingly estranged, they separated. The distance and tension between the two came to a dramatic and violent climax when a frustrated and drunk Penn staked out Madonna's Malibu house, scaled the fence, broke in, and confronted a horrified Madonna. After slapping her around, he bound and gagged her, then strapped her to a chair with twine. He berated and beat her for two hours, and *then stormed out of the house, only to later return and began tormenting her all over again. When she managed to persuade him to untie her to perform some sexual act, she dashed out of the house and fled in the vintage 1957 Thunderbird he had given her for her 28th birthday. She called the police. He was charged with felony domestic assault, but Madonna later dropped the charges and he pled to a misdemeanor.*

A week after the incident, on Jan. 5, 1989, Madonna filed for divorce on grounds of irreconcilable differences. In four years Madonna and Penn had gone from holy matrimony to unholy acrimony. She invoked the couple's prenuptial agreement concerning the division of property, allowing her to keep her personal income, which amounted to $30 million a year for each of the three years they were married, while Penn's salary was roughly $1 million per picture. Her estimated worth was $70 million compared to his net worth of $5 million. Under the terms of the prenuptial agreement, each got to keep what they brought into the marriage and the money they earned during it.

From the book "Madonna Unauthorized," by Christopher Andersen. Copyright 1991.

OPRAH'S INTERVIEW WITH PENN REVEALS THEY WERE DESTINED TO BE 'CLASSMATES,' NOT SOULMATES

Note: This interview appeared in the January 2005 issue of *O, The Oprah Magazine*. The dialogue printed here contains only excerpts from that interview.

Oprah: *What did your marriage to Madonna teach you?*

Sean: *… It was a miserable marriage, but it got me … knowing what I wanted.*

Sean: *She was a phenom … Frankly, I don't recall having a single conversation in four years of marriage. I've talked to her a couple of times since, and there's a whole person there. I just didn't know it.*

Sounds like a clearly more mature Sean Penn is saying Madonna was a great date, but despite their chemistry, wasn't meant to be his soulmate. They both made the mistake of marrying each other.

INDICATORS THAT PREDICT LONG-TERM RELATIONSHIP SUCCESS

To best predict your relationship's future, consider the findings of world renowned marital scholar Dr. John Gottman. His ability to predict marital outcomes accurately is legendary. For example, in a 1992 study, Dr. Gottman predicted with 93.6 percent accuracy which couples would divorce. Voted one of the 10 most influential therapists of the past quarter century, Dr. Gottman has authored or co-authored over 40 books based on the research with thousands of couples he and wife, Dr. Julie Gottman, have conducted at his Love-Labs housed out of the University of Washington department of psychology, and he has identified specific behavior patterns in couples that predict whether they become what he termed the "Marriage Masters" or "Marriage Disasters."

(As mentioned earlier in this book, Dr. Gottman's work was so impressive I elected to complete his Level I, II, and III training programs.)

While he received his Ph.D. in clinical psychology, Dr. Gottman received his master's degree in mathematics from MIT, and in his book, *The Mathematics of Marriage*, he employs mathematical modeling to identify traits and behavioral patterns that are reliable predictors of marital success and failure. One of his theories, "the Four Horsemen of the Apocalypse," identifies four traits and associated behaviors that are the proverbial serial killers of relationships and highly predictive of divorce. The four negative behaviors he described are contempt, defensiveness, criticism, and stonewalling.

First, contempt is feeling as though you have a superior argument to your partner, which allows you to feel as though you have taken the moral high ground in your arguments. From a Transactional Analysis perspective, contempt is taking an "I'm

OK. You're not OK" position toward your relationship problems. Your communications and interactions have a condescending flavor to them, as you treat each other with disrespect whereby one or both of you typically feels despised or worthless.

Second, defensiveness is seeing yourself as the blameless victim. Consequently, instead of addressing each other's concerns, you engage in defensive behaviors, such as a) cross-complaining: instead of addressing each other's concerns, you respond with a complaint of your own; b) ignoring your partner altogether; c) "yes-butting" your partner. You start off by seeming to agree, but inevitably you disagree; or d) repeating your point or complaint without acknowledging each other's complaint, almost as if his complaint were never made.

Third, criticism is attacking each other at the core, in a deeply personal fashion. For example, "You never think of anyone but yourself. But, your behavior is affecting everyone in the family. I don't think you are forgetful; I think you don't care. You're just selfish. You never think of our children or me."

Finally, stonewalling is withdrawing from the relationship to avoid conflict. You simply don't respond to your partner and shut down the interaction. You may think you are being neutral, but in reality you are expressing your disapproval and creating distance, separation, and disconnection. You are being smug. A second aspect of stonewalling involves increased heart rate. Despite a detached appearance, these partners' pulse readings typically register well over 100 beats per minute (or, above 80 beats per minute for conditioned athletes). Normal resting heart rate is typically 60 bpm to 100 bpm. Studies have shown after the heart beat rises above 100 beats per minute, we lose our ability to take in or process new information. For this reason, stonewallers can no longer hear their partner and don't react to new information, but remain fixed on their previous understanding of the conflict. Accordingly, it's not uncommon to ask a stonewaller to repeat her partner's point in an argument, and she simply can't, because she didn't hear him in the first place. Conflict resolution skills go out of the window until the partner is in a calmer state.

No matter how justified you feel about being critical, contemptuous, defensiveness, or stonewalling, they are relationship killers, and you and your man won't live happily ever after. Soulmates find a way to saddle these four horsemen.

WHAT NEWLYWEDS CAN TEACH YOU ABOUT YOUR RELATIONSHIP'S FUTURE SUCCESS

In a study of 130 newlywed couples in his Love-Lab, Dr. Gottman discovered that positivity expressed during conflict discussions predicted the newlyweds' relationship stability over a six-year period after the wedding and their overall happiness. Of the 17 couples who later divorced, all started off their conflict discussions with significantly greater displays of negative emotion and fewer expressions of positive emotion, when compared with couples who remained married over the course of the six-year study.

In *Making Love Last*, Dr. Gottman predicts the future of your relationship should you bridle negative behaviors like the four horsemen of the apocalypse that undermine positivity, or you allow them to trample through your relationship. To predict these couples' futures, he used an observational coding system to assess couples' interactions while having 15-minute conflict conversations, placing these couples behaviors into one of three categories based on their discussion: The "Nice" box, the "Neutral" box, and the "Nasty" box.

In the "Nice" box, he placed all positive emotions and behaviors, such as laughter, joking, smiling, validation, compliments, and empathy; and affirmative body language, such as leaning forward as your partner talks.

In the "Nasty" box, he housed all negative emotions and behaviors, such as anger, criticism, contempt, defensiveness, stonewalling, fear, disgust, disappointment, sadness, and bullying; and negative body language, such as crossing one's arms and leaning back or frowning.

The evaluators placed all other emotions and behaviors in the "Neutral" box.

Dr. Gottman found that happy couples spent more time in the "Nice" and "Neutral" boxes. At the same time, he recognized that even the happiest couples didn't always remain in the Nice box. Perhaps here is where couples' future outcomes are distinguished. When happy couples' tempers flared, they were more likely to either go to the Neutral box (and avoid the Nasty box altogether), or if they went to the Nasty box, they remained there for a shorter period of time than unhappy couples. Further, happy couples exhibited an almost surgical precision during critical junctures of the conflict discussions to successfully direct the partner's behaviors back toward the Nice box. He described these interventions as "repair attempts." For example, while in the midst of a conflict, one partner might make a self-effacing joke, make a concession, or offer a compromise. In return, the other partner demonstrates their trust in their partner by accepting this repair attempt, and diffusing the tension long enough to change the discussion's tone so that it is redirected to the Neutral or Nice box. In contrast, if a couple's conflict discussion escalates despite a partner's repair attempt, then couples remain ensnared in a downward spiral toward the despair associated with the Nasty box.

He next discussed the Neutral box, which he surprisingly described as the source of some of his "most exciting findings." At first glance, Dr. Gottman writes, it seemed as though these couples would bore each other to death or weren't particularly invested in helping each other resolve their conflict-related concerns. Nothing could be further from the truth. Despite the fact that they didn't use repair attempts too often, it seems like they didn't have to. In a study of couples aged in their mid-forties and sixties, Dr. Gottman found happy couples spent 65 percent of their time in the Neutral box when they disagreed, compared to 47 percent for unhappy couples. You won't find videos of Neutral box couples' fights that go viral on YouTube because they simply don't possess the emotional fireworks, dramatic breakups, and makeups shared by couples in dramatized love that you see on Reality TV. Yet, these couples are far likelier to live happily ever after than our more dramatic Nasty box couples.

Finally, unhappy couples spent far more time in the Nasty box. While all couples spend time in this box at some point, unhappy couples spend so much time here they end up feeling an impenetrable state of negativity, cynicism, and contempt, which frequently leads them to what Dr. Gottman calls the "roach motel for lovers." Couples check in, but rarely check out.

Couples I encounter in the Nasty box frequently say they don't like to fight, but their partners give them no choice and they rationalize their decision to reject their partner's repair attempts. They also seem to take relief in the notion that their partner metaphorically drove them to the roach motel, made the reservations, or decided to make their visit an extended stay. Candidly, if you are at the roach motel, it doesn't matter who's responsible for how you got there. Whether you ignored your partner's repair attempt, or didn't make a repair attempt of your own, your relationship will suffer all the same. Dr. Gottman's extensive research predicts roach motel dwellers are far more likely to fail — be it remaining in an unhappy marriage or ending in divorce.

TO GET A GLIMPSE INTO YOUR FUTURE TOGETHER, SIMPLY NOTE IN WHICH BOX YOU TWO SPEND THE MOST TIME

Be honest with yourself here. If you are in the Nice vs Nasty box at a 5:1 ratio, I imagine you have a happy relationship; conversely, if the ratio is 1:5, I imagine you are unhappy. While being in the Nasty box doesn't doom your relationship, I recommend you consider talking to a professional if you and your partner can't independently stem this tide. In short, if you and your partner have a tendency to reside at the roach motel, I suggest you consider closely studying Dr. Gottman's predictions for your relationship's future.

While they may visit from time to time, soulmates don't do extended stays or take up permanent residence in the roach motel, no matter how good the rates.

(This brief summary of Dr. Gottman's work scratches the surface. I highly recommend you get a copy of his landmark book, *Making Love Last*. It's a real game-changer.)

THERE ARE TWO SIDES TO EVERY STORY— AND IF YOU WANT LOVE TO LAST YOU NEED TO UNDERSTAND BOTH

Soulmate lovers understand they must develop the ability to resolve their conflicts effectively and get out of the Nasty box for their relationship to stand the test of time. Of the Five Cs (Choice, Commitment, Communication, Conflict Resolution Skills and Coach-ability) that distinguish happy from unhappy couples, conflict resolution skills will ultimately determine if your romantic love matures into soulmate love. Thankfully, it is one of the more coachable skills. To compromise in relationships, partners have to accept that it is a myth that there is only one perspective: yours. In reality, there are at least two truths: yours and his. Only in math is there one absolute truth: 2 + 2 = 4. In life there are always at least two sides to every story, and both have some validity. For example, if I call a businessman in Asia for a meeting, and afterwards I say "good night" only to be corrected by him "you meant 'good morning,' right?" Both of us are correct. Truth be told, our perspectives reflect our relative position from to the sun, which determines whether it is rising or setting. Other than in math, there are always two truths.

As self-evident as the Law of Two Truths might seem, partner after partner in therapy insists they alone hold the one truth and are right, and their partner is completely wrong. Their sense of feeling right is further justified when they share their distorted version of the truth with their friends, who co-sign on it. Instantly, their truth becomes legitimized, and thus, mysteriously truer. Next, they make the mistake of believing that if their friends agree with them, they must be right. And deep down, their man must know she is right and he is wrong, but some character flaw stops him from doing the right thing. It's hard to admire a man with such obvious flaws and selfish tendencies, so the fertile seeds of discontent, contempt, and resentment are sown.

In reality, the Myth of One Truth is a fallacy.

Some aspect of his truth must be valid. How could he be your Mr. Right if he were truly so wrong so often? Sabrina came in to a group therapy session for women, and told us what an ingrate Jerry was because he refused her offer to cook for him on Super Bowl Sunday. All of the women in the group co-signed on him being an ingrate and a self-absorbed narcissist. They showed him little mercy. Later that week, Jerry came to couples therapy with Sabrina and explained that he loved his wife's cooking and appreciated her gesture. However, he informed me that her anal-retentive tendencies would ruin Super Bowl Sunday for him. "Doc, if she cooks, the whole family must get up early Sunday morning to thoroughly clean the kitchen and dining room, prep the food, and join in on the cooking. If we get up at 8, we won't have food ready until 11:30. Once we finish the family meal, we must thoroughly clean the kitchen and dining room, mopping all the floors down and putting the food away in vacuum-packed storage containers for the week. By the time this rigorous process is completed, it's 3:30 p.m., and my daughter and I have missed the pre-game show. We just want to enjoy the pre-game festivities and watch the game. Hell, we can eat chicken wings or pizza for all I care."

When partners operate under the assumption that there is only one truth, they tend to avoid looking at their role in the conflict. Because they squarely place the blame on their partner's shoulders, they tend to remain angry. Think about it: Have you able been able to forgive someone when you truly felt they were wrong and you were right? Conversely, have you ever been able to remain mad at someone when you knew they were right and you were wrong? Soulmate lovers have the uncanny ability to acknowledge both truths. That is, they trust each other enough to hear where he is "kind of right" and to get him to hear where she is "kind of right" and go on to discover where she is "kind of wrong" and where he is "kind of wrong." Recognizing and acknowledging both truths is the only way you can truly forgive your man (and be forgiven by him) and move on so the conflict stops emerging in subsequent fights. Accepting the Law of Two Truths empowers partners to meet each other's needs during conflicts and is reminiscent of Transactional Analysis (see Chapter 1), which empowers partners to meet each other's needs during conflicts by acknowledging "You're OK" and "I'm OK." Accordingly, they acknowledge each others' side holds a valid truth. Both are OK in some important respect. Besides, if you didn't truly feel your man is OK, you would certainly not be fighting for the relationship.

All the same, many partners in unhappy relationships insist their truth is the only truth and that their partner "Is not OK." In conflict conversations, these partners tend to use what Dr. Gottman labeled "harsh start-ups," where one partner starts the conversation by showing contempt for their partner's position. For example, a woman who slapped her man's daughter said to me in our martial therapy session, "He's just a pathological liar and a wimp, doesn't know how to honor his wife, and won't accept his daughter is a sociopath." (Yes, I hear this type of stuff all the time.) I asked her if this were true, why would she still want him? "I love him. He is a good man," she said. It didn't sound like soulmate love to me. I shared with her that I wasn't sure how to help her. "I can't make a pathological liar truthful, transform a wimp into a strong man, nor can I fix his daughter if she is indeed a sociopath, or get him to abandon her if she were a sociopath," I said. "Even worse, I can't undo the damage caused by the Nasty box insults that wounded his manhood and made him want to hide his beloved daughter from you."

Herein lies the danger of buying into the Myth of One Truth: Very few partners will agree that "You are OK" — and they "Are not OK," even if the facts are overwhelmingly on your side. Nevertheless, let's say you are right—"he's not OK, but you're OK." Why stay? Leaving should be a no-brainer. Who remains with a man who isn't OK and has a sociopath for a daughter?

No one. Worse, instead of him making the changes you desire, your harsh start-up has resulted in him disagreeing with you, at best, and resenting you, at worst.

To avoid such a disastrous outcome and to get him to buy into the changes you desire, I recommend you attempt what Dr. Gottman termed a "soft-startup," which invites you to first authentically acknowledge precisely how he is OK, and talk about those positive aspects of his position for three minutes before offering any criticisms. For example, "I recognize you are a good father and husband who is trying to raise his daughter the right way and love his wife, even though the two of us haven't figured out how to work through our differences just yet. This must be a difficult position to find yourself in. I admire your commitment to both of the significant women in your life. Let's figure out how to make this a teachable moment, find a way to resolve this conflict, and create peace between your daughter and me." Researchers agree with the effectiveness of using soft start-ups and avoiding a harsh start-up, as studies have found 93 percent of conversations that start with a criticism in the first three minutes end in an argument. Drs. S. Carrère and J.M. Gottman found that the tone of the startup employed during the conflict discussion was key to predicting divorce or marital stability.

Always consider which box you are communicating from. If you aren't coming from the Nice or Neutral box, remember happy couples find a way to pivot from the Nasty box to the Nice box. In stable marriages, both husbands and wives express less negativity and more positivity during the first three minutes of these conflict discussions.

IS HE JUST A GOOD DATE—OR IS HE MY SOULMATE?

CHAPTER 4

Seven Steps to Using the Law of Attraction to Attract Mr. Right—and Repel Mr. Wrong

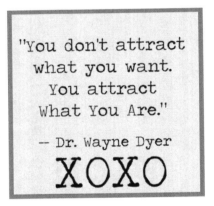

"You don't attract
what you want.
You attract
What You Are."

-- Dr. Wayne Dyer

XOXO

"We are like magnets—like attracts like. You become *and* attract what you think."
—Unknown

"Nothing is impossible.
The word itself says "I'm Possible."
—Audrey Hepburn, Actress

"Don't chase anything.
Be yourself, do your own thing, and work hard.
The right people—the ones who really belong in
your life—will come to you. And stay."
—Will Smith, Actor, Rapper, Husband, and Father

Years ago a women's group invited me to speak at their book club after hearing me do an interview on the law of attraction in relationships. They were reading *The Secret* by Rhonda Byrne. After the book discussion, the women read their lists describing the men they wanted and asked for my professional input on their ideal mate. I agreed that the men they described in their lists would be good catches. Then, I asked them how similar they were to the Mr. Right they described. Not to my surprise, I got some icy stares.

MISPERCEPTIONS ABOUT THE LAW OF ATTRACTION

One woman asked why it mattered that they be alike—"Don't opposites attract?" she asked.

Yes, opposites do attract. Nonetheless, it is a myth that the law of attraction gives you whatever you ask for; rather it gives you more of what you are. Put simply, you have to be what the other person is asking for, too. In a nutshell, like attracts like. Not wanting to lay a wet blanket on their desires to manifest their Mr. Right in their lives, I shared a quote my older brother had once given me, "Alas, I finally found the perfect woman, only to find I wasn't the perfect man." Next, I observed the men on their lists looked like Denzel Washington with LeBron James' body, Bob Johnson's financial acumen (and bank account), Chris Rock's blend of intellect and humor, Steve Erkel's (from "Family Matters") sense of honesty and loyalty, and Malcolm X's integrity and respect for women. "How many of you could be that man's Ms. Right, right now?" I asked. A middle-aged woman insightfully responded as she sucked her stomach in and poked her butt out, "I might have to do a little work on me first."

We chuckled.

This approach to the law of attraction is all too common, and it seems somewhere along the way this law has gotten a bad rap. In addition to those willing to put in the work to provide an even exchange for what they are trying to attract, many believers have developed a sense of entitlement.

Another myth about the law of attraction is that it is a newly discovered concept pioneered in *The Secret*. On the contrary, it has been around for centuries, if not since the beginning, when God forbade Adam and Eve from biting into the apple from the tree of knowledge (Genesis 2:17). God knew the power of man's thoughts to manifest both good and evil. Another biblical example, "As a man thinketh in his heart, so is he," from Proverbs 23:7, which inspired the critically acclaimed and widely popular essay, "As a Man Thinketh," by James Allen, published in 1902. Jesus describes the impact our thoughts have on our health: "And He said unto her, Daughter, thy faith hath made thee whole: go in peace, and be whole of thy plague," Mark 5:34. Consistent with Bible, Wayne Dyer refers to discovering earlier uses of the power of our thoughts 2,500 years ago in the *Tao Te Ching* which is written by Lao Tzu. Lao Tzu says, "If you live from these virtues, then all that you could ever need or want could be provided for you."

No matter what you call it, the law of attraction, self-actualization, or pro-active visualization, all have been around for a long time. And all instruct their followers to employ the intention to attract their desires into reality.

A helpful way to think of the law of attraction is to think of your thoughts as seeds in a garden. You first plant those seeds, and over time, they begin to grow and one day manifest fruit. The fruit produced is determined by the nature of the seed planted. If you plant an apple seed, you will produce an apple tree, but if you plant an acorn you can expect it to grow into an oak. The type of seed or thought you plant will determine the fruit you bear. Further, as in nature, you need to nourish the thoughts you plant, give them time to grow, and prune the weeds. You can't keep digging it up or nourish it in a fashion contrary to its nature. For example, you can't shower a cactus with water. Your actions will determine if the seed takes root, dies, or lives and one day blossoms.

Similarly, your thoughts will eventually manifest themselves into the man that is drawn into your life and your relationship with him. Initially you will still attract the type of men you don't want, which will seem to contradict the law of attraction, but just stick with it and prune the undesirable men quickly. Even if it means you may be alone, you must remain clear that you are no longer open to toxic relationships. Hold out for the man you asked for, keeping your thoughts and behaviors consistent with the type of man you hope to attract. Most followers of the law of attraction want things, and they want to force them to happen now; they become demanding. The universe doesn't work that way. You have to start (and continue) to think and behave in a manner that allows the things you want to happen.

The law of attraction is also more accurate than many suspect. You need to ask for and think about precisely what you want, not what you don't want. As much as thinking about not falling off the balance beam in gymnastics will make you fall, you have to think about completing the next trick in your routine, and staying on the beam. Likewise, thinking about not being alone or hurt again will likely materialize a far different man than thinking about what type of relationship will make you happy. Think about what specific type of man you want to attract into your life, what specific behaviors you are going to start to engage in to attract him and eliminate pretenders, and what specific type of relationship you want to have with him once you attract him.

SEVEN STEPS TO HELP EMPOWER YOU TO MATERIALIZE THE MR. RIGHT YOU DESIRE – AND REPEL MR. WRONG

Step 1. Decide Whether Fear or Love Will Govern Your Choices in Men

If you are asked to choose between selecting a man because of love or fear, your answer seems obvious. Of course, you will choose love! But that's when you are answering this question about a hypothetical man. The reality is that when faced with the task of making decisions about our personal relationships, many of our decisions are all too often governed by fear, consciously or not.

So ask yourself, "Did I choose him or stay with him because I love the way he makes me feel, or because I fear there is a shortage of men, so I better take what I can get?" Shifting your perspective of the universe from a pond of shortage to the ocean of surplus could prove revolutionary. As Dr. Wayne Dyer says, "Change the way you look at things and the things you look at will change." Fearing the universe is in short supply of men makes you more likely to accept or hold onto Mr. Wrong who doesn't meet your basic needs. In contrast, trusting the universe has a surplus of men makes you more likely to hold out for Mr. Right who does meet your needs and standards. You will know you've made the transition from a shortage to a surplus perspective when you start making your relationship decisions based on what you love versus what you fear.

Disclaimer: Before I go too far into the shortage versus surplus approach, let me recognize there is a real problem in terms of the ratio of African American women to men. Here is one place in the book where I'd be remiss if I didn't acknowledge that my being a Black male presents a limitation. As an African American man, I've grown up with the reality that another together Black woman is out there – if I haven't already met her. I have never experienced a shortage. It's one of the few privileges I have as a Black man in America. That said, I can share the experiences of the Black women clients who I've worked closely with in my practice. Together we've found the law of attraction applied to them whether there were two men to choose from or none.

Ironically, we've found, if anything, it means because of the ratio you have to be shrewder about selecting a man, because you are less likely to be bailed out of the emotional and financial consequences stemming from choosing a bad partner than your non-Black female counterparts. And, if you are dating along racial lines, it still applies because you still have to choose a good man over a bad one.

As Dr. Dyer says, "You cannot always control what goes on outside. But you can always control what goes on inside." In the same way, while you can't control the ratio, you can control your reaction to the options created by it. That is, either you trust there are many people out there you could fall in love with and hold out for a worthy man, or you can hold onto an unworthy one. Part of the challenge stems from thinking about soulmates in limited terms, such as Mr. Right Now versus Mr. Right—for me. There is more than one option. Whether you explore your options or not, once you have made your choice, you and your children are wedded to it, even if you elect to divorce him.

Of the 5 Cs (Choice, Communication, Conflict Resolution Skills, Commitment and Coach-ability) that will determine your relationship's fate, the man you choose most dramatically determines whether your relationship ends with you two living happily ever after or unhappily and over. Your choice of a partner is the one element relationship therapy can't correct. Further complicating matters is the reality that both partners adapt destructive behaviors to remain in a dysfunctional relationship. Unraveling the damaging ways he has learned to treat you, and you have come to accept, can be problematic.

For this reason, I ask are there really blameless victims in relationships? Or do you get treated in life the way you teach people to treat you? Because should you choose to remain in the relationship with this man you played a role, if only the role of enabler. For therapy to have a real chance of success, not only should the disappointing partner be held accountable for their destructive behaviors, but the disappointed partner also needs to be held accountable for teaching the disappointing party that their behavior is acceptable. In therapy, disappointed women frequently want me to treat only the disappointing partner. I almost always insist on treating them both. It takes two to tango!

When Fear Masquerades as Love

Partners in dysfunctional relationships don't choose each other by accident; rather, these partners complement each other's emotional pain in some fashion. They are co-dependent. There are no accidents or voids in nature, and the universe will meet you where you are. Much like if you place a banana on a space craft and send it to the moon, as the banana begins to rot, fruit flies will magically appear. While the moon doesn't support life (or fruit flies, for that matter), nature dictates that when fruit decays, something must be there to consume it. That something is fruit flies, complying with the law of nature. Similarly, if you are making decisions to remain with a partner based on fear or pain, you will attract a partner that feeds off that fear and pain. Ultimately your blind spots will enable you to rationalize bad behavior so you can remain with him, despite the dysfunctional relationship causing more pain than the threat you originally feared and were trying to avoid: being alone.

Meet Kathy and Donte. Kathy is a 32-year-old married mother of two, who received her master's degree in social work from Howard University. Donte is a 36-year-old, street-smart police officer with a streak of womanizing bad boy in him. From the beginning, Donte cheated — first getting busted in bed with her cousin, and subsequently getting busted with a string of other women. Kathy always forgave Donte and blamed the other women. She took him back with open arms, no matter how much she swore this better be the last time. Although his infidelity clearly hurt her deeply, she never left or otherwise imposed consequences on Donte.

During our first session, Donte admitted to being involved with another woman. "You want honesty: I love her," he said. At that point, I turned to Kathy and asked her what else she needed to know. She responded, "What type of man puts another woman above his own family? And why is he letting her poison his mind against us?" I agreed their family should be a priority.

"Nevertheless, what else do you need to know to make a decision, Kathy?" Sobbing, she didn't respond. I said, "He's made his decision. Either you are going to accept the situation and stay, or reject it and walk." She said: "But he should put us first. I'm his wife. I want to fight for my family." Again, I agreed he should put his family first, but gently reminded her she couldn't fight this fight alone. She could only fight the good fight within herself. That is, either she could respect herself and reject the abuse, or stay and teach him once again there were no consequence for mistreating her.

Kathy agreed she needed to quit sending Donte that message. To this end, she committed to stop having sexual relations until he agreed to break the triangle with the other woman.

During the next session it was clear my words had fallen on deaf ears. The family was enjoying quality time together and Kathy thought they were turning things around. But after three days of great sex, on the fourth night Donte disappeared. Kathy called and texted him repeatedly, but he didn't answer. She tracked him down at the other woman's house. Kathy was devastated. When Donte came out to his car the next morning (to find she had camped out by his car all night), she begged him to leave the other woman alone and just come home and let her love him. Donte told her he needed time to wean himself off the other woman. Ignoring our agreement to quit sending him the message that it was OK to mistreat her, she asked Donte how long he need to wean himself off that "whore." Her emotional blind spots and entrenched fears obstructed her ability to opt out of the triangle or otherwise impose consequences on Donte. When asked about her reaction to his rendezvous with his mistress, she vehemently blamed him for choosing the woman over her again and refused to take ownership for any role in her mistreatment.

(Note: Please don't mistake my highlighting her fears and role in their relationship's dysfunction with my thinking he isn't wrong for abusing her. Nothing could be further from the truth. He is totally wrong for his bad behavior and repeatedly breaking her heart. If he can't treat her right, he should be man enough to leave her alone. Nonetheless, she is the one in distress here. He is having his cake and eating it, too. So he appears to have little motivation to change. Therefore, I am focused on empowering her to make a change. Next, I asked them what they needed to do to become a healthier couple. She insisted that if Donte would only get rid of the other woman, they would be happy. Surprisingly, Donte disagreed and stated they both needed to work on themselves if they ever hoped to have a healthy, mutually fulfilling relationship. "I am not letting her be my soulmate," he said. "I need to be a better man and a more involved father, too. My sons are watching and learning, and I don't like what I'm teaching them. Not proud at all. She needs to start loving herself and quit accepting so little.")

Fear as Teacher

If Kathy and Donte remind you of your relationship, you may be romantically involved with a classmate instead of a soulmate. (This concept was introduced in Chapter 7, "Determine If He Is a Classmate or Soulmate.") Classmate in this situation represents someone with whom you share a definite soul tie, but their purpose or role is to teach you (and learn from you) an important life lesson(s), and maybe help prepare you for your eventual soulmate. As Caroline Myss writes in *Sacred Contracts*, spirits travel in packs and often have prearranged agreements to meet up in this life at critical junctures to teach us important life lessons, or to prepare us for or assist us in an important purpose. Although both classmates and soulmates may elicit strong emotional feelings and attachments, they are not one in the same. Soulmate love doesn't characteristically make you feel unhappy or miserable, like the relationship is too much work. In soulmate love, you don't argue and fight all of the time, repeatedly humiliate yourself by compulsively calling someone who doesn't respect you enough to return your calls, feel in a constant state of anxiety, or feel too embarrassed to share relevant aspects of your relationship struggles with close friends. By contrast, soulmate relationships characteristically uplift, strengthen, empower, enhance, and expand you. They feel right, are mutually fulfilling, edify your spirit, and love you back. Period!

Letting go isn't quitting. Letting go may be asking yourself, "Am I sticking it out, or am I staying stuck?" Ask your spirit for a revelation about your relationship. Is he a classmate or a soulmate? Be still and accept the answer. If there is a lesson you need to learn from your classmate, then learn it, embrace it, and move on with it. The soulmate love he's preparing you for may be around the corner.

Step 2. List Your Must Haves, Deal Breakers, and What You Will Give in Exchange. Be Clear, But Flexible

As the old saying goes, "If you don't know where you are going, any road will get you there." Clarity about what it is you really want and need is key. Why? You must be able to identify what you want and need when you see it and feel it. Furthermore, clarity will prevent you from being distracted by a man who clearly doesn't possess it. Imagine you felt the world were truly a place of surplus, where your imagination is the only limit. What kind of man would you ask for? How would he look? What qualities would he possess? (Don't worry about what you don't want for now, or how unrealistic this assignment seems. Indulge me.)

List everything you would like to have and everything you must have, and then prioritize your top three. After all of the qualities you just came up with, I'm sure you are thinking, "just three?" In *The Science of Happily Ever After*, Dr. Ty Tashiro explains why you only get three wishes. He supports this approach by hypothetically gathering 100 men into an auditorium for you to choose from. Then he looks at your list and eliminates men from the 100 gathered based on your list of qualities. Let's say your list indicates a man must be at least 6-feet tall. Then 80 of the men have to leave the room, leaving you with 20 eligible men. Next, if your list indicates your man must earn over $60,000, then 70 percent of the 20 men left have to leave the room, leaving you with six eligible men. Finally, if your list indicates your man must be moderately exciting, 70 percent of those six men left are ineligible, leaving you two eligible men despite having started with 100 candidates.

In short, be flexible.

Next, develop clarity on what you don't want—AKA the deal breakers. Make a list of your top deal breakers and prioritize them, narrowing the list to your top three. Be honest with yourself about what your deal breakers are. (See Chapter 6, When Mr. Right's Circumstances Make Him Mr. Wrong.) Keep this list short.

The next time you meet a man, remember the deal breakers on this list and your vow not to entertain men who possess them. In other words, "It doesn't matter how much I like you. You are married, so you can't have my number or otherwise contact me. Goodbye!" For most men, women who smoke and do not work out or engage in some sort of physical activity aren't a big deal. But I have bad memories of a mother who died prematurely of cardiovascular-related complications, and I've never enjoyed kissing a woman after she's just had a smoke. Accordingly, these two traits are on my deal breaker list, but smoking isn't on my prioritized top three list. What are your deal breakers? Prioritize your top three. Live by them, and let men who share these behaviors die by them.

Finally, now that you've identified your wants and deal breakers, make a list of what you are willing to give in return for such an ideal partner. This third list may be the most important one. He's not coming into your life to rescue you, save you from unhappiness, or make you whole. A soulmate is someone who will love, nurture, and support you while you do the same for him in return. List the unique gifts you will be sharing with the man you are hoping to attract. You must be in the process of becoming similar to, or complementary to, the man you are trying to attract. One way to think of it is if you haven't found the right person, it could be the case that you haven't worked hard enough on becoming the right person. This includes starting the process of soul searching, clearing out, forgiving yourself and others, making peace with your past, and facing your fears. It also includes beginning the process of learning to fully love and accept yourself so you can recognize and accept his love, too.

To plant the seed for the relationship you want to blossom in your life, repeat after me: *"I, _____ (say your name), fully commit to welcoming my soulmate into my life and growing myself into the kind of person I want to attract."*

Step 3. Embrace Your Fears by Shifting the Context

Courage is not the absence of fear. Courageous is what we become when we learn to face our fears in spite of being afraid. It's easy to ignore our fears and hope they'll just go away. Unfortunately, they rarely do. When our fears start affecting important life decisions, something's gotta give. We are all afraid of something, but being afraid has little to do with our capacity to overcome fear. Rather, overcoming our fears is ultimately determined by our decision to quit avoiding the terrifying behemoths we imagined, and instead face them head on so we awaken the sleeping giant within us.

Years ago while watching the Johnny Carson show on late-night television, I remember a Black celebrity being interviewed. Carson said, "You are an Olympian, a civil rights activist, a movie star, and a comedian who performs in front of large audiences regularly. Do you still get nervous when you speak?" The celebrity responded, "Yes, and if I ever stop getting nervous, I will quit. It's the nervous energy that propels me to succeed. Years ago, I had a debilitating stage fright, which almost ended my career before it started. One night, before talking myself out of going on stage, I ran into a colleague who had wrestled with the same demon. She told me to accept that getting butterflies was an important part of being a successful entertainer; furthermore, that I'd always get them no matter how hard I resisted." She instructed him to "shift the context" by focusing on getting his butterflies to fly in formation.

That simple adjustment launched his career.

Similarly, I ask you to list your fears when it comes to relationships. Besides your fears, write precisely how you might shift the context so your butterflies can be trained to fly in formation. For example, the fear of being deceived and cheated on can be a rather traumatizing and debilitating experience, frequently resulting in the betrayed person isolating themselves emotionally, or taking on a distrustful and angry persona to protect themselves from being hurt again. Both of these reactions is like building a brick wall around your house. True, no one can get in to hurt you, but you cannot get out, either. You become a prisoner in your own home. Facing your fears provides the closure you need to be set free. You have handled being cheated on before and survived, but you may be ill-equipped to handle growing old alone, which might be a substantially more painful reality.

In addition to putting your fears in a different context and facing them to get closure, be open to freeing yourself up psychologically by forgiving yourself for having been afraid or hurt. Recognizing the need for closure requires you to accept that just because you are done with your past doesn't mean your past is done with you. In *The One: Finding Soulmate Love and Making it Last*, Kathy Freston discusses the importance of making peace with your past. She writes, "As important as it is to request forgiveness, it is equally crucial to grant it—whether or not someone asks you to do so. Just as unresolved guilt will block the flow of goodwill and fulfillment, resentment will stand in the way of experiencing deep and soulful love." I totally agree. Providing couple's therapy has taught me we don't necessarily forgive others for them, but for ourselves so that we can release ourselves from the burden of carrying all that cumbersome baggage around. Ironically, resentment inadvertently causes us to focus on and attract more of what we don't want.

While some wrongs can simply be forgiven, other wounds are too deep and complex to salve with a simple "I forgive you" or "just get over it." Freud's Repetition Compulsion (see Chapter 1) is one such case. If you suspect your choice in men and relationships is plagued by some unconscious factors related to childhood trauma with your opposite-sexed parent, I suggest you talk to a professional to help make peace with your past so you can begin to make healthier relationship choices.

Welcoming your soulmate into your life requires you to begin the process of removing all the emotional hurdles that are interfering with or distracting you from having the relationship you truly desire and deserve. Whether it's a troubled relationship with a parent, someone you're still in love with, or any past relationship in your life that is still unresolved, holding onto this person, either consciously or unconsciously, is akin to having a third passenger sitting in your gorgeous two-seater convertible sports car.

No matter how excited you and your new partner are about cruising around with the top down, there won't be room for him to take a seat, much less enjoy the ride! You don't have to stop loving them, but you have to find a new space in your heart for them, a special chamber where you store all the people you have loved in the past.

Alternatively, you could be unwittingly alienating your soulmate by making lifestyle decisions that occupy the space Mr. Right will need to join your life. Perhaps you are a workaholic and don't make free time for a relationship; or you have a friend with benefits who is meeting your sexual needs; or you're so focused on helping your grown children, siblings, or others that you haven't left room for a man. Not making emotional room, time, and space for your soulmate is sending out a message to the universe that you're not ready to welcome him into your life. If you want soulmate love, you have to consciously make room for him, from a lifestyle and emotional standpoint.

Meet Kenya. She is a recently divorced, 35-year-old mother of twin boys. Before describing her current relationship dilemma, she elected to tell me about her ex-husband. Kenya described him as a sensitive but macho man who dressed meticulously and was a great dancer. He was close to his mother and very involved with the church. She fell heads over heels for him. "Yes!" was her immediate response when he proposed after just three months. She didn't give their never having had sex much thought; after all he had been celibate for years based on his commitment to the Lord.

During their wedding, she couldn't help but notice he and his best man, Derrick, were acting strangely and appeared to be quarreling. During the wedding party photo shoot, she caught a glance of them staring at each other intensely and found it unsettling. Shortly after arriving at the reception, Derrick left early, without giving the best man toast. When she asked why, her husband said he had recently been promoted and needed to rush back to Orlando, Florida, to meet his new sales team. Although she thought his sudden departure was odd, it was her day, so she dismissed it. Besides, his mother gave a stirring toast welcoming her into the family as the daughter she always dreamed of having. She was very excited about the marriage and the prospect of doting over her grandchildren. Kenya adored her mother-in-law, and was happy to have her visit during the pregnancy and after the birth of their twins.

"Unexpectedly after the birth of the boys, sex with my husband drifted from infrequent to non-existent," she says. They became distant. Initially she thought it was because she hadn't lost the baby weight and he was no longer attracted to her. Surely, things would return to normal once she lost the weight or he settled into the reality of being married with kids. Right? She worried about their newfound marital estrangement constantly. Then out of the blue, one of her bridesmaids called and invited her to meet for happy hour at the Holiday Inn where her friend had just started a new job as a hotel manager. She didn't think much of her insisting that they sit facing the lobby as they drank. However, shortly after their drinks came, Kenya thought she saw Derrick go to the front desk and check in around 4:30 p.m. She remembered initially thinking he must be back in town from Florida. Shortly, thereafter, she saw her husband come in the lobby and go to the elevator and head up to a room, although he hadn't checked in. Unsurprised by this chance encounter, her friend escorted her to Derrick's room 30 minutes later. Knocking on the door she shouted, "room service." A nude Derrick came to the door and peeped out. She waited in the hallway for her husband, and she confronted him. He admitted he and Derrick were lovers and that he was gay. She filed for a divorce and was granted full custody of the twins.

Afterwards, Kenya used men strictly to meet her sexual needs without making any emotional investment. Out of sight, out of mind was her motto. Two years after her divorce was finalized, she was out line dancing with her girlfriends one night when she met Leo, who really turned her on emotionally, intellectually, and physically. A passionate dancer, well dressed, charming, and smart, he captured her attention as they danced all night. Against her better judgment, she dated him, they made love, and they started to develop feelings for each other. Leo also had custody of his young daughter and was very busy with his job. Nonetheless, they made time for each other, introduced their children to each other, and were talking about getting serious. As she began to develop deep emotions and vulnerability, Kenya wanted them to have sex every time they saw each other and felt insecure if they didn't. In contrast, Leo had a lot on his plate and didn't desire sex so frequently. He insisted their relationship meant much more to him than sex, and he couldn't understand her insatiable need for sexual validation. She freaked out when he didn't pick it up in the bedroom, fearing he must be seeing someone else because when her ex-husband stopped having sex with her it was because he didn't desire her and was involved with someone else, and she missed the warning signs. She deeply feared being duped again and decided to stop taking his calls.

She was done!

Avoidance Keeps You in Emotional Bondage, Closure Sets You Free

In session, we discussed Kenya's relationships, and how she abruptly ended things with Leo. Based on our conversation, it was apparent she wasn't over Leo. While the breakup left her feeling less vulnerable, she was struggling to answer the "what if" questions. Leo remained perfect in her imagination, and she lit up when talking about him. Fearing she might meet and fall for another man, she became a recluse. Kenya was stuck and alone. At least, if he cheated and she found out, she could say, "Thanks, but no thanks. You're just not the man for me." She could be set free. Yes, it would hurt, but nothing will ever hurt like the pain caused by her ex-husband's betrayal and double life. Conversely, if she never faces her fears, she will likely remain stuck and alone indefinitely.

After several sessions, Kenya decided to get out of her self-imposed prison and go to a wedding with some friends. She ran into Leo and danced with him. Although it had been over 18 months since she last saw him, her heart raced, and all of those feelings she stuffed re-emerged. She was stunned when he didn't hit on her or subsequently call. We discussed her evening dancing with Leo, including how she felt when they were together. "My heart skipped a beat when he grabbed my hand and took me to the dance floor," she said. Despite her fears, she decided to give him a call. She apologized for abandoning him, and met him for lunch. During the session after their lunch, her smile was much sunnier than before, and it remained permanently affixed during our remaining sessions together.

Shifting the context from the fear of the familiar pain of betrayal to the more excruciating reality of missing out on a man she loved ultimately empowered Kenya to embrace and confront her fears and break out of her self-imposed prison once and for all. I suggest you try the same and that you remain open to talking to a trained professional for help if need be.

Step 4. Use Visualization and Feng Shui to Attract and Make Room for Mr. Right

The concept of manifesting your Mr. Right into your life has enjoyed increased notoriety as evidenced by Rhonda Byrne's bestseller *The Secret*, which has a cult following. This book is based on using creative visualization, which employs the mind's extraordinary powers to manifest thoughts into reality. Although it may sound like the power to create your reality is too good to be true, this fact is well documented. For example, studies on Olympic athletes have shown that less successful competitors train only physically; in contrast, athletes who couple physical training with creative visualization exercises medal in their events more frequently. Like the Olympians who win more medals, creative visualization can help you win in your romantic life.

Visualization Exercise

Here is a visualization exercise to help you with the law of attraction once you've completed the exercise described in Step 2. To do this exercise, you will need to enter into a light meditative state. Accordingly, I want you to identify a peaceful and quiet place where you are unlikely to be disturbed. Go to this place, have a seat, remove your shoes, and get comfortable. Once you feel comfortable, turn your attention inward toward your breathing. Begin by taking deep breaths, breathing in 1, 2, 3, 4 and breathing out 1,2,3,4, 5, noticing you are feeling more relaxed with each breath. (As you attempt to relax, random thoughts will pop into your head. Acknowledge them and let them float by.) Once you're in a relaxed state, you're ready to begin visualizing.

First, imagine you are in a theater room where there is a large movie screen with a movie playing. Upon closer examination of the movie, you notice it features you and your leading man, starring in a movie you wrote, edited, and directed, from beginning to end. At any point you can cut, edit, or add a scene. You have full creative license to record any scene or special effect you desire. After viewing this movie, I want you to recall the movie you just witnessed as vividly as possible. The more details the better. Namely, how did you feel physically (e.g., what was your breathing and heartbeat like)? What was it like to be in a man's arms who made you feel safe, comfortable, at ease and loved? What was the sound and tone of your voice during your interactions with a man who had your top three qualities and no deal breakers? Answering these questions in vivid detail is important. For example, if you were sailing, try to recall how the wind felt when it blew in your face, the smell of the salt from the ocean mist that sprayed you, the motion of the boat as the waves rocked it, the sound of the splash created by the school of dolphins as they sliced through the water on their swim by your boat, the sense of calm and security you felt, and the respect you felt for him as he adeptly navigated the high seas.

To successfully use visualization techniques to manifest the relationship you desire into your life, you will need stick-to-it-tiveness, imagination, and patience. Do this exercise daily and, if possible, in the same place and at the same time. At first, it may be difficult to complete this exercise without finding it a bit silly. Stick to it! Also, at first you will find it seems as though nothing is changing. That's par for the course. Persist! In time the man you desire will appear on the movie screen. This exercise will not only help you attract him into your life, but it will also help you eliminate impostors, as they just won't feel right. You will know this exercise is working by virtue of the fact that you start quickly eliminating impostors. In matters of the heart, knowing what you want (and don't want) is half the battle. Starting to change your life to reflect what you want to attract is the other half.

Use Feng Shui to Make Room for Love

I've had positive results with clients combining visualization and feng shui to attract Mr. Right. A former client, Crystal, had been involved in one failed relationship after another, yet she believed in love and wanted to manifest a mutually fulfilling, stable relationship. She was single, so I didn't get to meet her current or former partner. To get more objective insights, I had her describe past relationships and bring in photos of her two-bedroom loft-style condo. As we reviewed her pictures, the way she decorated her apartment jumped out at me as her interior design contrasted feng shui principles for singles looking to attract a loving relationship. First, her paintings exclusively featured single women, or women with children but no man present. Next, all of her paint and wall coverings were tan or green; she slept in queen-sized bed that was squeezed into a corner surrounded by two walls; she had only one nightstand, which had a vase on it containing a dozen dried-up roses; she had one chair on her balcony that faced the sunset; and all of her closets and dressers were filled to the brim with her clothes, shoes, and other items. Lastly, her bedroom doubled as her office, where all of her papers and books lay scattered. Also there wasn't a sound system to be found, despite her liking to dance. According to feng shui principles, she would have trouble making Mr. Right feel comfortable in her space because she hadn't made room for him—physically or emotionally.

To help make her home more inviting, she agreed to some feng shui couple-friendly changes to the interior design of her condo. First, she put up new pictures, some of which included couples; got matching nightstands; purchased a sound system; changed some paint colors to pink or red (which represent romance and sensual energy, respectively); and put out matching candle sets and a pair of giraffes whose necks were intertwined. She also threw out the roses and cleaned her closet (donating old or unused clothes and an ex's hoodies to charity). Next, she cleaned her bathroom drawers and replaced a solo chair with a matching set on her balcony so she and a prospective partner could one day look off into the sunset together.

As we began discussing her previous relationships, she admitted to still having sex with the ex, Mr. X, who had given her the dried roses on her nightstand. She also revealed that he was married. She knew they could never have more, but enjoyed their sexual trysts. (Poignantly, she mentioned he never complained about her condo's design during their rare sex-filled afternoon rendezvous.) Believing this illicit relationship would force her to deceive any new partner, or her honesty would likely do irreparable damage once he discovered she was in a relationship with a married man, she agreed to end the relationship promptly and make room for a soulmate. Prophetically, she told me about one promising man who completely changed the way he treated her upon learning about her involvement with this married man, Mr. X, although she tried to explain to the new man that the affair was about sex only and he shouldn't feel threatened or judge her. Soon, he, too, just wanted sex from her and gradually came to blatantly disrespect her.

She recognized this scenario represented everything wrong with her approach to relationships. She just didn't get men. The men she dated didn't have the basic qualities she needed for long-term success, and she ignored red flags that were all over the place. She lacked clarity. She epitomized the saying that if you don't know where you're going, any road (or man in this case) will get you there.

We decided she would complete the exercises listed in Steps 2 and 3 and refrain from dating until she had clarity. During these exercises, she began to recognize she wasn't just a victim or just a perpetrator. She had hurt men and had been hurt by them, too. Like the man who really adored her — he was crushed when he discovered she was still sleeping with her married ex. Through these failed relationships and heartbreaks, she had, in fact, learned a lot about what she did and didn't want. Based on this realization, she completed the exercises and committed to being shrewd about whom she would and wouldn't date going forward and what she would give in exchange.

Combine Visualization and Feng Shui—It Will Likely Seem Like Synchronicity!

When Crystal completed her lists, she began doing the creative visualization exercises regularly and committed to feng shui. Topping of her list was a sense of humor, intellectual stimulation, and how he made her feel. During the visualizations, her movie script rehearsals grew from 30-second commercials to a four-to-five-minute feature films. She did these exercises most days, adding and subtracting items as she gained more clarity. The success of this process became more apparent when she first started to exercise discipline in her dating life. She began saying thanks but no thanks to men who didn't fit her criteria or who possessed the listed deal breakers. She also became excited when her visualizations resulted in her museum visits and personal development classes. The men she met while at these events enabled her to go from fearing there weren't any worthy men out there to realizing that the more she put herself out there, the more worthy men she encountered. This shifted her approach to men from shortage to surplus. It was like night and day!

The changes Crystal experienced in her dating life can best be described as synchronicity. This term was coined by psychiatrist Dr. Karl Jung, and it refers to the occurrence of two or more events or phenomena that suddenly occur and appear to be meaningfully connected to each other; but one event didn't necessarily cause the other. Namely, did Crystal start to get clarity about dating worthy men because they suddenly appeared, or did worthy men suddenly appear because she got clarity about what type of men she wanted — and did not want — to date? This is the proverbial debate about which came first: the chicken or the egg?

After dating a string of men, Crystal started dating a man who possessed two of her three wish qualities — and some bonus qualities she hadn't realized belonged on her list. Even better, he didn't possess any game changers or deal breakers. They have been dating happily for the last 18 months, which she admitted was a bit scary at first. Nevertheless, she enjoyed entertaining him at her newly decorated condo. "We fit comfortably on my king-sized bed, and it was nice to see him leave his personal items in his nightstand. And, frankly, it was a major relief not to have to explain or lie about the roses. After three months together, I gave him his own closet and drawer space, too," she said. "He has a decent two-step, so we enjoy dancing, and listening to romantic songs during lovemaking. On weekends, we relish going out on the balcony and having good conversation as the sun rises or sets. We are happy in the relationship that closely resembles the one I visualized: although he isn't 6'2", we are good friends, make each other laugh and I definitely feel loved."

If you are ready to attract a new man, I recommend you give the creative visualization and feng shui a try. I also recommend you pick up a copy of read *101 Ways to Transform Your Life* by Dr.

Wayne Dyer. I recommend an audio instead of a written version of this book.

Step 5. Start Telling a New Story of Your Romantic Life

"You can't start the next chapter of your life if you are too busy re-reading the old one."
— Unknown.

The story we tell determines the life we live. If you are reliving your past, you are preparing yourself to live through the sequel; alternatively if you are re-writing the script, you are the master of your fate. How would your internal dialogue change if you realized today's self-talk is writing tomorrow's movie script? What kind of man, relationship, and ending are you writing with your dominant thoughts — a romantic comedy, a thriller, a drama, or a tragedy? To forecast your future, take a fierce inventory of your current thoughts about men and relationships, recognizing you are manifesting that reality into your future.

In *The Power of Intention*, Dr. Wayne Dyer writes, "The average person thinks 65,000 to 75,000 thoughts a day. The problem is they are the same thoughts." We have spent years and years thinking the same thoughts over and over again, based on past situations and experiences — and many of them are not even our thoughts! We have formed rules of thumbs that shape our actions and reactions based on these thoughts and our entrenched life patterns. Seldom do we stop and challenge our beliefs or their origins. For example, you tell the same old story over and over again about how men are dogs and how you were a victim in your last relationship, or how you're too old to find love.

True or untrue, the more you tell this same old story and are consumed by it, and the more energy you devote to it, the more you're blocking love from coming into your life. Why? Thoughts are things. Accordingly, it becomes a self-fulfilling prophecy. On OWN (Oprah's TV network), all of the millionaires, athletes, philanthropists, singers, and celebrities I see who came from poverty learned to ignore the reality of hard times and under-privilege and instead told themselves a new story that included a happily-ever-after ending. You often hear these well-known figures tell how they imagined themselves on the big screen, in business cutting a deal, or playing in their respective Super Bowl from an early age. They repeated this new story over and over and spent years practicing and perfecting their stories, in spite of the realities that surrounded them.

In time, their new story became their success stories.

Recognize that we live in a universe where reality is first created in the non-physical, which includes your mind and imagination, and then in the physical, which includes your life, partner, and home. The more you focus and give energy to your new story, the more you'll attract men and relationships that perpetuate your success story.

CHAPTER 5

Seven Rules of Engagement When You Earn More

"Married college-educated Black women earn more than 60 percent of their household income, which is the same estimated percentage earned by the average White husband."

What's Love Got to Do With It?

Author Donna Franklin

"College-educated Black women are sometimes the sole earners in their family, as more than one out of ten married, college-educated Black women has a husband who is unemployed." "Women, Men, and the New Economics of Marriage." Pew Research Center, 2010

Prior to the African American experience, the expectation for a young African female was to be swept off her feet by an initiated, highly skilled, family-oriented, and socially appropriate young African alpha male warrior, artisan, or chieftain. He was to marry her and bring home the bacon, provide for his family and live happily ever after. There was no such thing as a shortage of men in the dating pool, and one of the determinants of an African family's wealth was the number of children they had, so family was everything. For her part, she cooked the bacon, reared the kids, kept house, and was an adoring wife and mother.

On the contrary, today's African American woman is far less likely to have such a fairytale life. As Ralph Banks discusses in *Is Marriage for White People?*, African American woman today "are more than three times as likely as White women to never marry. And when professional Black women do marry, they are more likely than any group of women to marry a working-class man. In fact, more than half of college-educated Black wives have less educated husbands."

Queens without kings.

Well-documented historical factors (e.g., slavery, Jim Crow, limited educational and financial opportunities, the forced separation of children's parents by the welfare system, and an unjust criminal justice system) have contributed to the African

113

American woman's plight. Nevertheless, few of these factors account for her experience once she chooses a mate, particularly when she makes more than him, which by all statistical accounts is an all too realistic prospect. According to a 2010 Cornell University study, men who are completely economically dependent on their female partners are five times more likely to cheat than men in relationships with women who earned similar amounts. In contrast, in relationships where women earned about 75 percent of the men's income, men were the least likely to cheat, according to the study's author, Christin Munsch, a sociology Ph.D. candidate at Cornell University.

One explanation Munsch offered for these findings: "It may be that men who make less money than their female partners are less happy and cheat because they are unhappy, not necessarily because they make less money." Munsch pointed to research in *The Effect of Relative Income Disparity on Infidelity for Men and Women*, which suggests any identity important to a male or female that's threatened may result in them engaging in stereotypical behavior to re-establish their place in that society. Put another way, men are more likely to cheat when they are unhappy about their financial standing and can no longer meet their and society's expectations of them being the breadwinner. To compensate, they use sexual conquests to shore up their fragile sense of manhood and feel like the man again.

Before you hit the panic button, it should be noted that this study found a man who makes significantly more money than his girlfriend or wife is more likely to cheat, as well. Collectively, these findings suggest that despite the historical lessons Black women have learned, it may be the case that neither she nor her man can be expected to remain unaffected once either becomes the one who earns the lion's share of the income, yet is expected to divide it evenly and respect each other's contributions equally. As Dr. Gottman indicates in *How to Make Love Last,* once we start making "negative comparisons" between what we expected our life in the relationship to be like and what our life ultimately became, the seeds of discontent, resentment, and infidelity have been planted. When working with couples, I've found it is just as difficult to love a partner you perceive as a deadbeat as it is to feel loved by a partner who perceives you as a deadbeat. Accordingly, if one partner views the other partner as not pulling his or her weight or as a burden, and begins to think, "What do I need you for?", then the seeds of contempt and discontent will soon blossom into relationship or martial problems.

MONEY CAN'T BUY YOU LOVE—OR EXCLUSIVITY

Meet the Browns. Susan is CEO and president of her hugely successful interior design firm. She received her BS in architecture from Michigan State University and is a multi-talented 44-year-old woman. She is always meticulously and creatively dressed, interpersonally sophisticated, artistically talented, and possesses an uncanny business savvy and shrewdness. A devout Christian, Susan is a virtuous, Proverbs 31 woman: " ... her price far above rubies, will do him good and not evil all the days of her life, and a woman that fears the LORD."

Her husband, Rodney, is not the husband referred to in this bible Proverb, although he might be described as the proverbial screw-up who over achieved this one time in life — marrying Susan. Yes, he is smart, articulate, and educated, having received his undergraduate degree in finance and religion from Rutgers University. Originally, he had a job as an investment banker at a top-tiered brokerage firm; however, the SEC revoked his license after a hearing revealed he had committed several ethics violations by engaging in unscrupulous practices. Subsequently, his poor decision making cost him a series of professional opportunities, and he is currently self-employed as an unsuccessful day-trader.

Despite Rodney's professional shortcomings, he and Susan are best friends who have been together forever. They met at a summer school bible camp when they were 14. He was captivated by her knowledge of the bible and commitment to God. He went after her, and they quickly became sweethearts, dated through college, and married at age 28. They have two children

The Browns came into my practice requesting a marriage tune-up, as they were rarely intimate despite professing a profound love for each other and all outer appearances leading everyone to think they were the perfect couple. To justify not approaching Susan sexually any longer, Rodney discussed how professional failures had him depressed, leading to erectile dysfunction, weight loss, and a subsequent lack of energy, which had zapped his sex drive. Heartbroken and dejected by his sexual desertion and flaccid penis during the infrequent attempts at intercourse, Susan's esteem plummeted, leading to her own melancholy. During therapy it became apparent they had emotional turbulence brewing beneath the surface based on her success and his failures. To reduce this tension, she let him manage all finances. Susan loves him and is keenly sensitive to the hits to his ego and wanted to boost him up as head of household.

Once Rodney became the CEO of their marriage, he quickly declared the need for a new budget, allocating her a meager allowance. After several months of heart-wrenching marital therapy, all finally seemed to be well in paradise again. They were courting each other again and making love. Both reported feeling less depressed. He had regained significant weight and increased energy, and he seemed 100 percent committed to getting their marriage on track—though the hard copy of the budget never surfaced. Still, she was surprisingly apprehensive about terminating therapy, fearing things seemed too good to be true and insisting that Rodney might get too comfortable or otherwise find a way to screw it up.

During the next session, I was stunned to learn Rodney had traveled to Orlando, Florida, over the weekend with his buddies for a golf trip, and upon returning he left his gmail account open. She noticed an email entitled "a hole in one," with a video clip attachment sent to his fraternity brothers. Although struck by him not mentioning his golfing triumph to her or including her in the email chain, she unsuspectingly clicked on the video to discover live footage of his fully erect penis shoved down a prostitute's throat, and him subsequently penetrating and remaining erect long enough to provide the woman with multiple orgasms — all recorded without him wearing a condom.

Devastated and betrayed, she couldn't maintain her composure. Sobbing uncontrollably, she asked out loud, "Who have I been married to?" In addition to the sanctimonious Deacon Brown having sex with a prostitute (and there weren't any signs of erectile dysfunction), he had used her money to pay for the trip and the prostitute. Equally hurtful was being publicly humiliated by him sending the video to his fraternity brothers. While that betrayal was painful, she was almost broken by the fact that she had submitted herself and her finances to a man she didn't respect or trust. Her worst fears were confirmed when she later did a computer search and discovered he hadn't provided her a copy of the budget because he was squandering her hard-earned money away on sex websites, porn, and prostitutes. He had spent thousands of dollars on prostitutes. Even worse, she was petrified about the prospect of either of them having been exposed to HIV/AIDS, and the thought of her children losing one or both of their parents.

Despite Rodney's pleas that his deep sense of inadequacy lead to his sexual antics and not a lack of desire for her, his reminders that marriage is for better or worse and promises to start sexual addiction therapy didn't move Susan to remain in the marriage. She simply couldn't get past the visual images of him having sex with prostitutes, or the anger with herself for blindly giving up financial control, and was on the verge of an emotional breakdown.

Susan subsequently came into my office alone.

She shared that she had heard various rumors over the years that he was cheating, which was why she didn't want to terminate therapy. Next, she stated, "I felt horrible because I played a role in his infidelity. Doc, I can be a real ball buster when angered, and I emasculated him on occasion. I made it clear I was the star and he was lucky to be my moon. Angry about his screw up and the thought of him cheating, my sharp tongue let him know it was my house, and if he ever wanted to get his name on the mortgage, he'd have to pay his fair share of the bills. Otherwise he could take his broke ass back to his grandmama's house, which was the best he could do without me. Nonetheless, I love him deeply and miss our friendship. He always made me laugh. I know I shouldn't have said those things, but sometimes I felt, like, 'why do I need him, if he isn't going to carry his weight?' I was frustrated, and now I'm confused."

Rodney also contacted me, inquiring about sexual addiction therapy. I told him to pick up a copy of *Out of the Shadows*, by Patrick Carnes, Ph.D., which is the premier classic on sexual addiction. He also agreed to start sexual addiction and group therapy.

(Note: While I recognize members from all cultural groups and ethnic races find themselves struggling with sexual addiction and hate to have brothers feel I am throwing them under the bus, I would be remiss if I didn't mention African American, African, Caribbean, and Latin males' sense of machismo and male identity have frequently been overly sexualized during our emotional development and rites of passage into manhood. These cultural phenomenon and other historical factors play a major role in these men being over-represented in sexual addiction clinics.)

Ladies, Rodney's betrayal of Susan's love and trust (and her role in it, if any at all) should serve as no more than a cautionary tale. I've worked with 100 men who, like Rodney, made less than their partners and everything worked out perfectly. In fact, I cannot think of one couple where her making more money was the sole reason for their breakup, and there is little data showing these particular types of money conflicts lead directly to divorce.

SEVEN RULES OF ENGAGEMENT WHEN YOU BRING HOME THE BACON:

Rule #1: Revaluing Attributes That Don't Appear on the Balance Sheet

After hearing Susan describe her experience with Rodney, I thought of Farnoosh Torabi's groundbreaking book, *When She Makes More*. Torabi suggests that when a woman earns more than her man, the odds are she is less likely to marry him, less likely to have a happy marriage if she does, and more likely to get a divorce. In addition, Torabi speculates that when a man and woman relinquish stereotypical gender roles, and instead she takes on the breadwinner role, both suffer emotionally and sexually. This can play itself out in the form of impotency, lack of intimacy, and a loss of attraction. Even more dangerous, the breadwinner may develop feelings of resentment, contempt, and anger toward her man, resulting in her starting to wonder if she is better off without him. Torabi concludes to be happy when you make earn more, you must learn to come to terms with your new financial reality and remain keenly aware of the trade-offs your man provides.

Subsequent conversations revealed that Rodney provided Susan with tradeoffs that were important to her, and she had lost sight of them. Namely, he was a stabilizing force in her life who had financially and emotionally supported her while she was in architecture school, including buoying her flagging confidence when she received Cs during her first year and feared she didn't have what it took to make it at the highly competitive architecture program. He also was instrumental in her leaving corporate America and starting her own interior design business. Rodney had been key in many of her wins, and he was the love of her life. (No, I didn't let her take blame for his sexual addiction, and reassured her that his sexual addiction was independent of her being a "ball buster" or a breadwinner.) However, when we sat down and did a balanced inventory of the risk, rewards, and tradeoffs of life with Rodney, we came up with some insightful ways that Rodney added value. I encourage you to do the same.

More often than not, I've found women who earn more than their men have in fact chosen their mates wisely, as their list of rewards are frequently more compelling than the tradeoffs. Frequently they chose salt of the earth, intelligent, fun-loving men — great dads who made them happy. On the other hand, I typically find their list of tradeoffs are frequently short, and that subsequent apprehensions about their men are largely influenced by the opinions and standards of others. Society's views of who should earn what amount or where they should have gone to school play a role in women breadwinners losing sight of virtues that don't appear on the balance sheet. Money is only one aspect of relationship happiness. And when we are able to put money into perspective, I've found we were frequently able to answer Torabi's question ("Why do I need you?") in a more balanced way. The women say, "No, maybe I don't need you to pay an equal portion of the bills, although it would be nice; however, there are other critical ways you contribute to my life that make me feel taken care of, and that is more important." Empowered with a more balanced answer to this question, many women were able to re-evaluate what happily ever after means for them when they earn more.

Rule #2: The Michelle Obama Approach

Years ago, I spoke at Congresswoman Eleanor Holmes Norton's brain trust on "What Happened to Marriage in the Black Community?" at the Congressional Black Caucus. Also on the panel was the distinguished Audrey Chapman, who has enjoyed a 20-plus-year relationship radio show at WHUR and a distinguished career as a marital therapist. Insightful, experienced, and pragmatic, Chapman noted when selecting a mate it is important that a women choose someone at her eye-level to achieve long-term relationship happiness (that is, he needs to be your financial, educational and social equal). While I agree with the aspirations created by her eye-level test, I recommend women use their peripheral vision, too — that is, how to identify a man with a great upside based on his current plan and behaviors. No doubt, you are probably tired of hearing about why and how you should lower your standards. I get it.

However, I'm not asking you to lower your standards, but to trust your full sensory capability when applying your standards to choosing a man.

The Obamas: I'm sure everyone looks at Michelle's choice of Barack as a soulmate and thinks it was a no-brainer. But that was not always the case. During the summer of 1989, Michelle Robinson was an associate at Sidley & Austin when she was assigned to mentor a summer associate named Barack Obama. In interviews and speeches, she frequently talks about her early impressions of Barack. His name struck her as odd, and so was the fact that he grew up in Hawaii. Predicting he would be strange and overly intellectual, she assumed she would dislike him. Even if she did somehow like him, the fact that she was assigned to be Obama's mentor made her feel much too self-conscious to ever consider dating him.

Clearly his good looks, sound character, academic pedigree, quick wit, and intellect made him worthy of consideration. However, she was a highly regarded third-year associate at the prestigious Sidley & Austin corporate law firm.

A rising star who was paid handsomely to manage blue-chip clients' trademark protection, distribution rights, intellectual property, and entertainment law, Michelle was the breadwinner who earned considerably more than Barack. Conventional wisdom wasn't on the side of a man whose primary goal was to work as an underpaid community organizer, write a book, and, yeah, one day run for president of the United States. Right?

Based on those financial incompatibilities alone, he may have failed Chapman's eye-level litmus test. But Michelle combined what she saw at eye-level with her peripheral vision, which revealed some attributes that weren't on the balance sheet. Instead of relying strictly on the timing of where they were financially, she valued the trajectory of where Barack was headed, and what influence his trajectory would have on her life.

For his part, Barack wasn't deterred. "I asked her, she refused," he says. "I asked her again, she refused again."

On their first date, while driving to check out Spike Lee's "Do the Right Thing," she couldn't help but notice "his first car had so much rust that there was a rusted hole in the passenger door. You could see the ground when you were driving. It would shake ferociously when it would start."

After learning more about Barack, she said to herself, "This brother is not interested in ever making a dime. He had no money: He was really broke. His wardrobe was kind of cruddy." On one early date, he took her to a Chicago church where he was meeting with a group of people he had worked with as a community organizer before he started law school. She observed, "The people gathered there together that day were ordinary folks doing the best they could to build a good life. They were parents trying to get by paycheck to paycheck; grandparents trying to get it together on a fixed income; men frustrated that they couldn't support their families after jobs had disappeared."

To her amazement, Barack wasn't interested in parlaying his presidency of the Harvard Law Review into a prestigious clerkship for a U.S. Supreme Court justice, which would inevitably lead to a lucrative career. "Here I am, knowing the power of his position: 'You're not going to clerk for them? You're kidding me!'" Upon graduation, Austin & Sidley offered Barack a well-paid job. He turned it down, and instead accepted a less illustrious low-paying job at a Chicago civil rights law firm. Barack spent his first six months working Project Vote, which aimed to get low-income African Americans registered to vote.

Barack's idealism and desire to empower poor African Americans ultimately swept Michelle off her feet.

His commitment to service had a profound impact on Michelle's career trajectory, too. In spite of the prestige of her corporate law job (which didn't provide the same sense of fulfillment) and being on the high-profile partner track, the year before they married, she left Sidley & Austin to begin a life of public service. There was no need for Michelle to leave Sidley & Austin just because she was marrying Barack, because he was coming back to Chicago after graduation from Harvard, and she easily could have stayed with the firm. Yet, three years after representing Barney's and Coors, Michelle was working to bring new jobs and vitality to Chicago's neighborhoods. It was a turning point in her career and life, and would later frame her life story. *This story has been adapted from Michelle: A Biography (Liza Mundy).*

Being a woman who earned substantially more than the man she was dating, Michelle, too, had to wrestle with Torabi's question ("What do I need him for?"). From hearing her story, it seems like she responded with an unequivocal, "I love and value you for the man you are." Nonetheless, I'm sure many of her close girlfriends must have wondered about her decision to be with the eccentric, high-minded Barack from Hawaii. Imagine your parents' response (and they love you unconditionally) if you left a partner track at a top law firm to work for pennies on the dollar, only to marry a man who wanted to work with poor folk. This decision would raise some eyebrows. Ultimately, however, her assessment of his value as a man outweighed him not being the breadwinner, even when Michelle was earning close to $300,000 as vice president of community and external affairs at University of Chicago Hospitals. Michelle Obama remained the breadwinner for the first 10 years they were together.

While the eye-level test alone could have motivated her to make more practical choices that probably would include her being a partner in the law firm today, her peripheral vision inspired her to marry Barack Obama and make a very gratifying career change — ultimately leading her to "1600 Pennsylvania Avenue" and untold fame and fortune — and, more importantly, living happily ever after with Mr. Right.

Rule #3: Financial Compatibility

*"**Money** can't buy you love,*
but fighting over it can bankrupt your relationship."
— Michelle Singletary, Author of *Your Money, Your Man*

Money is a very emotional: It has both the potential to unite or divide the best couples. In many respects, financial compatibility is as important to your relationship's long-term success as intellectual, sexual, or romantic compatibility. To help you gauge your financial compatibility, I recommend you both complete the "Financial Compatibility" test located in the workbook you can find at theBlackMAN-ual.com, and compare results. The more accurately you gauge how he manages his finances while he is single, the more accurate a glimpse you can get of what your future life will look like together.

Does he wear only the best clothes and expensive watches? Does he buy a new car every two years, even when it is a stretch for his income? Is he a winer-and-a-diner — and how often does he eat out? Does he take brown-bag lunches to work? Do his credit cards get declined? Are his shoes run over? Overall, you need to assess whether or not his lifestyle reflects his income, or if he is living beyond his means. Does he max out his 401(k) and other employer matching programs? Although you may not know his exact salary, try the salary calculator on Monster.com to get a general idea. Most importantly, based on his lifestyle and attitudes about money, how will the two of you afford the house you want, private schools, vacations, investing in a business, or retirement? Conversely, if he is significantly more frugal than you, are you prepared not to go on exotic vacations, make more practical clothing purchases, and live with other penny-pinching lifestyle choices?

As these two divergent financial management styles suggest, while large salaries are preferred to small salaries, a big salary isn't always an indication that you will have financial security or be financially compatible. Rather, how he handles his money, not how much he makes, is a much better indicator of what your financial future together will look like. In the final analysis, it may be more important that your financial values are compatible than who earns more.

In addition to helping you understand if your financial lifestyles, values, and goals are compatible, there are several important conversations you need to have before and after getting married. Before marriage, you will need to understand the dangers of co-signing for your partner, prenuptial agreements, the evils of overspending on a wedding, the role of joint and separate accounts, the importance of setting household budgets, and to establish "household rules" (for example, if a purchase is over $250, we discuss it together and both get a vote). Once married, you may need to prepare to live on one income, teach your children about money, and save for their education. Finally, you will need to make investments, do estate planning, and otherwise prepare for retirement.

Rule #4: Ensure Your Man Feels Like the Man

In addition to thinking outside of the box, ladies, when you earn more, sometimes you have to think like a man. Male self-esteem is often linked with their financial prowess, and ignoring that reality could prove costly.

Both partners must have skin in the game. That is critical for a relationship to survive long term, even if there is a disparity between how much skin (or money) you both have to invest in the game. For a man to maintain his dignity, he needs to be an integral part of the financial decision making, too. Yet, studies show that in marriages where the wife is the breadwinner, the woman is twice as likely as her husband to make all the financial decisions, compared to where men earn more. When that's the case, both partners share in the financial decision making. Honestly, if you don't respect his financial decision making enough to give him a voice on financial issues, then you probably should leave or not choose him at all. No matter how much you love him, you can't be his financial mama. The male ego will likely falter in this atmosphere in the long run; rather, you probably are unwittingly creating the breeding ground for resentment, passive-aggressive behavior, frustration, deceit, and betrayal.

Assuming you respect him and want to include him in financial decisions, you both have to think outside of the box to re-evaluate his contribution proportionally and find a way to make his contribution matter more. For example, while it may be unrealistic to ask him to pay half of the bills, it may be very realistic to have him pay off both of your student loans, pay off existing debt, be responsible for coming up with the down payment on your home, contribute more heavily to your retirement fund, or pay for the 529 college education plan you set up for your unborn child. Making him financially responsible for these types of expenses positions you both to experience him having the rewarding feeling of sticking his chest out and saying, "I got us in this house, I got rid of our debt, I helped us retire, or I paid for our kids' college education." This concept is demonstrated clearly in the Bible. Remember Mark 12:44 (NIV): "They all gave out of their wealth: But she out of her poverty, put in everything — all she had to live on."

Trust you me, thinking like a man will make him feel like "the man" and, in return, he will make you feel like a woman.

Rule #5: Think Like a Man: "It's Cheaper to Keep Her"

"It's cheaper to keep her," as Buddy Guy infamously sang about the wife he no longer wanted, yet refused to divorce. Here, however, I'm referring to the weekend housekeeper, laundry service, or live-in nanny you most probably need and should want. Mathematically and emotionally speaking, it is cheaper to keep her than to work the "second shift" yourself when you get home, especially considering your earning power as the breadwinner. Men have always made bottom-line driven decisions to protect themselves financially and emotionally. You can learn a lot about protecting yourself emotionally from your male breadwinning counterparts. Extreme situations aside, men would never put themselves in the position of being expected to bring home the bacon, cook it, serve it, and then clean up the mess, too. Why should you?

While women have earned more rights in the workplace (though you still aren't fairly paid for your work), they frequently don't have equal rights when they come home at night. Rather, women are still disproportionately held responsible for the burden of the second shift. Whether or not you earn the lion's share of the income, study after study has found women are expected to do the lion's share of housework and child rearing. Society's definition of what comprises women's work and not men's work is part of the reason for this chore gap. In spite of both the modern man and woman agreeing "if we both work full-time, then we should both share household chores," women spend three times as long on domestic chores as their partners or husbands. In fact, one in five men admitted to doing nothing at all around the home. This chore gap is further evidenced by studies that show even when women work the same hours as their partners, or are the breadwinners in the relationship, they perform nine more hours of housework per week than men.

Even worse, being the breadwinner and then coming home and working the second shift can lead to depression. In a study of women across the United States, Leupp found that working mothers can reduce their risk of depression by recognizing that while they can *have* it all, they cannot *do* it all. This study found that while working moms have lower rates of depression than their stay-at-home counterparts, woman who attempt to be supermoms are at greater risk for depression. Supermoms were described as working mothers who expressed the attitude that work and home lives can be blended with relative ease. Whereas, working moms were described as mothers who accepted that they would have to surrender some aspects of their career or parenting to achieve a work-life balance. Ultimately, Leupp concluded, "women can happily juggle relationship or marriage, child rearing, household, and a career, if they are willing to accept that they can't do it all."

If you want to know it all about having it all, then *Mogul, Mom and Maid* by Liz O'Donnel is a must read. She shares her story and the stories of hundreds of women she interviewed, many of whom are breadwinners, who balance the demands of a career, motherhood, marriage, and household. O'Donnel provides insights about the choices women are making and their options — and the impact these decisions have on their families, the businesses that employ them, and the employees they employ in their companies. In addition to recommending you get help, she helps you realize you are not alone and provides striking insights, empowering strategies, and resources to help you.

Rule #6: Financial Infidelity: The New Extramarital Affair

Partners deceive each other financially all the time, and with devastating effect. According to a 2014 survey by the National Endowment for Financial Education, one partner out of every three couples admitted to lying or keeping secret some of their financial undertakings. Of the couples with a secretive partner, 76 percent reported financial deception had negatively impacted their relationships.

Meet Sylvester and Rochelle. Rochelle, is a 35-year-old school teacher and mother of two. Sylvester is an educated, charismatic, and single-minded 35-year-old businessman who thought he was well on his way to becoming a real estate mogul, or at least ensuring his family would never want for anything. He loves his boys and would do anything for his family.

Sylvester: "Other than the birth of our two children, the happiest day of my life was the day I gave Rochelle the keys to a new Range Rover and told her to quit her job. I had acquired numerous properties and was taking the equity out and flipping them, making more per transaction than her annual salary. We were living the life for several years. Then the bubble burst and I was upside down, and the banks suddenly wouldn't let me take any more equity loans out on my houses. The dream quickly became a nightmare. I kept hoping I could fix it, but no one was buying houses anymore. I was stuck with several properties and looming mortgages, so I robbed Peter to pay Paul as long as I could, hoping to buy time for the market to turn around. Dangerously behind, I was too embarrassed to tell her how deep a hole we were in, so I kept my secret to myself until she started getting calls from the banks and I couldn't hide anymore."

Rochelle: "Yes, I liked the feeling of quitting my job, but I didn't have to. I was too young to never work again. I was completely humiliated when I had to go back to my former employer with my tail between my legs, driving an old-model minivan. All of the naysayers knew we had been brusquely awakened from our American dream. We were living large. But, who needs a fully loaded Range Rover, a Jaguar, and a SL550 Mercedes Benz-Brabus? He would just show up with a new toy, without getting my feedback. Unbeknownst to me, he was purchasing some of these cars, houses, and getting equity loans in my name. When I discovered he had forged my signature, I felt completely betrayed. How can I ever trust him again? The empire he built was a house of cards, and his real estate ventures caused our marriage and family to come tumbling down, too. Today, we our living at an extended stay, our children's college fund is gone, and they are in public school. We had to short-sell our house and had to go through bankruptcy. It's hard not to be angry and feel totally violated by his clandestine real estate philandering."

Sylvester: "You didn't say that when we were on top; now that I'm down you want to kick me. You ingrate!"

Prior to the financial collapse of 2008, the data related to financial infidelity was both scarce and inconclusive. Today, however, researchers are finding that financial infidelity may be more damaging to relationships than sexual infidelity, as economic factors have negatively impacted the financial stability of U.S. households. In a recent online poll of 23,000 adults, "Today"/*SELF* found 60 percent of respondents view financial infidelity as harshly as sexual infidelity. Specifically, they found one in four spouses wouldn't tell their partners about "financial difficulties," shining a harsh light on the lengths some partners will go to hide financially damaging secrets from their spouses.

Couples Who Committed Financial Adultery

I have worked with numerous couples and families devastated by financial adultery, especially after the recent financial collapse. Working with these couples reveals that money is an emotional lightning rod, and the initial shock of infidelity is made much worse by the subsequent lies or cover ups to prevent their partner from discovering their financial hanky-panky — even if it was committed only to buy more time to solve the problem.

Preventive Maintenance

This is one of those times where an ounce of prevention is worth a pound of cure. To help partners avoid deceiving each other financially, I advise couples to consider putting in place some preventive maintenance ground rules to avoid financial infidelity before it occurs. For example:

- Agree to make financial decisions as a team, setting a dollar amount (let's say $250) where both must discuss and you both have to vote yes before making the purchase.

- Agree on a discretionary monthly sum of money that each partner can spend, "no questions asked," as long as it fits within the budget.

- Agree that creating an environment for transparency is a top priority. Namely, the consequences will be minimal if a partner confesses to having hidden money, compared to the consequences if their financial indiscretions are stumbled upon. Note: Studies show transparency builds trust and strengthens relation-ships.

- Agree on a policy regarding lending money to family members, grown children, and friends.

- Agree on who will pay which monthly expenses, and make it a habit of reviewing these accounts online, together.

- Agree on how to take care of aging parents.

Telltale Signs Your Partner May Be Committing Financially Adultery

- Your partner wants to clandestinely control the finances, without your input.

- You notice suspicious withdrawals from investment accounts.

- Your partner changes the subject when money discussions come up.

- You are made to feel like you are being intrusive or disrespectful to ask about your family's finances.

Three Scenarios That Place Couples at High-Risk for Financial Infidelity

1. **Couples With a Strong Connection, but Vastly Different Outlets**

   Typically these couples love each other dearly and are committed to the marriage, but their tastes, interests, or hobbies are different in some unresolvable way. While they can talk about most differences and resolve conflicts effectively, they cannot get on the same page when it comes to why she is willing to spend $1,800 on a Chanel designer bag, or $600 on a rare autographed copy of Frederick Douglass' autobiography; or why he spent $3,000 on a new set of tires with ceramic ball-bearings for his $6,000 all-carbon aero-road bicycle. Unless they can agree to disagree and allow each other their vices, they will likely have a difficult time remaining financially faithful.

   When working with couples confronted with this particular challenge, I try to emphasize that A) basically they are happy, which is most important, and that getting the partner to surrender a pet indulgence would likely result in a win-lose outcome, and, consequently, that would lead to a lose-lose outcome. As a result, they would inevitably experience relationship discord if they continued to insist these purchases represent a character flaw or that their partner should give up the hobby, rather than accept that these purchases are simply important to their partner's feelings of happiness. They don't have to get it. B) At the same time, we emphasize transparency around purchases related to their vices, and we agree these purchases cannot interfere with joint financial goals, such as paying scheduled bills and saving for a home purchase, children's college fund, or retirement. C) Next, I encourage the partners set up a "yours," "mine," and "ours" savings account to accommodate these indulgent purchases.

2. **Couples Who Are No Longer Happy and Harbor Feelings of Betrayal and Resentment**

   Ironically, as with emotional and sexual infidelity, the financially unfaithful partner frequently felt betrayed before they strayed. (See Chapter 7: When Soulmates Cheat.) Once a partner's predominant sentiment about the relationship comes to reflect feelings of disappointment from unmet expectations, all bets are off. In view of that, it certainly isn't a stretch for one partner to start to think, "How do I take care of myself in case this doesn't work out?" or "Given how much you've screwed me over, it is only fair I even the score a little." In these cases, it's not uncommon to find sexual infidelity is present, too.

   When working with these couples, I emphasize that they A) must start financial counseling immediately, B) should both decide they still want the relationship and demonstrate an openness to work through their trust and betrayal issues, and C) explore the possibility that some compulsive spending behaviors have developed as a coping mechanism created by the void created by their relationship tension. If one partner has developed an expensive, compulsive spending habit, or one partner has acted solo in a series of business deals that have soured (like Sylvester in our case study), then it may make sense for the other partner to stash cash away to feel prepared for a rainy day, especially if they have young children.

3. **One Partner Has a Relative Who Needs Help or Has Grown-Up Kids**

Sometimes blood is simply thicker than water. Siblings, children, grandkids, and parents who are in dire need can prove irresistible. Resisting these requests is even more difficult when the partner is the only successful member of the family, despite the fact that they are disproportionately asked to rescue their less successful relatives (and seldom reimbursed). While I've seen partners pledge to stop violating the sanctity of their current relationship, when partners find themselves in a catch-22, these promises often prove too difficult to keep. These lose-lose situations frequently end in financial betrayal. As mentioned in Chapter 6: When Mr. Right's Circumstances Make Him Mr. Wrong, failure to resolve family feuds in a win-win fashion will *always* come back to bite you, no matter how on board your partner appears to be. I've seen couple after couple who were deeply in love with each other have the fabric of their relationship unravel from employing win-lose resolutions. Despite their good intentions, the blood of their interfamily conflict will be on their hands.

Meet the Smiths. Jerry and Sherri have been married for three years. Jerry is a 55-year-old Metro train driver who is the father of three. Sherri is a 42-year-old, master-degree level researcher at the National Institutes of Health who doesn't have children. This is her second marriage, and she blamed the demise of the first marriage solely on her ex-husband's extramarital affairs. Jerry's oldest daughter, Nadine, has returned to college after being placed on academic probation because she was working as a bartender at nights to help pay for school. Jerry never married Nadine's mother. She is the first in his family to attend college. He is very proud of her, and her getting a degree means the world to him — so much so that after withdrawing from school after her freshman year due to financial hardship, he convinced her to return to complete her degree. Nadine is in the second semester of her third year in a nursing program and has thrived academically since giving up her bartending job and dedicating herself to school full-time. However, when she went on campus to enroll, the comptroller informed her that she needed to pay $2,500 by the end of the week to register for that semester. Panicked, Jerry approached Sherri about helping Nadine out. He was stunned when Sherri said, "That girl of yours is a grown woman. Why won't she accept responsibility and get off her lazy ass, quit partying, get a job, and ask her unemployed mother to give her some money? Hell, she can get a job dancing on a pole for all I care. Besides, I was planning on using $3,500 to lay down some new hardwood floors to get ready for our Thanksgiving dinner, and you agreed to provide $2,000 of it. I'm your wife, and we need to focus on building our life together. We can't let them keep bringing us down with their problems."

Sherri also told me she called Nadine and told her to grow up, quit using her father, and stop sabotaging their marriage. Nadine hung up, and Sherri feels he didn't protect her when he didn't insist Nadine apologize. Sherri also said Nadine was no longer welcome in her house.

In couples therapy, Jerry had gone from conflicted and disillusioned to wanting to retain a divorce attorney, while Sherri insisted she loved him deeply and wanted the marriage to work. Her approach to resolving this family feud was to have Jerry accept he needed to be head of household and put her first. She also felt he needed to quit being manipulated by his children, which was causing her to lose respect for him. Jerry indicated he couldn't live with himself if he paid $2,000 toward new hardwood floors he didn't feel they needed before helping his daughter get her degree and pursue her dream to become a nurse. "Think of how it will impact my future grandchildren," he said. Sherri didn't get it. Instead, she responded, "I have nephews and nieces and know how to set boundaries. You need to set firmer boundaries, too, so that Nadine and her siblings get it. Why are we focused on your daughter and not our marriage anyway? I don't want to discuss her anymore, and shouldn't be made to feel that her happiness is more important than your wife's. That's not what heads of household do. Happy wife, happy life."

When working with couples confronted with this particular challenge, I emphasize that A) basically they are happy with each other and want their relationship to last. At the same time, I emphasize that maintaining their happiness is dependent upon resolving their partner's catch -22 in a way that gives that partner an out (including setting a mutually agreed upon discretionary amount, say $150, that the partner can give without asking permission). However, the partner cannot keep financial secrets, as they pose a serious threat to the integrity of the fabric of their long-term relationship's success; B) create win-win outcomes by having relatives respect their relationship by asking them as a couple (instead of asking the relative individually) for loans or gifts greater than the discretionary amount; and C) they agree these loans or gifts cannot interfere with joint financial goals such as paying scheduled bills or saving for a home purchase, children's college fund, or retirement.

Finally, numerous studies show that financial infidelity occurs evenly across all income levels and both sexes. In some ways it is more harmful than sexual infidelity — both financially and emotionally. Should this form of betrayal occur in your relationship, seriously consider getting relationship and financial counseling.

Rule #7: Love and the Law

While love can be an unpredictable emotion, the law is very predictable, spelling things out clearly in black and white. Divorce happens! I'm not trying to put a wet blanket on soulmate love, however, 45 percent of the time marriage ends in divorce, so it could very well happen to you. In the worst-case scenario, getting a friendly legal consult on the front end can save you from having to lawyer-up on the back end.

First, before you get your marriage license, both of you need to get your credit reports from all three bureaus. Swap them and discuss them. Accept that how he manages his personal accounts is probably the best predictor of how he will manage your joint accounts. I know this doesn't sound romantic. It's not. Marriage and becoming a joint legal entity is a business decision, too.

Mr. Right: "But you love me, right?"

Ms. Right: "Of course, I do. If I didn't, your credit report wouldn't matter to me."

In addition to sharing your credit report, it's important that you be honest with what his report tells you. If there are red flags don't ignore them, because once you two are legally wedded you won't be able to avoid landing in the red. In community property states, you could be held liable for debt your husband accrued as a single man. If you don't live in a community property state, you are liable for repayment of debts you both agreed to be responsible for, such as a cosigned car loan, mortgage, or credit cards.

Next, the two of you should consider talking about a plan to get rid of all premarital debt before jumping the broom.

Finally, while only 1 percent of couples in the U.S. have prenuptial agreements, it doesn't mean the 99 percent of us couldn't benefit from the insider knowledge of the "one-percenters," especially when you earn more. Here are some considerations for prenuptial agreements:

- Coercion is illegal, so both of you should have attorneys present. Consider video-taping your agreement to prove you both participated consensually. Many states also require the agreement be signed six months before the wedding to demonstrate there wasn't coercion.

- Agreements biased toward one partner can be voided.

- Disclose all assets and liabilities, or state law can nullify, or void, the agreement.

- Know all state laws apply to your prenuptial agreement. For example, some states will not enforce an agreement that waives alimony or child support.

Divorce sucks. And, I go to battle with couples to prevent it. In marital therapy, I've not seen a prenuptial agreement determine whether or not a couple divorced or remained together. Moreover, 99 percent of couples don't have a prenuptial agreement in place, so most couples who divorce don't have an agreement. That said, it's been my experience that by time it gets to the divorce stage, that loving feeling is long gone. In its place is an intense, cynical and short-sighted focus on winning that borders on contempt, if not hate. Assets are a universal way spouses keep score. It just seems you need to take every precaution to protect assets on the front end to avoid financial devastation on the back end, particularly when you earn more and bring more to the party. If your earning potential is greater, you could wind up paying alimony (or palimony in California).

CHAPTER 6

When Mr. Right's Circumstances Make Him Mr. Wrong: 13 Ways to Distinguish Game Changers From Deal Breakers

"Often the key to success is recognizing a bad
situation early on—and getting the hell out."
—Dr. Mark Perrault

No man is perfect. You have to take the good with the bad in any relationship. At the same time, all bads aren't created equal: Some bads are potentially good; other bads are just, well, bad or game changers — and others are deal breakers. While it is definitely not my place to say who anyone should chose for their Mr. Right, I will say choosing a man with a game changer as a life partner makes living happily ever after a lot harder. Choosing a Mr. Wrong with a deal breaker may make it impossible. To help you evaluate your choice better, in this chapter I will share some of the insights I've gleaned from research and reading, years of providing relationship and marital therapy in private practice, and working with couples where a woman chose or married a man from this list of game changers and deal breakers.

You can take or leave them.

The majority of the couples that come in to my practice possess far more strengths than weakness. At the same time, a minority of them come in with behaviors that raise red flags I suspect didn't just appear out of nowhere. Rather, these red flags were overlooked, rationalized away (perhaps because one or both partners were projecting some of their dreams, fantasies, and hopes onto their partner), ignored, or she thought she could change him — or vice-versa. In any event, it was clear to me the two people sitting on my couch clearly shouldn't have ever ended up together in a long-term relationship or marriage. And it is even more heartbreaking when these couples have children. Typically, they say something, like, "we don't like each other and aren't even friends (and never have been), but we've got kids, and have to work it out."

I truly admire their commitment to their families and desire to work things out in spite of this fact. The goal of this chapter, however, is to point out certain unalterable and undeniable game changers and deal breakers to avoid so they don't doom your reality. Rather, when you and your partner decide to sit on my couch — or any of my colleagues' couches — I hope it's because you want to make a good relationship even better! If this list helps one woman avoid a toxic relationship or marriage with Mr. Wrong, I will consider it a huge success. To this end, please allow me to share with you perhaps the most crucial lessons learned after working with 15-plus couples a week over the last decade.

As I've previously mentioned, there are five Cs that will determine whether your relationship is functional or dysfunctional: Choice, Commitment, Communication, Conflict Resolution Skills and Coach-ablity. While I can generally work around the middle three Cs, the first C — Choice — is a fixed variable. You either chose wisely or you didn't. Hopefully, this list will help you realize what deal breakers and potential deal breakers you might want to seriously consider avoiding. Often the partners we chose to drop are as critical to living happily ever after as the ones we chose to keep.

Choice is the key to reaping the good fortune accompanying soulmate love.

In contrast, a poor choice that leads to a lifelong union with Mr. Wrong could be the key to great misfortune. Choosing to remain with, have children with, or marry a partner listed on this list of game changers or deal breakers could set you up to live a life right out Charles Dickens' *A Tale of Two Cities:* "… the worst of times." The couples I've worked with have taught me that all flaws aren't created equal: Some are exasperating; others are toxic. If that sounds harsh or cynical, I apologize. Again, I am not saying who you should choose as a partner here, but I won't be disingenuous and pretend I don't think some partnerships are doomed from the start. And based on research and my clinical experience, often the key to success is getting the hell out early on.

That said, here is my list of 13 game changers and deal breakers:

GAME CHANGERS

Although traditionally associated with a positive thing, game changers as referred to here speak about dating or marrying where some aspect of your interaction will make living happily ever after a lot harder. To help you evaluate your choices better, in this chapter I will share some of the insights I've gleaned from research and reading, years of providing relationship and marital therapy in private practice, and working with couples where a woman chose a man from this list of game changers.

1. **Emotional Incompatibility.** Is your partner "needy" or "neglected"? You love each other intensely, yet tend to find yourself feeling unappreciated and lonely in the relationship or marriage despite your strong feelings for each other and best attempts to address each other's emotional concerns. The problem frequently is you are trying to meet their partner's needs in the way you want their needs met (instead of learning how your partner wishes their needs be met). Eventually, if not careful, you could easily come to resent each other for rejecting each other's attempts to be supportive. Underlying this problem is the reality that while we as people tend to hire the same and marry the opposite. That is, we hire employees similar to us, while tending to seriously date and marry partners that are opposites, yet expect them to respond to our challenges and needs in the same manner we would.

In particular, there are two different personality types that frequently find themselves drawn to each other, but inevitably spend a lot of energy arguing and feeling deeply wounded by their differences: dismissive types partnered with meta-processors; and introverts partnered with extroverts.

While dismissive types tend to internalize and compartmentalize their feelings and seemingly only need a quick fix or silver bullet to move on, meta-processors tend to want to talk about their feelings and the feelings about their feelings. The painful reality of these differences in emotional styles wasn't as apparent when they first met; however, now they leave each other feeling "neglected" or one partner feels as though the other partner is "needy."

141

In a similar fashion, introverts and extroverts find themselves initially drawn to each other, but ultimately feel unloved, alone, and unsupported in their relationships. We tend to think of introverts as being shy and loners and extroverts as outgoing and gregarious types who never meet a stranger. In contrast, Meyer-Briggs distinguishes introverts from extroverts based on a different criteria: how they recharge their batteries. Introverts recharge their batteries through isolation and me-time, while extroverts tend to recharge their batteries through interactions with others. This difference can result in introverts coming home after a long day with co-workers and wanting to be left alone, while the extrovert partner may be eager to discuss their day and start enjoying an activity together. In addition, come Friday night, the introvert may want to spend the evening at home, enjoying a quiet dinner, rather than out with her friends. Finally, the extrovert's need to interact with others while she is out may be seen as flirtatious and rude, while the more reserved introvert typically lacks a need for social interaction that may cause him to be seen as rude, aloof, or even mean.

I've met several couples whose happiness was undermined by the perpetual gridlock caused by these differences in personality, and have witnessed more than a few of them be relegated from soulmates to roommates. Even more unfortunate, it is not uncommon for partners to share these different personality types in tandem, with an introverted, dismissive type being partnered with an extroverted, meta-processor.

No matter how much they try and talk about it, the words just seem to get in the way.

This tendency to misjudge your partner's needs results in emotional blind spots that prevent you from recognizing there isn't a one-size-fits-all solution to meeting your partner's emotional needs, and you and your partner's attempts aren't working for each other. Nevertheless, the problem isn't a lack of concern or effort.

For these reasons, if you and your soulmate find yourselves feeling "unloved, alone, and unsupported" based on these or a combination of these personality differences, know it neither means you are incompatible or are not meant for each other, nor does it mean that your conflict is coming from a selfish or mean-spirited place. Rather, you are just wired and experience the world in different ways. Accordingly, you two might benefit from talking to a counselor to educate yourselves about each other's interpersonal style and develop the skills needed to move from isolation, resentment, and anger to hearing and forgiving each other, and reconnecting.

2. **Family Feuds:** As Rosie Perez famously said to Woody Harrelson in the movie "White Men Can't Jump": "Sometimes even when you win, you lose; and other times even when you lose, you win." Resolving family feuds in a win-lose fashion will *always* hurt you. By family feuds, I mean entrenched, ongoing conflicts with step-children, parents, or siblings, and so on. The damage caused by these conflicts tends to be twofold: First, your partner is likely to feel bad about the loss of the family member involved in the conflict; and second, family members tend to be clannish, and therefore likely to rally behind the family member involved. Stuck in the middle of this catch-22, they would be damned for choosing you by their family member(s), and damned by you for choosing the family member.

I've seen countless couples that were deeply in love and otherwise happy have the fabric of their relationship unravel because they couldn't resolve a family feud in a win-win fashion. Whether or not his spoiled brat of a son went into your jewelry box and took your prized pearl necklace without your permission and you felt justified to slap him, your reasoning and perspective will likely be lost when the step-son's mother and grandmother retell the story to various family members. At best, your side of the story will remain untold; at worst it will be distorted. You will be demonized. For these reasons, if your partner is forced to no longer have his son visit your house on weekends he has custodial visits or holidays, this decision has the potential to cause significant unforeseen damage. Even if your partner appears on board with his son being wrong and had, in fact, told you it was OK to discipline him, he will likely experience major ambivalence once their estrangement results in him missing significant family events (such as birthday parties, holidays, and graduations) because he shouldn't go if he can't bring you. God forbid the grandmother (his mother) should die before the conflict is resolved.

The guilt he may feel for becoming and remaining estranged from his family could come back to haunt you, although you may have been right to punish her for disrespecting you. Getting this blood on your hands could ultimately mean you lose, although you feel right and are justified for teaching him a valuable lesson. Nonetheless, being right may prove to be a pyrrhic victory, which is akin to cursing out your boss for not giving you the raise you wanted. Although you may have been rightfully due a raise, you will likely be fired. To truly win here, you may have to give your spouse an out, even if that feels like you lose. No, I'm not suggesting you compromise your dignity, or concede a critical point, or otherwise create a lose-win situation for you, because that will only result in your becoming resentful. On the contrary, I'm suggesting you accept that in some instances he isn't going to be able to get his son to apologize to you, and that doesn't mean he is dishonoring you as a wife. You have to find a way to make peace, if possible. Consider a cost-benefit analysis, and weigh whether in the big picture this family feud is more important to you than the damage it can do to your relationship.

3. <u>Inter-faith relationships.</u> While America is becoming browner and browner as integration has led to a dramatic

increase in interracial marriages, Sunday from 8 a.m. to 1 p.m., America is as segregated as ever.

(Unlike any of the other game changers, I feel like addressing this issue is above my pay grade—literally! This is a complex topic. "God, I prayerfully ask that you please not let me mislead anyone here.") First and foremost, let me commend you for your openness and acknowledge that the two of you undoubtedly have a very special relationship, authentically respect and admire each other, and doubtlessly possess true chemistry to even consider taking on this challenge. These are all the things of soulmate love. For the record, yes, I do believe soulmates can come from different religions. At the same time, I think it can be very difficult in some cases.

That said, while inter-faith marriages are rising fast, they are failing fast, too. The American Religious Identification Survey of 2001 found that inter-faith marriages are three times more likely to end in divorce or separation than same-faith marriages. To best respond to your interest in inter-faith love or marriage with Mr. Right, I think it is important to formulate a reply to couples without children (or plans to have children) and one for couples with children (or with plans to have children).

Without children or plans to have children. This is a simpler decision than when kids are involved, but that doesn't mean it's an easy one. You should be with the partner that makes you happy, especially given that same-faith marriages can end in unhappiness, separation, and divorce, too. However, I'd be remiss if didn't tell you inter-faith marriages can cause additional conflict and may result in your Mr. Right having access to a private world you can't enter. This could be a potential powder keg that can be ignited at any moment and blow up in your face. Of the inter-faith couples I've worked with, I've found the outcomes are reflective of their conflict resolution skills, philosophical and emotional flexibility, openness to differences, ability to laugh, and the support of family members significant to both partners.

Even if they possess the aforementioned skills, traits, and families, I have found traditions associated with holidays and spiritually significant rituals can be more difficult to negotiate than originally imagined, particularly as it relates to family. These events are as much about family (if you have an intact one), and couples must sometimes find a way to attend each other's events in spite of their personal beliefs. To this end, I've also seen it be a much easier process for partners that weren't as devout; conversely, I've seen more devout couples struggle with the reality that religion is a much more integral part of everyday life than they were consciously aware of in the beginning. Negotiating these differences could likely prove to be an ongoing process. Also, I've found that some religions may have more beliefs in common and comfort or familiarity with each other than others, while others don't even acknowledge each other's spiritual traditions, spiritual leaders, and symbols. Finally, and perhaps most concerning, some religions share a hostile history or are currently experiencing tension that impacts a partner's families and friends, which could impact the couple negatively.

With children or plans to have children. Everything mentioned above applies, coupled with the decision of how to raise your kids, which can prove to be the ultimate deal breaker for inter-faith marriages. Pre-agreed upon decisions, such as no religion, both, or the same must be made, and may seem like they will solve your problem. However, even when these foreseeable decisions are made, unforeseen issues inevitably arise, such as if my child doesn't get baptized will they go to hell? Throw grandparents into the mix and tempers of people you love can flare.

4. <u>**ADHD, depression, and bipolar disorder.**</u> If your partner has ADHD or depression, and is opposed to treatment, then your hands are tied. It likely won't work. On the other hand, if he is open to treatment, and has learned how to (and is committed to) manage the symptoms associated with ADHD and depression, he may still be a good candidate. If the latter is true, you two will need professional help, including a psychologist, psychiatrist, and/or a life coach. You two will not be able to navigate these murky and turbulent waters alone.

If he or you has bipolar disorder and you are questioning if you two are soulmates, everything above applies. In addition, there is no way to sugarcoat that an estimated 90 percent of marriages to a bipolar partner ends in divorce.

Finally, perhaps the biggest consideration you need to make when you chose a partner with ADHD, depression, or bipolar disorder is genetic transmission. Your chances of having children with these disorders and co-morbid disorders (anxiety, PTSD, and substance abuse) rise significantly when you marry a partner with one of these disorders. For some, psychological problems may be deal breakers instead of game changers. Ultimately, it depends on the intensity of symptoms and how they are managed, and the personalities of the partners involved.

5.   **Open relationships**. So you want to open Pandora's box? On the face of it, this could easily appear like you are requesting a triangle, but there is a very different trust dynamic in play here. Specifically, most of the damage caused by infidelity comes from deception, betrayal, and the cover-up that typically unravels the integrity of a relationship. However, that isn't the case here, at least not initially. Rather, couples appreciate being open, candid, and upfront with each other about their sexuality. Instead, the damage usually arises from having opened Pandora's box. What if one partner can't handle the new relationship or abuses some aspect of it? Once open, this box is very difficult—if not impossible—to shut. Herein, frequently lies the potential deal breaker. Specifically, what happens when one person choses to keep this arrangement and the

other no longer wants it? What happens when one partner engages with the third party without the partner's consent? What do you do should one partner develop feelings for a third party? What do you do when one partner can't deal with the images of seeing the partner pleasured by someone of the same sex? What do you do when someone gets pregnant? Any of these issues has the potential to be a deal breaker.

If you are feeling like most of my examples I've provided so far are negative, it's because that's a more accurate reflection of my experiences working with couples who have opened up Pandora's box. Let them serve as a cautionary tale. At the same time, both married couples and unmarried couples consider this scenario. First, I've seen couples say, "Hey this marriage is dead as it currently exists, and if we are going to keep it alive or give it a rebirth to save our family, then an open marriage is the ticket." Next, I've met very sexually adventurous and honest unmarried couples who negotiated open relationships in a mutually fulfilling fashion, where everyone's sexual and emotional needs and fantasies were met. In either case, you two will need to talk and think about it thoroughly, be brutally honest with each other about your needs and limits, and remember that no matter what may happen, you both agreed to this arrangement.

6.   **Financial incompatibility.** "Money can't buy you love, but fighting over it can definitely bankrupt you" — Michelle Singletary, author of *Your Money, Your Man*.

Face it, money is a very emotional issue.

Couples come into my practice with very conflicting views about money and relationships with money. Although these differences may have worked while they were dating, they have the potential to become very problematic once the two try to merge. For example, those nice designer suits Paul wears and that luxury car he picks you up in were quite a turn-on when he was courting you, but not so much when you discover he isn't willing to change his tastes or downsize so you can put more money into savings for a rainy day, buying a home, or retirement. Alternatively, you were considering a frugal man like Robert whose tendency to focus on the savings and cutting costs was impressive; however, you subsequently realized he was a cheapskate when he told you on Valentine's Day that "flowers die." (A client actually said this in therapy. I cringed.) So who should you — and how do you — chose? In my workbook, I offer a "Financial Compatibility" test, and I encourage you two to take it and compare results. (See theBlackMANual.com.)

Also, look at his debit-credit card entries (I used to say checkbook, but they've since become virtually extinct), and you will probably learn a lot more about his relationship with money. Finally, at some point before going too far into the permanently committed phase of your relationship, you will need to look at each other's credit reports from all three bureaus.

7. **Infidelity.** This is listed last only because I have a whole chapter dedicated to this important game changer. Infidelity doesn't have to be a deal breaker, but it definitely has the potential to be. If you are dealing with this issue, I thoroughly encourage you to read Chapter 7, When Soulmates Cheat.

DEAL BREAKERS

While choosing a man with a game changer as a life partner makes living happily ever after a lot harder, choosing a man with a deal breaker may make it impossible. To help you evaluate your choices better, in this chapter I will share some of the insights I've gained from research and reading, years of providing relationship and marital therapy, and working firsthand with couples where a woman chose a Mr. Right whose circumstances made him Mr. Wrong because of one of the listed of deal breakers.

8. **Characterological abusers.** In the article "Typologies of Intimate Partner Violence," Faniel Joseph Friends et al. defines (and provides a screening measure) to help you distinguish between characterological abusers (CA) and situational abusers, (SA). CAs commit severe emotional and physical abuse to dominate, control, and manipulate a romantic partner; and this type of perpetrator frequently displays anti-social or borderline personality traits compared to non-violent men. SA's violence is physical aggression between partners consisting of low-level violence (e.g., pushing, shoving grabbing, etc.). While psychological abuse exhibited by the SA is similar to that exhibited by the CA, it occurs less frequently and is absent of controlling and dominating behaviors. Finally, SA violent men do not exhibit borderline or antisocial traits any more than non-violent men.

In contrast with CAs, Jacobson and Gottman found SAs are in relationships characterized by reciprocal physical aggression between partners, and the levels of violence are less frequent and occur as a result of unmanageable conflicts that escalate in physical aggression. Further, the level of aggressive behaviors is less intense (for example, pushing, spitting, shoving, grabbing, etc.), and there is an absence of controlling and dominating behavior.

If these descriptions of abuse remind you of your relationship, I encourage you to accept that the depth of your partner's problems are beyond your power to heal, not your fault, and no matter how much you love him, this relationship could very well end tragically.

(Note: Help with an abusive relationship is beyond the scope of this book. In addition, psychotherapy is contra-indicated for a characterological abuser. However, I encourage you to seek the help of a professional, non-profit agency, or program.)

9. **Substance-, gambling-, alcohol-, sex-, or porn-addicted partners.** I've worked with addicts for many years, providing psychological services for a methadone clinic for

heroin addicts and alcoholics at several VA hospitals as a pre-doctorial intern and while a graduate student at the Ohio State University. In addition, I worked with sex addicts and pedophiles during my internship at an off-site practicum at a training clinic affiliated with Johns Hopkins Medical Center during my year as a graduate student intern. These experiences taught me addiction is a disease, not simply a decision. Consequently, addicts are frequently self-medicating other co-morbid psychiatric disorders and require intensive specialized treatment. I am not excusing their behaviors, rather I am acknowledging the reality that their problems are a complex combination of physiological, genetic, emotional, and sociological factors. Accordingly, quitting frequently involves much more than "I love you, and will quit _____ to keep you," although you will frequently be told just that. We liken it in the addiction field to making love with a gorilla: You aren't done until the gorilla is done. Likewise, no matter how much he loves you, there is over a 90 percent chance of relapse. At best, your love can be a part of their long-term success after he is well into his recovery, has substantial "clean time" under his belt, and is actively involved in an aftercare support group.

While being in love with or married to any addict is confusing and heartbreaking, being involved with a sexual or porn addict can have a particularly devastating effect on a partner's psyche. Sexual addiction is a powerful and frequently misunderstood addiction. A few years ago, in my blog in *Psychology Today* magazine, I blogged about "Why Would a Happy Tiger Woods Cheat?" when all indicators suggested he was happy in his marriage. Nonetheless, his addiction, obsessive cravings, and sexual predilections overrode everything he once valued, including family, friends, fortune, and fame—and even the "clean cut" image that came along with lucrative endorsement contracts. In the end, none of these factors stood a chance against Tiger's addiction to the hunt.

As a sex addict once said to me in group therapy, "If you asked about having sex with a giraffe someone in this group would know what to do with the legs. We see the world different than non-addicts." Sexual and porn addiction has nothing to do with their partner's performance in bed. In contrast, non-sex addicts who commit adultery are usually unhappy in their marriage, and the affair is typically a symptom of marital problems, not the problem itself. While both require counseling, sexual and porn addiction is unique and requires specialized sexual addiction psychotherapy. Jennifer Schneider's research finds that in 70 percent of couples in which one partner has a cybersex addiction, at least one of the partners will lose interest in their sex life together. I recognize porn can be a compliment to your sex life to enhance mutual pleasure during sexual intercourse with your partner. However, if one partner sneaks to view porn alone and keeps it a secret, porn can easily become a form of betrayal, particularly should it become a habit and take on a compulsive quality.

When it comes to addiction, please recognize and accept your love cannot save an addict from himself. Period!

(Note: Help with a partner with an addiction is beyond the scope of this book. I encourage you to seek the help of a professional, non-profit agency, or program.)

(Note: External influences aside, deal breakers #8 and #9 are the only two where the couple may actually have found their soulmate, and have what it takes to live happily ever after, but break up or divorce instead.)

10.   Emotionally unavailable men — married men.

"If someone is willing to cheat with you,
they will cheat on you."
— Unknown

If I had a dollar for every time I heard, "He's married. But he really loves me and she is such an evil witch. She's ruining his life. He hates her and is planning on leaving her any day now! Technically he's separated, even though they're still living together. He sleeps in the basement, while she is upstairs in their old bedroom, and he texts me all times of the night, so I know it's true." Yes, all men come with baggage, but this is more like the Zero-Halliburton indestructible type.

Statistics on relationships that start with an affair indicate only 7 percent of the men ended up marrying the other woman. Even worse, 75 percent of those marriages end in divorce. Unsurprisingly, the reasons given for this high divorce rate include distrust of the other person, a general distrust in marriage, guilt over hurting children and former spouse, and challenges associated with blending the family. Finally, perhaps the biggest challenge these marriages born out of fantasy face is the disappointment with the reality of the actual relationship compared with the imagined relationship.

One famous example is Deion Sanders, who left his wife for Pilar, and married her. Their subsequent high-profile celebrity divorce was almost as high profile as their marriage. Yet this outcome (minus the Reality TV show audience) typifies what happens when the "other woman" gets her man. Perhaps a worse example of the likelihood of infidelity once he leaves her for you is presented by former GOP presidential candidate Newt Gingrich. Newt left his first wife for the second, and then left the second wife for his third wife, Callista Gingrich, to whom he is still married. Nevertheless, there are other famous exceptions to the rule that men who leave their wives for the other women inevitably cheat on the other women, too. For example, former GOP presidential candidate John McCain is still happily married to Cindy McCain, for whom he allegedly left his first wife. Brad Pitt, who was married to Jennifer Aniston, left her for his now-wife, Angela Jolie-Pitt. As far as we know John McCain and Brad Pitt have been faithful to their second wives, and from the outside looking in, these marriages appear happy.

Cindy McCain and Angela Jolie-Pitt aside, statistics suggest you may have a better chance of winning the Mega-Millions lottery than ending up living happily ever after with the man you've taken from his wife.

11. **Emotionally unavailable men, unmarried.** Unlike women who are dating their married counterparts, women who date single, yet unavailable men find themselves in a completely different situation. First, no studies have been conducted on these men, so I can't tell you the statistical probability of a better or worse outcome than dating an emotionally unavailable man. However, my experience with these women in therapy suggests the chances of you two living happily ever after are rare, even if you should marry him. (Personally, however, I recommend you purchase that lottery ticket and take the proceeds and find your own, unmarried Mr. Right.)

Meet Ashley. Ashley, age 32, is a practical, smart, outgoing, and meticulously dressed, actuary at a top insurance company. Having majored in mathematics at Spelman College, she is great with numbers and people and is on the fast track at her company. Although she frequently finds herself without a date on most weekend nights, it isn't for a lack of suitors, as men find her approachable, witty, and charmingly sweet.

But she is smitten with Mr. Right, Nick, an alpha-male, and is 100 percent committed to him.

Nick is a very successful and suave, workaholic entrepreneur, who, at 42, is well on his way to becoming a confirmed bachelor. Designer suits and expensive watches, exotic cars, and a stately house in the Gold Coast (an upscale Washington, D.C., neighborhood) are just a few of the things that make him irresistible to her, and, as Ashley fears, to other women, too. While Ashley may be in denial about it, Nick is fully aware that he loves living the good life and is a bit of a sexual addict who has no interest in being committed or exclusive. He doesn't want to risk parting with any portion of his hard-earned wealth, either. He was born into poverty and went to school at Tuskegee on a baseball scholarship. That said, he acquired his wealth the old-fashioned way: He earned it.

Quiet as it is kept, Nick is a bit Machiavellian. He has no interest in becoming Ashley's prince charming, much less searching about for a Cinderella with a glass slipper in hand. Shrewd and a bit opportunistic, if he marries at all, it will be to a well-heeled woman who brings at least as much as he does to the party. While a philanderer, he's no philanthropist. Financially speaking, he and his spouse will be equally yoked. He's a businessman through and through, and not given to emotional decisions or fairytale endings.

Fearful of him abandoning her if she brings up the status of their relationship, his unavailability, and inability to commit, or her concerns that he may be womanizing, Ashley avoids confronting him and instead internalizes her apprehensions to avoid scaring away such a "good catch." Instead, she remains in denial and rationalizes his unavailability to his work ethic, despite several of her friends seeing him around town with different women and hearing rumors about him having strippers at his boat parties. Of course, she doesn't complain to him about never being invited to his boat parties.

Ashley insists one day Nick will realize there is more to life than making more money, want kids, and be ready to slow down—with her, of course. Despite her intuition screaming, "run, Forrest, run" and her friends' warnings, she's planning on waiting him out. She is hopeful he will put a ring on it one day. Who wouldn't, right? I mean, they have been dating for over seven years now, and who else could he really trust besides her? All of these other blood thirsty women just want him for his money, but she met him before he accumulated his assets. She's been there for him. Right by his side. Yes, Ashley is definitely the one.

INTERVENTION

In therapy, Ashley and I talked about her dream of marrying Nick. She was initially hesitant to share they had been together for seven years and he had never proposed or officially agreed to upgrade their relationship status to committed, much less become exclusive. When asked about how she felt about him not committing and his unavailability, she said, "Nick has been through a lot in life" and I would have to know him like she does to truly understand. I responded, "You are right." I requested she invite him to attend a session so I could get his perspective on their relationship.

After three no shows, he finally called during a session.

When I asked how he saw their relationship, he responded, "Ashley is my boo, and she knows what that means to me." As Ashley melted upon being referred to as his "boo," I couldn't help but notice he didn't respond directly and it sounded like he was placating her. When I asked him help me understand what precisely being his boo meant, he responded: "Ummm, you know, my boo. Doesn't that speak for itself? Have you ever had a boo?" I asked, "Does this mean you want to commit to her one day?" He chuckled and said, "Ashley knows I love her and can't commit right now."

"Right now?" I repeated.

He said, "Look, I'm not trying to string anyone along here, but committing isn't an easy thing when you've worked as hard as I have to make it. Why would I risk potentially giving half of my assets up, should things go south? That could ruin me financially. Do you know what it's like to be poor, and go from rags to riches?"

"No, but I get that," I said. "You just said love. Do you love Ashley?"

"Love her? Yes, of course, I do."

"Great. Are you in love with her?"

"In love? That's a strong notion," he said.

I agreed. Then I told Nick he was too bright and successful a man not to be able to communicate with me directly, so perhaps he was purposefully choosing to be vague and avoidant. I then challenged him to be a man and love her enough to set her free if he wasn't going to do right by her. "We both know what time it is," I said. "How would you want your sister or daughter to be treated by a man?"

After an extended pause. He said, "Look, Doc I've been straight up here. Ashley knows we just kick it. I've told her over a hundred times, 'I don't see marriage in the cards for us — er, I mean me — right now.'"

"So you aren't marrying her?" I asked.

"I know what this looks like, but I've not played games here," he said. "Clearly, if I haven't committed in seven years, I'm not looking to marry her. Don't my actions speak for themselves? How clear do I need to be? Ashley is trying to make a come-up, and I don't roll like that. I ain't mad at her; she's trying to get hers but I ain't the one."

Ashley was absolutely devastated, and it took me a while to console her. However, the next week she was at a different place. Steeled and relieved, she said, "I needed to hear that. I never would have confronted him. Candidly, I'm madder at myself than him, because I knew things didn't feel right, but was too scared to confront him."

We talked about her fear of confrontation and where it originated. She said she saw her mother and father fight all the time as a little girl, and vowed not to run her man away like her overly confrontational and angry mother did to her father.

"I was a daddy's girl, and I needed my father. I missed him so much."

But why would Ashley wait for the clearly non-committal, womanizing Nick?

As I discussed in Chapter 1, there is a subset of women who remain involved with men who are unavailable, in part, because of unconscious phenomenon, such as the repetition compulsion, or because their life experiences have developed within them an "I'm not OK. You are OK" life position. Unwittingly these subconscious and historical forces often converge to play a role in these women developing an uncanny attraction or unconscious radar for unavailable men.

In a manner of speaking, Ashley was re-enacting a familiar relationship pattern, which allowed her to return to the scene of the crime with the hope of better understanding what went wrong before, or somehow changing the outcome: "This time around I will win his love." In many cases, the subconscious sense of familiarity (and by-proxy safety) associated with these relationships is inexplicably compelling, despite the inherent pain and rejection associated with them. Accordingly, Ashley was willing to endure the negative feelings associated with Nick's unavailability, lack of commitment, and womanizing to avoid her fears of confrontation. That way she could avoid his obvious rejection, and remain in denial of the reality that "Nick just was not that into her."

Should this sound like you, I recommend you consider talking to a professional to determine what subconscious or historical forces—if any—might be influencing your decision to remain in such a frustrating and painful relationship, particularly if you have seen this pattern before. No, I don't think you necessarily want such a one-sided relationship. However, I have learned, as with Ashley, within you lies the solution and ability to find a mutually fulfilling love.

12. **"I'm OK. You're not, but I can fix you" or "I'm not OK. You are OK!"** There are four ways to resolve a conflict: 1) I'm OK. You're OK, 2) I'm OK. You're not OK, 3) I'm not

OK. You're OK, and 4) I'm not OK. You're not OK. However, only one approach works over time: I'm OK. You're OK. If your basic interaction dynamic with your partner is "I'm OK. You're not OK, but I can fix you!" or "I'm not OK. You're OK," then you are involved in a dysfunctional relationship, and chances are this isn't your Mr. Right—at least not right now. Soulmate love is based on the fundamental assumption that "I'm OK. You're OK," which will empower you and your man to have the foundation needed to establish and maintain a mutually fulfilling relationship that stands the test of time. (See Chapter 1 for more details.)

13. **He wants kids; you don't (or vice versa).** A catch-22 defined: damned if you do, damned if you don't. This is a lose-lose situation (See #4 from game changers, above). Deep down, you know what you want your future family to look life. You know he wants kids (and lots of them) and gets excited at the mere thought of having a house full of pitter-pattering little feet running around, while the only thing you like about kids is leaving them with their parents when it's time to go. You can't imagine the thought of having kids trampling around your meticulously neat and well-decorated house, much less consider the thought of giving birth. If you can get your man to say he is on board—and, trust me, you won't be able to get him to stay on board—with your vision, this union will be replete with resentment. No matter who wins, the other will lose, which will ultimately result in you both losing. While couples always have to compromise, even on the number of kids they might want, if his idea of family life is the polar opposite of yours, I don't see a win-win outcome in your future.

14. **Triangles.** You, she, and me. As Kenny Rogers sings in "The Gambler": "You got to know when to hold 'em, when to fold 'em, when to walk away and when to run." Here is a situation where a good run is better than a bad stand. It's a no-brainer! I imagine triangles work for some people.

Perhaps the couples it works for just don't need therapy, because I've never had a couple come to therapy saying it worked for them. Honestly, if you are the spouse and find yourself the third wheel, it's time to roll. You have to accept sometimes nothing is better than too little. This is one of those situations where there just isn't a winning angle. You will lose respect for yourself, he will lose respect for you, and she will look like a more appealing option in comparison.

Triangles are different than open relationship in important ways. Triangles typically include betrayal, rejection, and deception or a lack of consent in some fashion; whereas, open relationships and the boundaries associated with them are candidly discussed, and both parties mutually consent before the relationship is entered.

I don't do clients who do triangles, either!

Summary: Whether reading through this list made you feel your relationship fit in the game changer or deal breaker group, membership here dramatically reduces the likelihood this man is your Mr. Right or that you two will live happily ever after. Alternatively, you are probably better off talking to a trained professional to determine if your game changer can be changed, or if it's indeed a deal breaker that will lead to broken dreams and hearts — and it's time to bolt.

WHEN MR. RIGHT'S CIRCUMSTANCES MAKE HIM MR. WRONG

CHAPTER 7

When Soulmates Cheat

Should I Stay or Go ....

So you and your soulmate have decided to give it a try. The stars are in alignment, and it just feels right. Congrats!

You two are very excited about each other, your special love, and your future together. Over time, however, the electricity and spark of romantic love wane a bit, and your relationship gets tested in ways you two likely hadn't foreseen. You two will be forced to work through challenges spurred by your differences — differences that have the potential to cause you both deep emotional pain. Yes, your views, attitudes, and behaviors on issues important to you both will be diametrically opposed at times, and, consequently, some of your partner's most critical needs will go unmet.

Yes, the prince and princess both have warts. How dare they be so human and selfish, too?!

Didn't Cupid see this one coming?

In her chart-topping song, "Exclusively," Jill Scott brilliantly describes the shock of discovering what appears to be a soulmate love being abruptly exposed as a deception. After a long night of surreal love making, she euphorically strolls to the grocery store to get food to cook her man breakfast, only to discover fate has drawn her to the register of a cashier with whom she has way too much in common. After ringing her up, the new cute cashier sniffs, sniffs, and sniffs again, then blurts out their Mr. Right's name, Raheem. (If you haven't heard this song before, Google it.)

But why was she so blindsided? Wasn't Raheem happy? She was ecstatic, and exclusive.

HOW TO SAFEGUARD YOUR RELATIONSHIP FROM AFFAIRS BEFORE THEY OCCUR

While most couples can resolve day to day logistical conflicts, like dividing up household chores or saving money, when emotional differences arise, conflict resolution skills are tested in a unique fashion. As blind spots and clashes in interpersonal style begin to emerge, disagreements become more painful by each invalidating, dismissive, or defensive response.

Far worse than the original fight is how we resolve—or don't resolve—our differences. At the center of this conflict is what I call the Law of Two Truths vs. the Myth of One Truth. Only in math is there one universally agreed upon truth: One plus one always equals two. In contrast, when it comes to emotional conflicts, there are always at least two valid opinions—the ones held by each partner. Yet couples vehemently insist there is only one valid perspective: theirs. Further damage is done when they began to believe not only is their truth the only truth, but that deep down their partner recognizes this truth and some character flaw prevents him from acting on this truth in an appropriate fashion. Feelings of betrayal, loss of respect, resentment, and anger begin to develop when they tell friends their version of the story and those friends cosign, of course, without hearing the partner's side of the story. Now their truth has been validated and has magically become even truer. Worse, the sanctity of their relationship has now been violated, and their friends, who have their own biases and experiences with men, have an unauthorized influence on their relationship. The seeds of betrayal are sown.

Meet Bernadette and Harry. Their interpersonal styles transformed them from soulmates to roommates. Bernadette is what we call a "dismissive type" when it comes to emotional issues, while Harry is a "meta-processor": that is, she internalizes and compartmentalizes her feelings and moves on, while he wants to talk about his feelings and the feelings about his feelings. The painful reality of the differences in their emotional styles weren't as apparent until Harry's mother died, and he needed Bernadette to be his emotional rock. After six months had passed, Harry, a self-admitted mama's boy, still found himself grieving inconsolably, which frustrated Bernadette to no end. She barely was affected by the death of her own absentee father and appeared to struggle to empathize with his inability to let go. By month seven, Bernadette started to call Harry "needy" and felt "frustrated, drained, and overwhelmed" by her futile attempts to address his "excessive" need to process his feelings and his inability to "let go." In response, Harry began to feel "unloved, alone, and abandoned" in the relationship.

"You do not care about my mother or my feelings," he shouted. "What type of soulmate are you? Perhaps I met your representative. When we first met, you were so attentive and supportive; now you are insensitive, self-absorbed, and narcissistic. This isn't what I bargained for. My friends are far more supportive, especially Brenda, who lost her mother two years ago and agrees with me you are aloof, self-absorbed, and unsupportive."

I find this combination—dismissive types and meta-processors—frequently attract, and frustrate each other to no end. While they typically have a deep love for each other and partner together in many practical ways, if they don't find a way to hear and meet each other's needs, they can really end up resentful, angry, and isolated. Frequently, this is where the seeds of infidelity are sown. During my training at Dr. Gottman's Institute, I learned infidelity begins when "negative comps" emerge and remain unspoken or unheard. Negative comps are comparisons about your relationship expectations that are significantly, or even grossly, unmet by your partner, whether these needs were expressed or unexpressed before the commitment. Although you initially are hopeful things will change and your soulmate will hear you and do something about it, should these needs remain unaddressed over time, some partners start to question if this is really soulmate love at all.

The extent to which these seeds of discontent take root and are cultivated frequently depends on how well the original problem is resolved. If resolved in a meaningful and timely fashion, the feelings of mutual admiration and love are restored, and infidelity is likely avoided. However, if the partner's feelings aren't heard or addressed and left unresolved because the other partner is in denial, defensive, or the couple has poor communication or conflict resolution skills, these negative comps could result in the unhappy partner developing a cynicism that negatively colors all of their partner's past and future interactions. Even worse, the unhappy partner may begin to feel betrayed. As ironic as it may seem, the unfaithful partner frequently feels betrayed by the partner long before they actually commit infidelity. It is the couple's ability or inability to resolve these feelings of betrayal that is most likely to seal the couple's fate.

While sexual infidelity is the worst-case scenario when there are negative comps, other forms of infidelity are more likely. For example, an emotional infidelity may occur where the unhappy partner harbors resentments, or a financial infidelity occurs where the unhappy partner creates a secret just in case rainy day savings account.

In therapy, I frequently ask couples about their negative comps and what conversation they should have had before the affair, and at what point should they have had it. Typically, the unfaithful partner says, "I tried to talk about it, but my concerns were dismissed, denied, or minimized." In contrast, the hurt partner says, "I just thought you needed to get over it." Next, I ask about their current negative comps and what conversations they need to have right now. I've found these conversations to be critical in the beginning to develop the communication skills needed to start addressing and meeting each other's needs and expectations, and ultimately to restore positive feelings of love and admiration.

CAN SOULMATES SURVIVE INFIDELITY?

In her landmark book, *After the Affair*, Dr. Janis Spring asks and answers the quintessential question: Can a couple survive infidelity? She answers yes.

I agree.

Recovering from infidelity and re-establishing trust and a healthy relationship is possible; however, not every relationship can or should be saved. If you are to save it, know that it will take a lot of patience, pain, and perseverance — from both of you.

Unless conflicts are resolved in an "I'm OK. You're OK" fashion (see Chapter 2) within any relationship, soulmates aren't exempt, infidelity is a real possibility. Estimates of infidelity vary widely from study to study, with as many as 37 percent of married men and 20 percent of married women reporting having been unfaithful. Upon hearing these percentages, clients always tell me these number seem low. I'm not sure what the actual statistics are, as it's reasonable to suspect if an unfaithful partner is willing to deceive his or her spouse, he or she may be likely to deceive researchers as well. In addition, responses may not include emotional affairs, work wives/husbands or virtual infidelity.

ARE ALL INFIDELITIES CREATED EQUALLY?

In my 11 years of working with couples each week, I am always confronted with the reality that what constitutes infidelity and betrayal varies widely among partners. For some, infidelity is receiving a text from an ex, for some it's returning that text, for some it's calling them, for some it's having lunch, for some it's dinner, for some it's kissing, for some it's having sex, for some it's having sex and not inviting them, for some it's inviting them but appearing to enjoy the other party more, and for others it's contacting the third party after a ménage-a-trios without the spouse's consent. As such, couples struggle to get each other to agree and recognize their infidelity-related boundaries and feelings of vulnerability.

More important than how infidelity is defined, I've found that if a partner or spouse felt hurt, rejected, or betrayed, infidelity has occurred — at least in their emotional and psychological world. Their trust and sense of security has been compromised or completely violated, so Houston, we have a problem.

Over the last few years, the experience of infidelity has been further complicated by virtual infidelity, or e-affairs. It's one thing to come home unexpectedly for lunch and discover your partner or spouse in bed having sex with his lover. That's an open and shut case; either you can deal with it or you leave. But with most virtual affairs, there is only circumstantial evidence and no real smoking gun. You might uncover a text or email from an ex or co-worker that says, "nice seeing you last night." However, you don't know what came before or after that text. After all, your partner's responses of "Yes, we ran into each other in the parking lot at the dry cleaners, but it wasn't special for me at all," or "Yes, I naively overvalued my friendship with her, met her for dinner, but I declined her advances" could be true.

While you lack the closure needed to leave the relationship or make an informed decision to stay, you may feel just as betrayed and unprotected as if he has had sex and begin to treat your partner as though he has been unfaithful. Perhaps he has. Problem is, it's very difficult to leave a partner or spouse with such a molehill of evidence, especially if you have children. This is further complicated by your partner being far less likely to feel contrite because he hasn't been caught red handed, or hasn't done anything akin to infidelity in his world. Though he may be guilty of being inappropriate, he doesn't equate that with infidelity. You will need a mountain of evidence to break up your family.

But a molehill of intuition can feel like a mountain of evidence, and you know it in your gut, so he is guilty in your courtroom. Suspicion rather than closure is all that is required to do major damage to your relationship when you feel betrayed. You don't want to feel vulnerable or be made a fool of, so you shut down emotionally or sexually and begin to become argumentative. You're pissed. Now the bond uniting a good, or even bad, relationship is compromised, just as if the partner was caught in the throes of passion. The distrust from the misplaced suspicion of a virtual infidelity presents challenges to the strongest of couples, particularly when there is a history of betrayal—with each other or residual distrust from previous relationships. At the same time, just because the hurt partner is being described as "paranoid," it doesn't mean the unfaithful partner wasn't indeed deceiving them. I've seen this, too.

Your inability to move on until you have closure is known as the Zeigarnik Effect. It is the tendency of people to remember and replay incomplete, interrupted, or unbelievable stories over again and again compared to complete, seamless, and credible stories. The autonomic system signals the conscious mind that a previous activity was left incomplete or doesn't feel quite right. It seems to be human nature to finish what we start and, if it is not finished or doesn't feel right, we struggle to accept the story at face value and move on. Instead, we keep replaying it in our head in hopes of it making sense when told from a different angle. Accordingly, I've seen many clients that didn't plea to obvious facts associated with the misdemeanor, get charged with the felony. That is, because you feel if he won't admit to small, obvious transgressions (and you can't distinguish truth from deceit), then he is probably guilty of the worst possible offense(s). You decide, I'd rather be wrong than duped again.

THREE STAGES OF HEALING FROM INFIDELITY

Whether an affair was virtual, emotional, or sexual, my experiences in private practice has identified three distinct stages of the healing process: 1) reacting to the affair, 2) reviewing your options ("Should I stay or leave?"), and 3) recovering from the affair ("How do we rebuild our life together?")

Stage One: Once the affair comes to light, this stage automatically begins. Both the hurt and unfaithful partners have to figure out how to react to the affair. Each is likely to be overwhelmed and confused by a series of conflicting emotions and choices. The hurt party is thinking: 1) How can I still love someone who deceived and hurt me? 2) I thought he was open, honest, and the person I can trust most in life. 3) I don't know who he is now, much less how to deal with the loss of what I thought was my Mr. Right. 4) Do I want to start all over? 5) Why do I feel so inadequate when he was the one who cheated? 6) How can I ever feel special or trust him again? For the record, you are not alone; it's normal to feel unstable and surprised by conflicting and confusing emotions and questions that arise during this phase.

On the other hand, the unfaithful partner is wrestling with conflicting and confusing emotions, too. 1) This relationship didn't work and I was happy with the other person. 2) I don't want to be separated from my children. 3) Why can't you just get over it? Can't you see I'm now done lying? 4) Why do you need my passcodes? It feels like I am dating a detective. 5) How can I be in love with two people?

While you both are likely to feel your perspectives are valid, and they are, your partner is unlikely to agree with you or see it your way. He is hurt and neither cares why you were unfaithful nor how important your "friendship" with the other man was to you. He also likely doesn't agree that you didn't play a role in the infidelity or agree that his infidelity should be held over his head forever. He definitely doesn't want you to stop having sex with him.

Finally, there are some significant differences in the needs infidelity meets for men and women. While it's very painful no matter who cheats, research on attitudes and behaviors surrounding extramarital affairs shows women are more likely to have affairs with partners that provide love and companionship, while men are more likely to seek out partners where sex is the primary attraction. Put another way, women seek out an alternative soulmate, whereas men seek a playmate. Women tend to believe if their affair is for love, then it is justified; on the other hand, men think if the affair didn't involve love, it was less wrong. Lastly, women tend to invest more emotionally in extramarital relationships and are more likely to feel the affair has complicated their life. In contrast, men tend to compartmentalize sex and love and value novelty, so are more likely to think the affair brought excitement to their life.

Yes, these are generalizations, and as such they may or may not reflect the dynamics surrounding your situation. All men and women aren't alike and all affairs aren't, either. Rather, I am providing insights that researchers have observed and that my experience corroborates.

<u>Stage Two:</u> After months of anguish, time for reflection, and ambivalence, you have to decide to work on the relationship or end it.

While the wild range of emotions and reactions makes it somewhat impossible, it is important that you find a way to be still, get in tune with your inner voice, do an on-balance inventory with all of your options on the table, and decide what you want and need out of the relationship — or no longer want and need. You have to answer two questions: All things considered, do I still believe in our love, and is this the right person for me?

During this second stage, you will be forced to accept that the relationship has to evolve from romantic love to mature love. In the transformation process, you will have to re-evaluate some of your expectations. For example, "Mr. Right will always recognize my needs and meet them," "I shouldn't have to work to be trusted or loved," "soulmate love is conflict free," "If I'm not feeling you right now our relationship is over," "I don't have to change; you should love me unconditionally," "If I'm not happy in the relationship, it's your fault," and "I'm right, and you are wrong."

As you wrestle with these questions about your soulmate, you must reassess how realistic and useful some of your beliefs about relationships are. If you don't want to re-evaluate your core beliefs about love and relationships, I completely understand; however, you must ask yourself if some of your preconceived notions about love are setting you up for further disappointment and failure. It might also be wise to ask yourself where these notions of love and relationships originated, and how relevant they are today.

If you decide to work on the relationship, you have the unenviable position of confronting your misconceptions, fears, and doubts. While this isn't an exciting or fun phase, many couples have told me they are able to take a sober and insightful look at their relationship dynamics and values in a fashion that they simply ignored during the romantic phase of love.

Several critical issues related to your and your partner's history when it comes to infidelity must be discussed, such as 1) Is this affair and subsequent cover up-related deception an isolated event or part of a pattern of repeated affairs? Past behavior is the greatest predictor of future behavior. 2) Is my partner or I highly secretive? 3) Has too much damage been done? 4) Can we hear, acknowledge and empathize with each other's pain? 5) Can we – and are we willing to – change in the ways necessary to meet each other's needs? 6) If we have children, can we do this for them?

Even if you've made the decision to recommit, you may feel overwhelmed by the thought of what lies ahead. Here are a few suggestions to get you started. 1) Restoring trust and addressing these questions will be tough if not impossible for you and your partner alone. Consider getting professional help with a therapist that specializes in relationship therapy. 2) Shrink the change. Instead of trying to answer all of the questions at once, consider attacking one question at a time and clearly identifying three specific behaviors you'd like your partner to do to meet your needs. 3) Engage in active listening, where you ask open-ended follow-up questions and simply listen. 4) I highly recommend you pick up either Dr. Spring's book, *After the Affair*, or Dr. John Gottman's book, *What Makes Love Last?*, for a research-based approach.

Stage Three: You have worked through some of the critical issues needed to recommit, and are ready to start the recovery stage, where you begin to figure out how to rebuild your life together. 1) If you are the one who has been unfaithful, you must say goodbye to your lover. Period. 2) Figure out the meaning of the affair and the role you both played in creating negative comps and not resolving them. 3) Re-establish trust and learn how to forgive (and be forgiven) — and forgive yourself. 4) Attempt to resume sexual intimacy and work through all of the related issues. 5) Manage your personality differences and expectations of yourself, your partner, and your relationship; identify specific behaviors that you would like your partner to do to meet the unmet needs and cause and effect underlying patterns uncovered in therapy. 6) Safeguard your relationship against betrayal by identifying clear boundaries and respecting them. 7) Take note of lessons learned from the affair. 8) Set and accept realistic expectations. 9) Work on staying in the Nice and Neutral boxes and keep your involvement in the Nasty box to a minimum.

Whew! I know that's asking a lot. But, no one said it be easy.

PUTTING YOUR RELATIONSHIP BACK TOGETHER

Why Do I Say One Thing But Do Another? Resistance!

You decided to work on your relationship and resume your life together. Let's face it: Change is hard, and re-establishing trust is infinitely harder. So let's look at some of the issues that lead to resistance to change, for they are bound to appear and have the potential to undermine the best intentions. Please know that because you are experiencing resistance, it doesn't mean you aren't committed or are resistant to change—or your relationship, for that matter. Rather, it means you are human and want to prevent being vulnerable in the future, and some of your beliefs, behaviors, and attitudes are likely to interfere with your ability to become a more authentic partner, especially after being betrayed.

Here are thoughts and attitudes that make up resistance and are hurdles you will likely have to overcome as you attempt to re-establish your relationship: 1) I don't think you should have the password to my social media and email accounts. 2) Either you trust me or you don't. 3) My partner should get what my needs are and I shouldn't have to spell them out. 4) My partner has his own agenda, so I don't have to really make changes. 5) I shouldn't have to give a round of applause every time my partner does what he should, like, make honest self-disclosures without me having to catch him. 6) My partner only wants it to look like he wants me back, but really he only wants our kids around, or to avoid paying child support—and not to be seen as the bad guy.

It will be very difficult, if not impossible, not to entertain many of these forms of resistance in your thoughts, and they have the potential to undermine your stage three goal of re-establishing your relationship. However, you are doomed if you don't change your thinking here. Candidly, one of Dr. Gottman's biggest predictors of divorce is rejected repair attempts. A repair attempt is an act initiated by you or your partner to repair the marriage. Rejecting them is detrimental to recovery for two reasons: First, your partner is trying to make things better the best way he knows how and rejecting that is a bad idea; second, after a pattern of rejecting his efforts becomes clear, he becomes less likely to make them and shuts down. Your theory that he really didn't care becomes falsely, albeit convincingly, confirmed.

Couples are encouraged to acknowledge some authentic aspect of the repair attempt, even if it's as simple as, "I appreciate you for trying to make me feel respected by bringing me roses," whether you wanted make-up flowers sent to your job or not. Next, the receiving partner is asked to identify specifically what repair attempts would work. Say, for instance, "I feel respected when you take time to hug me and ask about my day when we first meet, don't make jokes about our relationship to your family at family events, and put your phone away when we are enjoying quality time together."

Finally, this approach presumes the unfaithful party has acknowledged the affair. That may not always be the case, however. Unfaithful partners often wrestle with the question: to reveal or not to reveal the affair. Here are the three positions well known therapists and researchers take on this important question. The more conservative approach recommended by Dr. Gottman suggests not only must you admit the affair, but you should tell others (in-laws, friends, and even your children) that an affair has occurred and you are working on it. Not admitting to the affair isn't an option. In contrast, Dr. Frederick Humphreys believes revealing the affair prematurely alters — and sometimes has the potential to destroy — a relationship or the other person, and that couples have a better chance of success when partners first try and work through their conflicts and start meeting each other's needs. Dr. Humphreys is very critical of therapists who push their patients to reveal their secrets. Alternatively, Dr. Springs points out some disadvantages of admitting to the affair, such as traumatizing or crushing your partner unnecessarily, and the possibility that your disclosure will stop your partner from exploring the problems that led to the affair. She also lists some advantages of telling your partner, such as hearing about the affair from you is much better than your partner stumbling upon it in the future, increasing the chance of you staying faithful in the future and stopping the conspiracy between you and your lover from further trumping the bond with your spouse.

Whether you decide to reveal the affair or not, I feel Dr. Spring's approach forces you to be more deliberate about your decision and take a measured approach as opposed to a one-size-fits-all one. That said, I personally asked Dr. Julie Gottman (Dr. John Gottman's wife) about their approach after a Level I training I attended, and she said the problem with not revealing the affair is "the other person is left to think they are crazy or gullible and that you don't respect them enough to be honest. As such, you probably will never regain trust in their eyes if you don't come clean, and their level of resentment and disrespect for you will likely become insurmountable." Plus, you are being inconsistent by asking for forgiveness and looking for a fresh start, while still engaging in a deceptive cover up. Personally, I encourage honesty in all of my sessions, and find deception of any sort unacceptable and counterproductive in the long run.

PUTTING IT ALL TOGETHER:

The Law of Two Truths vs the Myth of One Truth, Revisited

To give you a better understanding about how this approach works in practice, let's get back to Harry and Bernadette. They originally came to see me after Bernadette discovered Harry had developed a romantic relationship with Brenda. (You remember the friend he confided in. That Brenda.) Bernadette was devastated, and Harry was unrepentant and angry, as he felt she had abandoned and betrayed him by dismissing him while he was grieving his deceased mother. After working through stages one and two, they decided to recommit and re-establish their relationship. However, he insisted on maintaining his "friendship" with Brenda.

During the third stage, we began to process his negative comps. He indicated things fell apart when Bernadette didn't measure up to his basic expectation for support. In response, Bernadette sincerely apologized and explained her side of the story. As a little girl, her father abandoned them. Her mother quickly remarried their neighbor and became pregnant within weeks with her twin brothers, Brett and Brent. As such, Bernadette never got to mourn the loss of her father, as her mother's focus was on her new husband and the babies. She simply never had a voice in the family and wasn't allowed to even mention her father, with whom she had been very close before he left. A rigid and sanctimonious woman, her mother pretended Bernadette's father never existed, and Bernadette learned to be stoic, internalizing and compartmentalizing her feelings.

When Harry's mother died, Bernadette was actually devastated and became depressed herself. She was the mother Bernadette never had. Simply put, she just couldn't find the words to express her despair and grief. In addition, she had tried to console Harry on several occasions early on, but she felt rejected and taken aback when he said, "You never had a good relationship with your parents and wouldn't understand." Out of frustration, she offered the only tool she ever mastered — tough love and a silver bullet fix: Let go, let God. When that failed, she felt hopeless, as she had as a child, and didn't know what to do, so she shut down. (Ironically, her outward aloofness was, in part, caused by Harry rejecting her repair attempts.)

We discussed how dismissive types frequently offer a silver bullet fix, like, "only the strong survive," in an attempt to provide one of the few tools they have in their toolbox. It's their form of support, and it is based on love in a way they know how to authentically accept and express.

Upon hearing this and recalling how she had reached out to him several times early on, while he was too depressed and grief stricken to receive it, he began to sob uncontrollably. She grabbed some tissue for them, and also began to cry as she put her arm around him. Recognizing that her silence and stoicism came from a place of pain and necessity, he immediately recalled how that trait had originally drawn him to her.

Upon accepting and validating each other's truths (in place of insisting there was only one truth — theirs, individually), they began to hear (and feel heard by) each other, and forgive (and be forgiven by) each other. In time, he agreed to end his involvement with Brenda completely.

CAN LIGHTENING STRIKE THE SAME RELATIONSHIP TWICE?

Clearly the thought of all the hard work required to go through the three stages of healing to recover from infidelity can be intimidating and even overwhelming, leaving the most remorseful partner thinking, "Perhaps I just blew it. She (or he) will never love me again. We all know lightning never strikes twice in the same place."

I appreciate your fears and concerns, and hope the very thought of losing your soulmate or family deters you from cheating in the first place. However, if you have been unfaithful, there is hope. Contrary to popular opinion, it's been my experience that like lightening, love has a greater probability of striking the same couple twice — in the case of soulmate love — than it does in nature. In nature, there are certain dynamics of physics (e.g., negative and positive electric charges, weather patterns, and lightning rods) that draw electricity, which frequently results in lightening striking the same place more than once.

Here's where the power of choice re-enters the picture.

In contrast to couples who never had "it," when couples have the dynamics of soulmate love (e.g., friendship, mature love, natural affinity and fondness, and compatibility) with each other, love can indeed strike again. This is precisely what happened to Harry and Bernadette. The last time we met, they reported having a richer and happier relationship and I discharged them from therapy. I have not seen them since. However, I thoroughly enjoyed the Christmas card I received from them with a picture revealing she was wearing a wedding ring, very pregnant, and smiling radiantly. It was signed, "Living Happily Ever After."

PART II

Being/Becoming Ms. Right

Part Two: "Being/Becoming Ms. Right" discusses ground rules and strategies for maintaining fulfilling soulmate love — with your partner, yourself, and your blended family, should you find yourself in that situation.

This part of the book is written for readers who may or may not be in relationships or marriage, or have ended bad ones or divorced and are looking to make changes to ensure their future relationships or next marriage is healthier and more fulfilling. Here I present strategies for loving yourself, uncovering myths related to soulmate love, blending your family should you have children or enter a relationship with a partner who has children. Finally, I conclude this book with a section on how it's never too late to live happily ever after.

CHAPTER 8

Spread Your Wings and FLY (First Love Yourself)

As Beyoncé's hit song, "Pretty Hurts," suggests, the journey toward self-love and being/becoming Ms. Right starts within. She sings about a young woman who aspired to be happy in life, and that her mother told her she was pretty and what was in her head didn't matter; rather, the outside is all that matters. Women try to fix the problem, but you can't fix a problem you can't see. In reality, surgery should be performed on the soul. (These lyrics are beautiful and I recommend you Google them.)

Similarly, self-help books, gurus, pastors, and elders alike always say you have to love yourself before you can love — or be loved by — someone else. While this is undoubtedly true, many clients ask me, "But how do I love me? Saying "first love yourself" (FLY) is easy, but the task of learning to FLY before entering into a romantic relationship is anything but easy. One client said it best, "Doc, are you saying that loving me is a prerequisite to receiving the love I need to love me? Isn't that like requiring a patient to get well before they are eligible to receive the medical intervention they need to feel better? If he loved me wouldn't I love me, too?" That's the million-dollar question. And there doesn't appear to be a simple answer. FLY-ing is kind of like chasing a butterfly; no matter how fast you run or how high you jump, it's almost impossible to catch. However, if you remain still long enough and are lucky enough, it might just deftly land on your shoulder someday.

Now that's straight talk. Right? No, but it's the best I can do. Part of self-love is knowing your limitations and feeling comfortable with them. You can't teach experience. If you try to explain wisdom, it will frequently sound like foolishness, said the wise man.

There I go being abstract, again.

To be more concrete, I will say that the word love is a verb. Just as your actions show your love for someone else, it's important to actively do things to love yourself. However, this is not to be confused with doing more. In contrast, I've seen the power of subtraction empower more women learning to FLY than I ever have seen addition, or through the accumulation of things. It's no accident the word subtraction ends with action: subtrACTION.

Love by subtrACTION is doing less to love yourself more.

Yes, less is more. Less negative self-talk and fault finding, comparisons and competition with others, unrealistic expectations of others, chasing things to make you happy, need for the approval of others, time spent in the past or future, compromising yourself, and neglecting your spiritual essence. Less time and energy spent on these counterproductive actions will give you the clarity to spend your time and energy on forgiveness and self-acceptance, appreciation, time spent in the now, and energy spent nurturing your mind, body, and soul. Finally, you won't find self-love and sustain it without God.

Throughout this book I have avoided taking a spiritual stand, but as a former self-described atheist, I've personally and professionally found that your relationship with God makes a profound impact on your relationships with others. I'm a Christian, but loving yourself isn't necessarily based on your religion or how you interpret your holy book. Loving yourself has more to do with your personal relationship with the Author. Only He can provide the clarity of mind to allow you to love and trust yourself. Only He can guide you and provide the discernment needed to become Ms. Right, recognize your Mr. Right, and maintain a mutually fulfilling relationship with him. Only He can turn your emotional vinegar into wine.

You need to embrace the Creator to embrace the creation. No matter the source of your spiritual pain or how you define your spirituality, it is almost impossible to reject God and accept and make peace with yourself. Making a man your god can be a dangerous substitution. While you can trust a man to complement you, trusting a man to complete the core of who you are is a major mistake. If you have a spiritual void, you never know what that man you trust will use to fill it. Prayerfully something good, but possibly something bad. Even if you end up with the man you love, ultimately he and you may end up loving and respecting you less.

Only He can guarantee your void is filled with the self-love you will need for soulmate love.

You didn't think the answer to the million-dollar question would be so simple, did you? But, it is that simple, natural, and achievable, which is much more than I can say for catching that fleeting butterfly. FLYing is easier to do once you lighten your load.

CHAPTER 9

Addition by Subtraction: Seven Subtractions That Will Help You FLY

*"If you want to change your life status,
focus your energy on finding Mr. Right.
If you want to change your life,
focus your energy on becoming Ms. Right."*
—Dr. Shane Perrault

Y ou don't need to search for self-love or get a guru to unveil

it to you on a retreat in the Himalayas. Learning to FLY doesn't require you to discover something deep and supernatural, but to uncover something already deep-rooted and natural inside of you.

Think about a baby. It has only two natural fears: loud noises and falling from a high place, which is why it won't crawl off a bed, fall and hurt itself. All other fears, all negative self-talk, and all messages to not love itself are learned behavior. Loving itself is all a baby knows how to do. (Well, other than pooping, crying, and keeping you up all night. But you get the point.) Otherwise, babies are a blank slate.

You, too, were once a blank slate. Loving yourself is about getting back to your natural state, re-examining the negative messages about yourself that you have internalized, and recreating the original self-love message born inside of you.

Babies don't dislike or want to hurt themselves, and we have to strip away that learned behavior. To reconnect with feelings of self-love, you have to start suppressing the distracting and misleading messages playing in your head long enough for you to get in tune with your original message again. Changing your thoughts will change your relationship with yourself and, ultimately, the world.

If someone showed up at your house, went into your living room, and dumped trash everywhere, you would kick him out (after you made him clean the mess up, of course). Yet, we routinely allow people to dump negative stuff into our mind and never consider asking them to leave, much less clean up the mess. Instead, we will invite them back to do it again and again.

Learning to FLY involves doing a hard reset and gradually firing the culprit who is dumping negativity in to your thinking on a regular basis, and reprograming how you think about yourself. Hitting the hard reset button doesn't mean get over it. (No, it isn't about minimizing your pain by putting some rosy spin on the misfortunes that haunt you. Rest assured, I'm not going to insult your experience like that.) Far from it. If the experience impacted you enough to traumatize you to this day, it was real and hurt you deeply. Of course, you can't just get over it, or you would have by now. God knows you have tried. I'm simply saying we have to help you learn to make peace with your past so you can start to get past the pain of reliving it over and over.

SubtrACTION 1. TUNE OUT THE NEGATIVE MESSAGES THAT INHIBIT YOUR ABILITY TO FLY

No matter how painful, the past contains valuable lessons, even if you shouldn't have had to learn them. The past informs us who you became in spite of the transgressions committed against you and adversity that faced you, which speaks volumes about your character, resilience, and ability to overcome difficult obstacles. Making peace with the past is accepting that once something is crooked, it will likely never be straight. I'm sure you have had the experience of trying to make something crooked straight, only to find that bending it backward and forward only resulted in it breaking. It likely never got straight. Candidly, the secret isn't making it straight, but uncovering and accepting the magnificence of its crookedness. For example, the Leaning Tower of Pisa would be unknown but for its crookedness. While tearing it down and rebuilding a new tower would have cost millions, accepting that it was crooked was free. Today it is considered a priceless national treasure, and tourists travel the world to see and photograph it precisely because it is crooked.

The same is true with the traumatic events in your life. You can't make them right or straight. Rather, you must find a way to come to terms with their crookedness. For example, perhaps you were the disadvantaged little girl who got teased because she wore hand-me-downs, your family caught public transportation and required government assistance, and you never were accepted by other kids. While it's hard to get over the painful memories of rejection and cruelty, you undoubtedly were also a real survivor who had to learn prematurely how to take care of yourself and your younger siblings, do more with less, develop the vision and tenacity to overcome obstacles, and develop a shield of armor to tune out the negative opinions of others. All of these traits likely fueled your future success in some critical way. (I know that's my story, and it made me who I am today, painful memories aside.) Making peace involves you coming to terms with the reality that you weren't just someone who simply got bullied, but you fought back even when outnumbered and knew it would end in pain, simultaneously demonstrating bravery, selflessness, self-determination, and resourcefulness.

Reframing your experience from a more balanced and detached perspective is an important aspect of making peace with yourself. Does making peace with your past erase it or ask you to just get over it? No. But recognizing you weren't just a victim, but are, in fact, a survivor who did the best she could, does move

187

you forward in making peace with your past and ultimately forgiving yourself for being human in a difficult predicament.

To hit the reset button, you will need to make peace with your transgressors. That is, forgiving them whether they actually deserve to be forgiven or not. Sometimes they truly don't deserve your forgiveness. Perhaps the rat bastards should "die slowly," as Tupac Shakur sang, and in lots of pain. I get it. I'm not suggesting you forgive them for them, but for you. It's a shame they get to live rent free in your head all these years. Forgiving them is the emotional equivalent of evicting them.

Why keep them as tenants? Only so they can re-offend you on a daily basis. Forgiveness is about freeing yourself and not allowing their negative messages to continually loop in your thoughts and prevent you from loving yourself. Once you forgive them, you can make a decision about what happens next. If you don't desire them in your life, you are right to banish them. Conversely, if you feel they have changed, are remorseful, and have sufficiently made amends to you, then you can decide their place in your life.

Forgiving others and yourself, making peace with your past, and finding your splendor in spite of the crooked things that happened to you will dramatically reduce the negative messages which prevent you from FLYing.

Listen to your self-talk, note it, and change it.

Are you repeatedly saying negative things about yourself, like, "I'm a screw up, and it's all my fault yet again. I keep messing things up"? No matter how normal it feels, bludgeoning yourself with those steel-toed boots is one of the least loving things you can do for yourself. To start the process of changing your self-talk today, commit to becoming more aware of your self-talk. Is it positive or negative? Note the messages about yourself that you've internalized, and which play in your head over and over. If you want to journal them, that's a great way to become more aware of what you are saying about you to you.

Next, try to restate the messages you send yourself. Consider making them less absolute, like, "I have made some mistakes and missed some opportunities, but so do others. Yes, I played a role in this mess, but so did he." I'm not suggesting you don't take responsibility for your role in your problems, but once you accept responsibility, learn to avoid the tendency to kick and berate yourself. Instead try forgiving yourself and moving on. While it sounds like a small change, big improvements almost always start small. As you reflect and replay your life experiences, try to get to the point where you don't say anything about you that you wouldn't say to someone else you love. Finally, start listening to positive affirmations, like, *101 Ways to Transform Your Life*, by Dr. Wayne Dyer, and consider listening to some of his audiobooks, like, *The Power of Intention,* or some other self-help books, such as *How to Stop Worrying and Start Living*, by Dale Carnegie. Also, be open to getting professional help, too. You wouldn't hesitate to see your dentist for a throbbing toothache, would you? So why not work with a therapist to heal the pain in your heart and mind, too?

You will be amazed at how having a less negative relationship with yourself will lead to more positive relationships with others.

SubtrACTION 2: TAKE AWAY HIS POWER TO WALK OVER YOU BY OWNING YOUR POWER TO WALK

Oprah: What is the most important thing you are going to teach your daughter?

Madonna: Self-respect!

Oprah: And, what are you going to teach her about men?

Madonna: If I teach her self-respect, I won't have to teach her about men.

Years ago, a self-described ladies' man who could also be described as an alpha male came into my office. Our conversation sticks with me to this day. We discussed women and how he determined the way a particular woman was to be treated — or mistreated.

Dr. Shane: How do you differentiate what woman gets treated how?

LM: Before I approach her, I ask myself how she carries herself. Is she physically fit (and likely to stay physically fit), and can I wake up to that face every morning? If the answer is 'yes,' it starts off good. As long as she isn't gauche or cheap or trashy, I can work with her on the wardrobe thing. I go into it with an open mind, listening to her and letting her inform me how she feels about herself. However, it can quickly go downhill should she unveil her riddle and I discover things aren't quite like they initially appeared.

That's how I decide to treat her. I let her teach me!

Dr. Shane: How do women unconsciously unveil their riddle?

LM: Mostly through their behaviors. Talk is cheap. I try to determine are her words inconsistent with her behaviors. She may talk a good game about having a solid moral fabric, and have it going-on on paper; but, it is never lost on me if she is willing to compromise that very moral code she initially paraded. For example, Tiffany was feeling me, and she was gorgeous, so I was feeling her, too. We had a few drinks and danced, and returned to the bar. She pulled out her phone and began sharing her pictures. I'm asking why I am seeing nude selfies of her on her iPhone only hours after having met her. Yes, I'm going back to her place, but I'm not staying the night and won't be calling her the next day.

Alternatively, take Staci, who I met at a cookout, and says she is devoutly committed to God. I'm feeling good about her, until I notice that she cheats on her expense reports and is writing our very expensive dinners off as client meetings. I'm loving the fine dining. But, she either lied about her beliefs and moral constitution, or she is willing to compromise them. I wonder what else she will compromise. So, I push the envelope and see what I can get away with. Why not?

Dr. Shane: Why are you so hard on these women?

LM: *I know these seem like small flaws. And, on the surface it may seem as though their true fatal flaw is liking me too much, too soon. Nevertheless, mothers are the first teachers, so I ask myself what she will teach my daughter about being a woman, or my son about how to interact with women. Her seemingly minor flaws could result in my kids having major character flaws. I can't have that and her fate is sealed!*

Dr. Shane: *Ironically, it sounds like despite the fact that you mistreat women, you actually hold them in high regard.*

LM: *Let me correct you, Doc. I don't mistreat all women. Some I actually treat very well. But to answer your question, yes, the role a woman plays in a man's life is crucial. Men are judged by the woman they keep.*

Take a guy I thought was kind of weak, and I see him with a together woman. I think, maybe I slept on dude. The opposite is true, too. Take a man I admired and I see his woman disrespect him, flirt with other men, get tipsy in public, or have inappropriate tattoos popping up all over the place. His stock drops in my book. I realize he is not what I thought, but deep down he is insecure or has low self-esteem, so I now know how to treat him.

A woman has to be consistent with a man's brand, too. If he's corporate, but is trying to take a woman to his office party or golf outing who is dressed with her breasts out and can't speak the King's English, then he has a problem. She doesn't match his brand. No matter how phat her ass is, or how nice or smart she might be, he's going to lose the respect and confidence of his colleagues, superiors, or clients.

Dr. Shane: *When did you first realize how to get women to share the secret to their riddle?*

LM: *With Heather, it was the way she would sing the lyrics to that S.O.S song, 'Just Be Good to Me.' She said she heard her mother sing this song as a young girl, and it had a catchy beat. It was like she was in a hypnotic trance. Those words rolled off her tongue like they were her anthem. I trusted what I heard her share with me, and I went with it.*

Dr. Shane: *So how did it end?*

LM: Let's just say I wasn't very good to her. She was very good with me not being good to her, however. Why mess a situation like that up? I'm no fool. She was the expert on her, so I trusted her when she told me how to treat her.

As I replayed LM's conversation, I thought about his rules of thumb, experiences, and insights. I also thought about how strongly he reacted to Heather's singing "Just Be Good to Me," by the S.O.S Band, so I went and looked up the words. They are eye-opening. You will be surprised when you Google them. I was! She doesn't care about anything as long as he's good to her. Doesn't mind if she's wasting her time, that he has a reputation for having many other girls, or that he uses other people. Rather, she rather have a piece of him than nothing at all because life is a game of chance. Even worse, in exchange for no commitment at she will give him her love and affection.   Written and produced by Jimmy Jam and Terry Lewis, "Just Be Good to Me" was released as a single in 1983. (Jam and Lewis also produced Janet Jackson's "Control.") While this is long before the proliferation of the Internet, the last time I checked, this song had 5,553,861 views on YouTube, and I doubt the majority of those hits were men. This song's popularity on YouTube speaks volumes about just how timeless this self-destructive message is to women.

Perhaps like you, I always liked this hit song and never stopped to think about the lyrics. Having read them word for word, I couldn't imagine it reaching number two on the R&B chart if sung by a man. Men would universally reject it. And, we all would wonder about the few men who embraced it. What type of man would need to sing that his woman should "just be good to me"? It would be a flop. It's just not socially acceptable for a man to accept so little, much less proudly proclaim it. Subsequently, I wondered if society was somehow complicit in a grand misogynistic scheme to set women up to be mistreated. No. Clearly not! Right? At least, I hope not! While I am not cynical enough to conclude society has consciously conspired to set women up for mistreatment, I recognize society has a double standard that contributes to women accepting mistreatment.

For these reasons, you must own behaving in a fashion that belies your words or core values, or compromising yourself to be with a man. For example, if he repeatedly cheats and you take him back time after time; or if he blows his portion of the rent and you cover it for him, again and again; if he hollers and curses at you in front of the kids and you accept it only to have him repeat this behavior, you are sending and reinforcing the message "just be good to me," and you will accept whatever he chooses to dish out. Let me be the first to say: He's wrong for mistreating you and should stop. Nevertheless, I would be remiss if I didn't point out only you can train him to treat you right.

Should you find yourself being mistreated in your relationship, try owning your role in training him to mistreat you, and begin to own and execute your power to train him to treat you right.

SubtrACTION 3: QUIT GIVING DISCOUNTS; KNOW YOUR VALUE AND DEMAND IT

"Your sense of self-worth is determined by the value you place on yourself and how you conduct yourself. If a man is asking you to discount it, he either doesn't recognize it, doesn't respect it, or can't afford it. He needs to shop elsewhere."
— Dr. Shane Perrault

Coming to know your value and not discount it is one of the most important realizations we can make on the journey of life. Before mastering this phase of your journey, you will find you give in to the temptation to settle for less than you deserve, allow others to take without giving (or even attempting to meet your needs), let his opinion and approval outweigh your own sense of self-worth, or are too intimidated by the thought of confronting him to speak up. Instead you mute your voice or opinion. These are all forms of discounting your value and self-worth.

I've had some amazingly successful, strong, and otherwise independent women come into my practice who inexplicably found themselves either discounting their value, not knowing their value, or not honoring their value to be in a relationship with a man who devalued them. Despite it being obvious early that their partner was a poor choice, they stayed in unfulfilling and even dysfunctional relationships way too long. Some of these women tolerated repeated infidelity, emotionally unavailable partners, and uncommitted partners, even when they wanted a commitment, and gave the upper hand to men who flat out were inferior to them in major ways. They made priorities of men who made them an option.

To help you determine what value you place on yourself and ensure you aren't falling into the same trap, despite your success in other areas of life, here are some questions you might want to ask yourself:

Do you ...

1. Pursue men who aren't available, either because they're just not that into you or are married?

2. Place his approval of you above your own approval of yourself?

3. Make a man a priority who makes you an option?

4. Engage in sex or sexual practices with him that you don't enjoy instead of expressing what you'd like?

5. Accept a causal relationship with a man when you want a committed relationship?

6. Allow your man's slights, words, or actions to determine your mood or sense of worth?

7. Settle for less?

8. Find yourself thinking "I'm not enough"?

9. Justify and minimize your man's hurtful, negligent, or abusive behaviors?

10. Let his personality limitations or feelings about your friends and family members determine who is in your life?

11. Mute your voice instead of confronting him on important issues?

12. Base your sense of worth on the mere fact that you are in a relationship—be it a fulfilling, unfulfilling, or dysfunctional one?

13. Let the thought of being single make you feel anxious?

If you answered "yes" or "occasionally" to four or more of these questions, you're likely letting either your man or society's perception of your value outweigh your own sense of self-worth.

Don't be discouraged!

Regardless of your score, the most important person on your journey to your sense of self-worth is you, and you have all you need to complete it. Besides, no one can make you feel inferior without your permission. Coming to appreciate your value and stop discounting it is a process, and frequently a gradual one. Your journey to self-worth starts with baby steps, and knowing where you stand is the first step you need to take. To help you successfully navigate the rest of your journey, there are many chapters, activities, and resources in this book; and in the workbooks located at theBlackMAN-ual.com.

Fasten your seatbelt, Dorothy. Next stop Kansas. Try to enjoy the ride!

SubtrACTION 4: INSTEAD OF EXPECTING HIM TO THINK LIKE A WOMAN, LEARN TO PROBLEM SOLVE LIKE A MAN

As Jennifer Hudson sang, "Act like a woman, but think like a man." I frequently hear women and men say men aren't emotional. That's simply not true. Men are very emotional. For example, I've seen men propose to a woman on the strength of how she looked in a dress and the way other men looked at him when he walked in the room with her on his arms. Nothing else appeared to set her apart from women who were far more impressive in many critical ways. When some men feel they're with the most beautiful woman in the room, nothing else matters. Based on that stroke to his male ego and sense of bravado, he's ready to stake a claim.

Now that's emotional!

Men just have different rules than women about how we express and manage our emotions. To better understand the emotional rules that men use to govern their emotions, especially alpha males, you might consider some of the books men read. Yes, we read. Unfortunately, we don't read relationship, romance, or communication books. We read books that help us compete and succeed in the game of life. One such book is *The 48 Laws of Power* by Robert Greene. I've read it cover to cover three times and have listened to it in audio form another three times. Why? Because learning the rules of power has taught me how to manage my emotions in ways that have been a boon to my professional success and personal relationships. This book has sold over 1.2 million copies and has been translated into 24 languages. Former drug dealer Curtis Jackson (best known as 50 Cent) said the book changed his life when he read it in prison. He later co-authored a book, T*he 50th Law,* with the author Robert Greene. This book has also been mentioned in songs by UGK, Jay Z, Kanye West, and Drake. Nevertheless, I must forewarn you this book, at times, is Machiavellian, shrewd, and harsh — definitely, not for the faint of heart.

Here is an excerpt from Law #9: "Win through your actions, never through argument." Robert Greene writes, "Any momentary triumph you think gained through argument is really a pyrrhic victory: The resentment and ill will you stir up is stronger and lasts longer than any momentary change of opinion. It is much more powerful to get others to agree with you through your actions."

A violation of law #9: **Meet Bernie and Josephine**. In a couples' therapy session Josephine was supremely disappointed because Bernie was checked out and refused to take her on a cruise with her family. Here's how the conversation went:

Dr. Shane: Why won't you take her on the family cruise?

Bernie: We went on one for our honeymoon, and she cursed me out every night. I felt trapped with nowhere to go. It was a nightmare, and I will never do it again.

Josephine: That was years ago, and you just don't value me or you would get over it. I'm tired of your excuses.

Dr. Shane: Seems like your husband had a bad experience. What happened on the previous cruise?

Josephine: He promised not to drink at all during the cruise, and I caught him drinking O'Doul's beers twice. I tore into him. Bernie wasn't keeping to our agreement, so I let him know about it every night and all night, and all the way on our three-hour flight back home. My father was an alcoholic, and many of our family events were marred by him being drunk and acting the fool. I wasn't going to have my honeymoon ruined.

Once we got home, and I realized the O'Doul's were non-alcohol beers, I apologized for cursing him out. Besides, he didn't get drunk and we had a great time, so my approach worked. That's all that matters and he should be over it.

Bernie: I will never get over it, and I will never be trapped with you again.

Seven years after their honeymoon, he was still scared.

In true pyrrhic victory form, Josephine won the argument, but lost her husband. I couldn't imagine how many women I've seen in therapy (men, too) who couldn't accept they could be far more effective by speaking with action instead of words. Mastering this law will help you avoid appearing angry, needy, and out of control. Appearing this way means you've likely blunted your point, and it will be lost, dismissed, or minimized. Anger and neediness are turnoffs that have proven themselves to be mutually exclusive with seduction. Arguing past a certain point is counter-productive, especially if tinged with anger. By contrast, action is compelling.

Besides, just because you are angry at a man doesn't mean you don't still love him. I've rarely seen a man remain in love with a woman who is always angry and hollering at him. The constant rejection frequently becomes a turnoff, in part, because he has a different version of the story where she shouldn't be mad at all, and in part, because he will either feel emasculated or like he simply can't make her happy. Even worse, the angry partner is likely setting herself up for further frustration as her man is likely to check out, which will only make him further reject and retreat from her. Instead of motivating him to fix the issue, he typically avoids the person he perceives as the problem — you. I've seen this wicked downward spiral become the source of many a breakup and infidelity, and is why I feel Law #9 is so crucial for partners to master.

While it may seem like I am letting the unfaithful man off the hook, I am not. If you can't make peace with your anger and move on, you might be better off cutting your losses by leaving, and sparing yourself further pain. However, staying and remaining enraged will likely end in your worst nightmare becoming your reality. I typically get major push back here; nevertheless, I've seen far too many angry victims of deception, infidelity, and betrayal crushed by this pattern. In contrast, I've never seen an angry person win.

Overall, *The 48 Laws of Power* offers amazing insights into how men think and manage their emotions, and I highly recommend it. I apologize to my brethren for sharing this particular insider tip, but it is a game-changer — in a positive way.

SubtrACTION 5: JUST LET GO! BE WILLING TO CUT YOUR LOSSES AND MOVE ON

The Good Witch: Are you ready?

Dorothy: Yes, I am ready now!

The Good Witch: Close your eyes ... and tap your heels together three times.

— "The Wizard of Oz"

Those of you who have seen "The Wizard of Oz" know the truth is Dorothy always had the power to change her situation and go home. She never needed the Wizard of Oz. And his perceived ability to solve her problems was a racket. The Wizard was cubic zirconia, a fraud!

Like Dorothy, learn to trust yourself. You have the answers to your problems. If you don't feel comfortable with your relationship, or it makes you act out of your character or constantly anxious, be willing to let it go. Refuse to be the kind of person who so desperately wants to be loved that you'll put up with anything in a relationship. You're worth more than that. Chase him if you will, but always let him catch you. Know a confused mind will always decide against you, because he will focus on the cons and not the pros. Wait for his desire for you to catch up with your desire for him. Believe that it's only a matter of time before he discovers how awesome you really are. If you don't believe that, then you can't seduce him. You have to internalize the notion that people naturally become attracted to anyone who we feel comfortable with, makes us laugh, and is slightly out of reach. Studies have found that a playful attitude and sense of humor makes people more attractive. By contrast, the tension created by pressuring yourself or him to close the deal will make him feel uptight, put him in anything but a playful or laughing mood, and make him wonder why you are so eager, anxious, available, and pressed, all of which accomplish the opposite effect. That's human nature.

As Maya Angelou said, "I do not trust people who don't love themselves and yet tell me, 'I love you.' There is an African saying: Be careful when a naked person offers you a shirt."

Similarly, if your relationship has come to resemble the dynamic inside a pressure cooker, and he appears somewhat indifferent or to be back peddling, then protect yourself from a man who just may no longer be into you. Instead of applying more pressure, which will only result in your being further rejected and disrespected, know you have the option to leave. Like the Wizard of Oz, he is not the answer, so click your heels three times and use those ruby slippers of yours to walk.

> LOVE WHEN YOU'RE READY, NO WHEN YOU'R LONELY.

I've had numerous women tell me their man doesn't want to commit, and then ask what should they do? I say, believe him. Accept you are in a no-win situation, thank him for his forthrightness and the get out of jail free card, and move on. The problem you face by not walking is two-fold. On the one hand, if he cheats, he has an airtight alibi because he said he wasn't ready to commit, so technically he could still be a man of integrity; accordingly, you will struggle to move on if you are in love with him. His only crime was a misdemeanor—being too honest to deceive you. He told you he wasn't committed to you. When it comes to infidelity, the felony is seldom the affair itself, but the lies and the cover up. While it's easy to despise a liar and leave him, his straight-forward candor is the perfect defense. On the other hand, if he tells you, "OK, I will commit if that's what you want," you won't believe him or feel secure because it wasn't his choice. Herein lies the problem. It's hard to be mad at a man or get over a man who simply was straight up with you. Dogs lie, but this man was honest. For these reasons, either way, you lose.

Again, the only way you win is to thank him for his honesty, and wish him the best.

Recognize the art of the deal by accepting you can't negotiate unless you are willing to walk away from a deal—or your man. Be willing to cut your losses. Know God's abundant kingdom has enough enlistees to send another Mr. Right into your life to replace him. And sometimes after a break, a previous man may return with a new commitment level. This isn't to be mistaken for not working through your problems, but accepting that it takes two people to make a thing go right. One hundred percent isn't you giving 60 percent while he gives 40 percent, but you both giving 100 percent.

Let go and move on. Invest your 100 percent where it has a legitimate chance to generate a positive return. If you do move on, don't let your focus on the destination cause you to stop enjoying the ride.

SubtrACTION 6: STOP FALLING IN LOVE; START GROWING IN LOVE

The temptation of soulmate love is a seductive one indeed, and only a precious few successfully combat the irresistible tendency to get swept away in the rapture of love. Nonetheless, soulmate love is a marathon, so you might want to pump the brakes a bit early on and really get to know more about this Mr. Right you are falling head-over-heels with to better understand your relationship dynamic with him.

But, why does it matter if you are falling in love or growing in love—and how do you know the difference? Falling in love is an essential part of an earlier stage of romantic love; nevertheless, no matter how deeply connected you two feel to each other, you will need to develop various relationship and conflict resolution skills to navigate life's ups and downs together and grow closer in the process. The most important distinction between *falling* and *growing* in love is that as you two grow closer together and your partnership gets stronger, you will develop the skills needed to begin to grow closer instead of growing apart together in times of conflict.

So let's look at the tell-tale signs below to help you distinguish the difference and significance between falling and growing in love:

Tell-tale Signs You Are Falling or Growing in Love:

Falling in Love	Growing in Love
Falling in love is effortless.	Growing in love requires continuous effort and developing your relationship and conflict resolution skills.
"Friend" is considered a bad word.	Friendship is the cornerstone on which your good relationship is built. Not having a strong cornerstone is considered bad.
You can fall in love with Mr. Wrong.	It is very difficult to grow in love with him unless he is Mr. Right.
Falling in love is a euphoric feeling, like being on an emotional high (much like drinking or taking drugs).	Growing in love is making a sober, sound-minded, balanced, practical, and emotional decision about the life partner you love.
Falling in love frequently means you have an illusion that Mr. Wrong is fairly perfect.	Growing in love gives you time to know your Mr. Right and have a fair understanding of his imperfections and love him anyway. There are no illusions.
The feeling of being in love usually last 6 months to 2 years.	Growing in love can last a lifetime, and get stronger as time goes on.

Conflicts haven't yet emerged or are avoided, and when they do, love will make everything OK.	Conflicts are adeptly resolved in an "I'm OK. You're OK" fashion to empower your partnership to accomplish a greater good.
You feel opposites attract.	You've taken time to recognize, speak, and become fluent in each other's emotional differences and love languages so you two can effectively communicate and grow together, avoiding becoming polar opposites.
Love doesn't have a balance sheet.	You accept fighting over money can bankrupt your relationship and take steps to assess the long-term impact of your different financial philosophies.
Love can conquer all.	You've made sure your relationship is free of any deal breakers and all game changers that love didn't have a chance of conquering have been discussed.

Whether you are falling or growing in love, this is an exciting time indeed. If you answered these questions positively, great. Don't be alarmed if you didn't feel "growing in love" best reflected your relationship in every scenario. Just know that before you get too attached to each other or decide to take your relationship to the next level, you will have to learn more about each other, so consider having some heart-to-heart conversations or talking to a relationship therapist or a psychologist.

In any event, enjoy the ride and all the best!

SubtrACTION 7: INSTEAD OF DOING OTHERS, DO YOU!

Years ago, while working at an alcohol and substance abuse clinic, I went to an Al-Anon meeting for partners of alcohol and substance abusers. (Al-Anon groups are for co-dependent partners of alcoholics.) The facilitator, Jay, instructed the participants to walk out to the parking lot and report back what their car's fuel level readings were. As Jay foretold, all of the participants reported their cars being on E — empty — which he said was symptomatic. The members painstakingly made sure their partner's needs were met, while their own needs were neglected.

To love yourself, it is essential that you stop focusing all of your energy on others and do you!

Here are four guidelines to help you start to do you:

1. Carve out space and time for you. One of the best ways to love yourself is to pay attention to what it is that you want and need — from your job, in your relationships, out of your friendships, and in life. Many accomplished women who come into my office were taught to disregard what they want and need. It is not uncommon for women to go through their entire adult lives living for others without stopping to ask, "What do I want or need here?" or "What's best for me?"

    No matter how many people you are responsible for at home or at work, if you don't start taking care of you, then you can't take others for long. Like the members of Al-Anon, you will have to learn to put gas in your tank, too.

    Develop the habit of asking, "What do I what? What do I need?" — and be honest with yourself about what relationships are and aren't helping you to get your needs met.

2. Set boundaries. Boundaries are about figuring out where other people's wants end and your needs begin. At first,

you may feel selfish, guilty, or embarrassed about the notion of setting, or needing to set, boundaries, particularly with the ones you love. However, loving without boundaries will frequently cause you to sacrifice your integrity and happiness, and disproportionately put your partner's needs over yours. Ignoring your boundaries will likely result in you feeling lost in the process, especially if you aren't receiving the same in return.

3. How to create and maintain healthy boundaries:

A. Identify the core values essential to your happiness, and fiercely guard them.

The first task is to identify what you value most. For instance, if you value being able to talk with your man and discuss your feelings and the feelings about your feelings, then set boundaries around this value. This means you need to avoid men who only talk about themselves, aren't good communicators, or who otherwise make you feel like your feelings have been dismissed or like your concerns are minimized. Accepting his inability to make you feel heard while dating is a sign he may not be able to meet your needs in the long run; and, therefore, he just may not be capable of being the man for you, despite his positive qualities. While you can change or positively accentuate traits he naturally possesses or desires to improve upon, don't buy into the notion or illusion that you can make over a grown man.

Make sure he is meeting your needs, too, and release men who do not offer an even exchange of some sort that is mutually fulfilling.

B. Notice how you react to others and how they impact you.

If you are an introvert and need me time to recharge your battery, determine which men can and can't comfortably honor that need. For instance, if he always needs to be on the go, on the phone, around other people, and doing so exhausts you, date men who have a positive relationship with your need for solitude. While opposites initially attract, over time he will come to see you as negligent and you will come to see him as needy.

C. Avoid taking responsibility for others' problems.

If you tend to date men you feel need fixing, and totally throw yourself into their problems to your own peril, you need to ask yourself what you are getting out of this relationship pattern. Avoid the deceptively wrong answer. It's not just because you are a good person. Consider whether it stems from a need to feel needed, or a sense of making yourself feel so indispensable that he can't leave or hurt you, which isn't true, either. Face the reality that if saving him didn't somehow benefit you, you wouldn't be saving him. Identifying what you are hoping to get out of it will allow you to possibly get that need met in a healthier way, saving your valuable energy to meet your own needs. Besides, he is a grown man with his own path in life, and learning to fix his own problems is a critical part of that journey. It's not your place to inadvertently rob him of that experience, and he may secretly resent you for doing so. While you are right to support and encourage him, learn to practice restraint when it comes to fixing him or taking on his problems. Accept that you are only responsible for you and yours.

D. Enforce your boundaries.

If creating boundaries is the first part of this journey, perhaps protecting them is the most critical aspect of maintaining healthy boundaries. Boundaries are meant to be enforced and will open the door for mutually fulfilling love. If you are honoring your own boundaries, others will, too. Enforcing boundaries is training others how to treat you.

E.   Analyze your boundaries.

Whenever you find yourself trying to figure out what choice to make, ask yourself, "Is what I'm about to do honoring my boundary of _____?" Make it a habit of always making decisions consistent with your boundaries.

Conclusion: As you honor your boundaries, men who are wrong for you will fall by the wayside, and you will be more available to notice more of the right men who start to show up — or who may have already been there but you were too distracted to notice. (Whomp, whomp. Yes, sometimes sistas sleep on the good ones! But men do, too!) Equally important, healthy boundaries will ensure you don't end up like the co-dependent Al-Anon members whose cars are always on E.

4.   Find ways to complete yourself. Nourish your mind, body, and soul.

A.   You don't have to become a competitive cyclist or run a marathon, pay off all of your debt in a year, learn a second language, complete divinity school, or save a fortune, but you will feel more complete if you find ways to identify and pursue goals that give you a greater sense of purpose.

Few of us feel as though our life is exactly where it should be, so there's no reason to beat yourself up over not being perfect. But taking small steps to start living the life you've always wanted is one of the best ways to show yourself love.

B.   Consider using the "IRS method" to accomplish a few goals that will make you feel your life is more complete: Identify, Reduce, and Schedule the goals important to you. Take out a sheet of paper and make a free association list, including every word that comes to mind when you hear the topics: personal life, professional life, social life, family life, financial life, and spiritual life.

- *I-Identify.* Based on your free association list, write down every goal you can think of related to these six areas.

- *R-Reduce.* Pick out one to two items related to each area on your list.

- *S-Schedule.* List and schedule the 3-, 6-, 12-, 18-, and 24-month interval steps you will have to take to accomplish these goals.

C. Finally, don't neglect your spirit. Even if you fellowship regularly, don't forget to slow down and take time to pay attention to what's going on within yourself. Are you happy or fulfilled? How are people affecting you? What types of spiritual goals would you like to accomplish, and what type of spiritual support do you need? Make sure you are replenishing the energy you exert investing in others by taking the time to pray, meditate, connect with those who reinvigorate you, and read meaningful books that nourish and enrich your life.

D. Live in the now. Being present is a surprisingly hard place for people to remain. Instead, we frequently slip back into the past, which may be filled with thoughts of glory or regret. Alternatively, anxiety and fear about the future draws us away from the present, too. The present is all we have, and it's the only resource we have to make peace with the past and prepare for a peaceful future. Being present is one powerful way to love yourself and make the most of who you are right now.

Consider taking a yoga class, or picking up a copy of Dr. Wayne Dyer's CD, *Getting in the Gaps*; or Eckert

Tolle's, *The Power of Now,* or completing the workbooks at theBlackMAN-ual.com.

Being present and loving yourself isn't selfish.

Consider your heart. It pumps blood to itself first before sending blood out to the rest of the body. Similarly, the more loving you are to yourself, the more love you'll be able to send out to others in your life — your family, your friends, and the men you date or the one you marry. So make the decision to be present and love yourself now, working to love yourself more fully day after day.

Again, learning to FLY doesn't involve you discovering some rare supernatural secret. Actually, it's often as simple as uncovering the you that loved herself so naturally before she was taught some of the negative messages you internalized over the years — messages that told you that you could not FLY.

I hope you employ these 7 Subtr**Actions** to lighten your load and start **FLY**ing soon!

CHAPTER 10

Nine Myths About Soulmate Love—and How to Shatter Them

"You don't want to be in love.
You want to be in love in a movie."
From "Sleepless in Seattle," Rosie O'Donnell's
character famously tells Meg Ryan's character

SOULMATE LOVE

Oh, how tantalizing and seductive we find the notion that in the entire universe there is only one soulmate love for us! Since the beginning of time, he has been eagerly traversing the cosmos on a quest to reunite with you. The prospect of such a rare and divine love appeals to us on at least three levels: First, it soothes the nagging wound stemming from the sense that we are all alone in the world; second, it fosters the hope that some majestic man will love us unconditionally — embracing us, warts and all; third, it makes us feel special to know that no matter how harsh and impersonal the world seems at times, the universe has a unique design on our destiny.

Shazam!

No wonder soulmates are so universally sought. Instead of working on your shortcomings, all you have to do is hail the coming of this anointed Mr. Right who can turn your romantic vinegar into wine. The perfect one whose love will magically erase all of your imperfections, transforming the ordinary into the extraordinary, carrying you on the back of his white horse as you two ride off into the sunset.

Thanks to movies, love songs, and romance novels, the concept of finding a soulmate has universally captivated aspiring lovers. These aspirations were reflected in research conducted at Rutgers University. During a 2001 National Marriage Project Survey, they found that 94 percent of the participants in the 20- to 29-year-old age range felt: "When you marry, you want your spouse to be your soulmate, first and foremost," and 88 percent felt: "There is a special person, a soulmate, waiting for you out there."

Many of the married couples I have worked with shared the same expectations. On their wedding day they envisioned living happily ever after — no arguments, no disagreements, one man, one woman, 2.5 children, and a white picket fence. Yes sir, till death do us part!

So what changed?

The easy answer is life! Yes, life happened to these couples, as my many case studies and staggering divorce rates give witness. The realists, the cynics, and the play-it-safe types were right about the fallacy of soulmate love. Ironically, while those types never cheer about anything, it's their chance to cheer and shout, "Don't believe the hype. We didn't!"

The hard, and more difficult, answer to accept is that somehow soulmate love got a bad rap, and being overhyped isn't the problem at all! Rather, the media and myths surrounding it were based on a faulty hypothesis. The hypothesis' fatal flaw was that romantic love is soulmate love, which ignores the reality that romantic love is an early stage of soulmate love. Only couples who endure life's ups and downs develop the mature love that becomes soulmate love.

Yes, the books you read and the affirmations you made to start attracting Mr. Right were on point, and you were wise to work on changing your thoughts and behaviors to attract him. That's the obvious part of the magical formula. The not-so-obvious part of the formula is becoming Ms. Right, so that you are his soulmate, too. The problem wasn't that God couldn't deliver. Perhaps, the problem was you just weren't in the place to receive—or be—Ms. Right. I've been very blessed to have had a front row seat while many women navigated their self-development journey to soulmate love. It's been amazing to witness them face their fears, make peace with challenging pasts, occasionally rid themselves of dysfunctional relationship patterns, and scale mental stumbling blocks to get ready for a soulmate.

Yet, it happened for them.

For it to happen for you, however, you must have a clear vision of what being in a relationship with Mr. Right—and becoming Ms. Right—looks and feels like. Only then will you start to avoid falling prey to the myths that shroud soulmate love and start resisting the temptation presented by its promises of grandeur. By overcoming those stumbling blocks you will be able to recognize the self-acceptance, commitment to personal and partnership growth, and appreciation for God's abundance needed for your relationship to mature into soulmate love.

What is a myth?

MYTH: Misinformation You Thought was Helpful. The key word is "misinformation." Myths that stand the test of time almost always have their roots in truth. Nevertheless, some modern myths are just that—myths. To help you look beyond these myths and start uncovering the truth, here is my list of the Top 10 Myths About Soulmate Love I'd like to shatter.

SOULMATE MYTH 1: PRINCE CHARMING WILL BE RIDING A WHITE HORSE.

Even if he isn't exactly on a white horse, can he still be your prince? The Lipizzaner is universally agreed upon as the most magnificent of all stallions in the equestrian kingdom. Although Lipizzaners are predominantly white once full grown, the foals are all born dark brown or black.

Their metamorphosis from black colt to white stallion takes seven years to complete. Ironically, full-grown black Lipizzaner stallions are the rarest and most prized members of this distinguished breed. Yet, the future majesty of the young black colt is regularly lost on the untrained eye.

Renowned for their bravery, agility, strength, and superior instincts, these regal warhorses were bred by the Moors of North Africa to conquer parts of Europe and Spain from the 7th to 16th centuries.

Like this deceptive pedigree, ladies don't let your potential soulmate's outer appearance or any other preconceived notions mislead you. Outside of character, which is a fixed variable, train your eye to consider non-fixed variables, like his present circumstance and life trajectory, to forecast his ability to make you happy in the long run.

(Note: Please, do not confuse this with rescuing a man without a plan, which is discussed in Myth #6.)

SOULMATE MYTH 2: YOUR LIFE WITH A HIGHER-PROFILE MAN WILL BE HAPPIER.

Stephanie: Look at him, girl (she said, as she eyed Wesley from head to toe when he walked into the bar where she and Dominique were enjoying Happy Hour). Did you see the Maserati he drove up in? And, he is *wearing* that custom cut Armani suit!

Dominique: Don't stare. That's the guy I met a couple of weeks ago. We went out to dinner (blushing). He does joint venture capitalism, or some high-finance stuff. Has a fantabulous house, too; and it's decorated like something out of an interior design magazine.

Stephanie: Decorated like a what? Now, exactly how do you know about the inside of his house? Nique, you didn't! Girl? Umm! (Realizing normally conservative Dominique had ventured out of her shell and possibly slid into the 800-thread count Egyptian cotton sheets on Wesley's bed, she burst out laughing. Falling to the floor, Dominique's eyes sheepishly gave her away. Accepting her worst sin was not sharing such a juicy story, she glanced at Stephanie and smiled. They high-fived.)

Stephanie: Why am I just hearing about this, Nique? What a well put together man. Girl, how was it?

Dominique: Like I'd ever tell you. (She smiled sternly.)

Stephanie: Whatever happened to Steady Eddie? Thought you were finally going to give him a chance.

Dominique: A chance? We were supposed go to NYC for dinner and a play, but he has been cutting back since the government sequester reduced his hours and cut all overtime. Damn Republicans! We laugh a lot, but I'm a bit out of his price range right about now. Physically, he's close, but the wardrobe needs attention. A good man, but no fireworks. Friends. Besides, looks like I've upgraded.

Stephanie: Wesley. Hold up! I remember you told me about a Wesley. Recently divorced, right?

Dominique: Yep. Just got it finalized last month. He says she was insecure and always accusing him of sleeping with his exes, friends, and coworkers. Had issues from a previous relationship. You know how that goes. He got tired of her snooping and paranoia and called it quits. Her loss, my gain.

Stephanie: She let a man like that slip away? Hmmm! Maybe where there's smoke, there's ...

Dominique: Shhhh! He's coming over. I will fill you in later. He might be The One.

Ladies, I'm sure this isn't the first time you've heard this conversation.

I'm happy Dominique has met a new, upwardly mobile man, but I'd be remiss if I didn't share some research on high-profile men. These alpha males are passionate, always composed, driven, dress-code smart, pose a challenge, clever and cunning, not afraid to face their faults, don't feel a need to prove themselves, dominant, physically fit, witty, and exhibit great body language and etiquette. They are smooth operators.

While studies have found no significant difference in happiness for couples who are attractive compared to those who are less attractive, they have found that high-profile men tend to be less happy in marriage than lesser attractive men.

In "Hot or Not? Why Women Shouldn't Pick Attractive Husbands," Vicky Larson blogs, "The more financially independent women become, the more they prefer good-looking men. But they don't just want their physically fit partners to be hotties, they want them to be masculine, physically fit, loving, educated, a few years older, and making the big bucks. Oh, and they also have to really want to be a hubby and daddy." She further writes, "Men with more testosterone are consistently rated more handsome than other men ... and are 38 percent more likely to cheat."

Larson suggests that the happiest couples are those where the woman is more attractive than her man.

Across the board, researchers on this topic agree with Larson, and further speculate these men possess a "grass is always greener" mentality that contributes to them feeling less satisfied and being less committed to doing the work necessary to maintain their marriages. And their wives feel less supported.

In contrast, studies find men with wives rated more attractive than themselves report higher levels of marital satisfaction. In her study of 450 newlyweds conducted over four years, Dr. Andrea Meltzer, a psychologist, posed the following question: Does a good-looking spouse lead to a more satisfying union? She found the partner's level of physical attractiveness played a larger role in predicting husbands' marital satisfaction than it did in predicting wives' marital satisfaction.

Interestingly, the wives who were more attractive than their husbands reported higher levels of satisfaction, because having a happy husband made them happier, too.

So, women if you are seeking a soulmate, you might be better served in the long run to choose the man a notch below you in the looks department. Why? Researchers suggest that in addition to men placing greater value on beauty, higher-profile men are more likely to place less value on doing the work to repair their relationship or marriage. I'm not trying to discourage any woman from pursing a Mr. Right that is easy on the eyes and suave, just sharing what researchers have to say. Namely, Dominique should precede with caution and probably not delete Steady Eddie's number just yet.

SOULMATE MYTH 3: WHO HAS TIME TO WAIT FOR A SOULMATE WHEN THERE'S A MAN SHORTAGE?

Numbers don't lie! There is definitely a shortage of Black men compared to Black women, and these ratios are further distorted when you consider the growing number of good Black men who date and marry outside of their race.

At the same time, choosing to be with Mr. Wrong is, well, choosing to be with Mr. Wrong. There just isn't any winning with Mr. Wrong, ratio aside.

Candidly, it's been my experience that due to the ratio, you definitely have to wait for a soulmate because you don't have the luxury of getting it wrong as often as your White female counterparts. You have to be more disciplined, shrewd, and keenly aware of what you want than other women.

Mr. Right isn't necessarily the unavailable or overly challenging alpha male you might be projecting your fantasies onto; rather, he's the one who is available enough for you to work through real problems on a day-to-day basis. The biggest challenge you two face is how to come together more effectively to work through life's ups and downs.

I know this doesn't sound romantic, but it is real talk based on what I see in private practice. Couples with the "it factor" are always the ones with a sound friendship. And, shortage or not, if you two aren't friends, then you are likely not soulmates.

Finally, the term soulmate has the word soul in it, which means spirit. Meaning this is a spiritual phenomenon as well, so trust in God's omnipotence. In His infinite kingdom, there is only surplus, no matter how high the deck is stacked against you in this world. Trust God's abundance is greater than any ratio by far. It just is! All you need Him to send you is one man who's right for you.

SOULMATE MYTH 4: THE ENDS JUSTIFY THE MEANS.

Trying to get a soulmate by hook or crook is oxymoronic. That is, the word soul indicates a spiritual connection, while resorting to hook or crook suggests the opposite. You may get your man, but you won't get a soulmate. Karmic law will bring these ill-gotten gains back to haunt you. For example, if you steal him from his wife, then you will likely have serious trust issues as his wife. Even more detrimental, his ex-wife will be at every significant event in his children's lives (should they have children), and she will not let you win over his children, nor will you likely ever win the respect of his mother. This will result in untold family feuds or catch-22s where he has to choose between you and his family. You will be damned if he chooses them over you, and damned if he chooses you over them. In the case of the latter, he will likely feel horrible for becoming estranged from loved ones and blame it on you, even if he doesn't say it.

Perhaps, the problems caused by getting your man by hook or crook are represented in the outcome statistics on relationships born out of an affair. Only seven percent of the men ended up marrying the other woman. Even worse, 75 percent of those marriages end in divorce primarily because actual marriage seldom lives up to the expectations of the fantasized marriage.

If you want to end up with a soulmate, you might be best served by being faithful to his marriage or your integrity — even if he doesn't want to be.

In short, why not remain his fantasy, and let some other woman be his mistress and failed post-divorce statistical casualty? Then become his soulmate after the rebound relationship fizzles, assuming you haven't already found one you can trust.

SOULMATE MYTH 5: ALL SOULMATE LOVERS LOVE ALIKE.

Just as all great minds don't think alike, all great lovers don't love alike. As Paula Abdul famously sang, "Who would have thought we could be lovers ... we come together because opposites attract." Contrasting personality styles breed excitement and can fuel romantic connections. At the same time, these divergent personality styles can be the source of perpetual gridlock. For example, after a long week around employees in the office, introverts tend to feel depleted and need to recharge their battery with some me time. By contrast, after a week around employees in the office, extroverts are energized and ready to enjoy quality time with their partner, laughing and joking, or spending a night out on the town. Unlike introverts who recharge their batteries with solitude away from people, extroverts recharge their battery by being around people. Although wildly attracted to each other, fights over the perpetual gridlock caused by these sort of hard to explain differences can feel personal, causing deep emotional wounds and feelings of isolation, in spite of both partners' attempts to love and support each other in the only way they know how.

To love and support their partner's divergent needs, happy couples find a way of recognizing, embracing, or, at least, depersonalizing each other's emotional differences instead of trying to change them. They ask questions to better understand and employ new ways to honor these differences in a fashion that creates win-win outcomes. This conflict resolution style is the romantic equivalent of turning lemons into lemonade.

Learning to create win-win outcomes with your partner in spite of your different personality styles will require you both to expand your definition of love, and become more adept at understanding and speaking each other's love and emotional languages. First, I recommend you consider learning to recognize, and become fluid in your partner's love language. In the *Five Love Languages*, Gary Chapman identifies five unique ways partners experience and express love, including words of affirmation, quality time, gifts, acts of service, and physical touch. For example, if he enjoys quality time and physical touch, and you simply try to make him feel loved by giving him cards (because your love language is words of affirmation), there could be trouble in paradise. He will likely feel neglected, while you feel you've tried to support him, but he is a bit of an ingrate.

Remaining positive during conflict extends to accepting that your man very likely speaks a different love language than you do. The law of two truths encourages you to accept all love languages are valid, especially if your man is speaking it to tell you how much he loves you. To resolve conflicts and recognize that some of your man's intentions and genuine expressions of love may have been misunderstood or unrecognized, your solution may be found by taking a closer look at your partner's love language. In therapy, couples are frequently amazed to discover their partner has been loving them all along, but because it was delivered in a love language foreign to them, they didn't receive it, and vice-versa.

For these reasons, if you or your man feel unloved, alone, and unsupported based on personality differences in spite of your partner saying he is trying to make you happy, recognize it doesn't necessarily mean you two are incompatible, aren't soulmates, or that your partner is selfish or mean spirited. Rather, you may just need to better understand each other.

SOULMATE MYTH 6: YOUR LOVE CAN FIX HIM.

Woman after woman has sat on my black couch with partners they were trying to fix — and more than a few have insisted I try and fix him, too. "Teach him to be a man. Tell him to get more 'ABC,' or do less of 'XYZ,' and otherwise man up," they insisted. Sensing their frustration, however, didn't change the fact that my hands were tied.

While I have witnessed a good woman help make a good man become great, I've never seen a great woman make a bad man good. However, a bad man can make a great woman bad.

You can't fix him, or change him, no matter how much you love him.

Change is hard. Face it, it's almost impossible to get a person to change dry cleaners, much less their character and approach to life. What's most likely to change is their sense of happiness being replaced with resentment and downright rebellion.

Ironically, the women who bring these men in claiming they are in need of repair are often highly resistant themselves. They frequently rebelled against me when I informed them therapy isn't about just fixing one partner. They need help, too, if for no other reason than because they picked such a clearly inept man to fill such a critical role and remained with him. Furthermore, it's not just the ratio, because many Black women who chose from the same dating pool of men come into my office with men whose lives were running smoothly.

If you are seriously dating or are married to a man who you actively dislike or feel is defective or inept — one who makes you feel the need to make major changes to who he is — ask yourself what is driving you to be with him. Is your choice based on love or fear, or some other historical factor, like the previously discussed Freudian Unconscious Repetition Compulsion? (See Chapter 2.) In either event, the solution to the problem may lie within you and not him.

If he just doesn't have what it takes to be Mr. Right, you might consider talking to a professional and uncovering what's behind your choice and how to precede from there.

On the other hand, if you genuinely like and respect him as a man, but you are trying to determine if he has the potential to make you feel secure, I encourage you to take the approach employed by insurance companies to set rates for applicants for coverage. They plug actuarial data into mathematical algorithms to predict the future likelihood of the applicant filing a claim. For example, they say if you are a 25-year-old male with one accident, and you are looking to insure a sports SUV in neighborhood Q, then you pay X + $250; whereas, if you are a 25-year-old female with a college degree and no accidents, and are looking to insure a basic SUV in neighborhood A, then you pay X - $150.

What do insurance companies know that you don't know? Insurance companies know the best indicator of future performance is past performance. Based on countless claims in their database, they can predict how much, or how little, risk these drivers represent with various profiles, and accordingly set their rates or elect to decline coverage.

Likewise, if a man has a good plan, and a proven record of overcoming obstacles and executing that plan, then he's likely a keeper. Conversely, if he's going through life on what war pilots call flying on "one wing and a prayer," then he likely might not be a keeper. A man will need to find a way to contribute to supporting his family financially to be a soulmate, otherwise he likely will feel emasculated or like a burden. No matter how great your love is, either of these sentiments has the potential to bankrupt your relationship.

This doesn't mean he can't earn less, be less formally educated, or have some other challenges. It just means you have to genuinely admire and respect him in some major ways, or there will be trouble in paradise. For example, let's say you went to college and he didn't. Not a problem. There are different ways to be smart. In fact, IQ may not be as important as EQ (emotional quotient) when it comes to real-world success. Also, I've worked with many couples where the less educated partner earned more. Just be clear on what his strengths are and how he hopes to employ his skill set to add value and be accountable in a way that works for both of you and your family.

That's not rescuing or fixing. Fixing doesn't work. That's being flexible; that can work. By contrast, rescuing never works in the long run. Instead it frequently leads to resentment on both parts, and sometimes infidelity on both parts.

SOULMATE MYTH 7: HIS LOVE WILL FIX YOU.

I dated my last boyfriend for seven years and I'm not getting any younger. My last boyfriend cheated or was physically abusive. I'm ready to start a family. I don't trust men. He does very well financially and we can afford the type of house my parents would admire.

These are just a few of the situations from which I've heard women describe they wanted their Mr. Right to rescue them. (Don't get me wrong; men come to my office wanting a relationship to save them, too.) A soulmate's purpose in your life isn't to rescue or complete you, because that wouldn't make you his soulmate. Instead I've seen men retreat, feeling the pressure of these demands and fearing it's too tall an order for them to fill. Accordingly, it is vital that you start the process of completing yourself and becoming Ms. Right.

In soulmate love, two wholes make a whole, not two halves.

There is no one person who fits us perfectly, who completes our missing half. The nature of soulmate love requires two whole people that counter balance and complement each other, helping each other to fulfill their purpose. Your soul is complete and independently whole, desiring another whole for mutual support and love.

While you don't have to be perfect to find soulmate love, it's much easier to keep your soulmate love relationship alive if you both are committed to working through your imperfections. Great relationships function like great cars. The transmission and the engine depend on each other for the car to run, but they both must function independently of each other if the car is to perform up to its potential. Similarly, soulmate lovers are inter-dependent.

If you are aren't feeling whole, accept you can only feel that remaining half with self-understanding and forgiveness, personal growth, self-love, and, more importantly, God. Accepting that only these components can fill your void and make you whole will stop you from expecting a man to do something he knows he can't do—complete you.

SOULMATE MYTH 8: SOULMATE LOVE DOESN'T REQUIRE A MAINTENANCE PLAN.

This myth can be dispelled with one question. Would you drive your car until your dying days and never take it in for maintenance? Clearly not! Then you are saying you are willing to invest more in the car than the driver and passengers. If he isn't open to working on improving or maintaining your relationship, he probably isn't your Mr. Right—unless you feel the same way. If you both are in agreement here, I recommend you keep an attorney on retainer, and you might want to wait awhile before deciding to have children.

This reminds me of a couple I worked with briefly, Herb and Vivian.

Wife: I want him to be more romantic. At least, give me roses on Valentine's Day.

Husband: Roses die!

Wife: See what I mean?

Husband: They do die. She doesn't complain when she looks at our savings account balance. A healthy nest egg and retirement plan is sexy to me. Speaking of money, how much is this costing me to hear her complain about freaking flowers? Really! If that's her worst complaint, did she really need to drag me in here, Doc? I'm sure you've seen couples with real problems.

This isn't soulmate love at all. This can't even pass the romantic love test. This is two unhappy souls who merely live together, share complementary rings and matching names.

SOULMATE MYTH 9: SOULMATE LOVE LASTS FOREVER.

"Letting go doesn't mean that you don't care about someone anymore. It's just realizing that the only person you really have control over is yourself." — Deborah Reber.

Rare, precious, and definitely a girl's best friend, soulmates are kind of like diamonds, but they don't necessarily last forever. Nor are they always meant to.

Contrary to the myth that there is only one Mr. Right for each of us and if we blow it we'll never have another chance at soulmate love, the truth is we all have many potential soulmates. We will have soul ties with all types of people who will come in and out of our lives: some to spur our awakening, some to foster our development, some to help prepare us for another purpose, and one or some will be your soulmate for a reason, a season, or a lifetime — it's not always initially clear.

When their purpose in our lives has been served, it's time for them to move on, for their good and ours. For these reasons, you are best served loving the men you have soul ties to with an open fist, understanding that you are together by choice, not coercion or even contract. Yes, even a soul tie that seems like it will last forever can unravel as quickly as it came together. Instead of growing old together, sometimes couples grow apart. Holding on to a relationship with a tight fist after its time has passed will only bring you anger, resentment, mental bondage, and probably block you from being able to receive a more valuable gift. Learning to release him in a loving way will set you both free.

A soulmate may be meant for a moment in time or a lifetime, while some men you share soul ties with are meant to share your journey as long as they are needed. Just because it did not last forever and you are single again does not mean you didn't share a true soul tie. It's time to master the lesson he was meant to teach you and move on.

Perhaps, he was part of your preparation for your next soulmate.

CHAPTER 11

Dating With Kids: Strategies for Beating the Odds!

"These are the situations that separate women from girls."
—Jada Pinkett-Smith, on blended families

HOW JADA PINKETT-SMITH PLAYED THE ROLE OF A LIFETIME TO BLEND HER FAMILY

In an open letter to friend on Facebook, Mrs. Jada Pinkett-Smith shares her thoughts on blended families:

> *"Blended families are NEVER easy, but here's why I don't have a lot of sympathy for your situation because ... we CHOOSE them. When I married Will, I knew Trey was part of the package.... Period! If I didn't want that ... I needed to marry someone else. Then I learned if I am going to love Trey ... I had to learn to love the most important person in the world to him ... his mother. And the two of us may not have always LIKED each other ... but we have learned to LOVE each other.*

> *I can't support any actions that keep a man from his children of a previous marriage. These are the situations*

that separate the women from the girls. Your behavior is that of an insecure child who needs to recognize her own weaknesses that MUST be strengthened to take on the task at hand. We can't say we love our man and then come in between him and his children. THAT'S selfishness ... NOT love. WOMAN UP ... I've been there ... I know. My blended family made me a giant.... Taught me so much about love, commitment and it has been the biggest ego death to date. It's time you let your blended family make you the giant you truly are."

Jada Pinkett-Smith's candid thoughts on blended families draws advice from her own experience with her husband, Will Smith, his eldest son, Trey, and Smith's first wife, Sheree Zampino. It also follows a photo of Pinkett-Smith and Zampino with their children, Willow, Jaden and Trey, several years back.

Her approach to making her blended family work was spot on. And, if this picture represents the happiness they share, then her exemplary choice to morph into a giant undoubtedly played a critical role in their celebrity marriage standing the test of time. Their 17-year marriage seems like an eternity when you consider both celebrity marriages and blended families are on the endangered species list, renowned for having a short shelf life.

In many ways, her success in blending her family stemmed from her ability to let her ego die and accept the differences in the biological and step-mother's roles, which can perhaps best be described as the contrast of being cast as a leading lady versus a supporting actress, as far as the child is concerned. Stellar performances by both actresses are essential for the movie's success. Either can play a heroine or villain, and both actresses' performances can potentially grab an Oscar nomination. Nevertheless, the biological parent's name will always appear first on the screen credits. The key to the blended family having a happy ending is each actresses and actor knowing, accepting, embracing, and playing their roles masterfully.

But do you share Smith-Pinkett's desire to, or ability to, *woman up* and embrace your role, Ms. Right? If you are like most, no! And, don't want to, given the way she's treated you. Right? That's fine. Frankly, you likely feel like you do for good reason. You are exactly who this chapter is written for because family feuds over issues children from previous relationships are one of the few deal breakers that can result in soulmates who love each other deeply breaking up or divorcing.

STATISTICS YOU SHOULD REVIEW BEFORE GETTING MARRIED IF YOU HAVE KIDS

With divorce rates rising, the remarriage rate is rising as well. Accordingly, today's blended families and second marriages are more common than ever before. There are 1,300 new step-families forming every day, and over half of American families are blended. Over 65 percent of Americans are a step-parent, a step-child, a step-sibling, or a step-grandparent.

The bad news is less than one-third of these new families will last.

While the U.S. divorce rate hovers around 45 percent, the divorce rate for second marriages, when only one partner has children, is over 65 percent. When both partners have children, the rate rises to 70 percent and the divorce rate for third marriages is 73 percent. These are startling statistics, but they are even more alarming because most of these couples are unaware of the difficulty of the challenges before them. Many think they will be more successful the second time around because of lessons learned from their previous marriages, and because they have a new presumably better partner. Unfortunately, these assumptions don't hold true, nor do these couples appear adequately prepared for the unique challenges associated with blending their family.

While you and Mr. Right are likely to approach a new relationship or remarriage and a new blended family with great joy and expectation, your or his children may not share your excitement and be uncertain how the merger will impact their future. They wonder what the new girlfriend or wife really will be like. They are also probably anxious about living with new step-siblings, whom they may not know, or worse, may know and not like. They worry how the new coupling will change their relationship with their mom and dad.

Everyone wants this relationship or marriage to be their last and to be healthy and strong. Yes, we want the "Brady Bunch," like we saw on TV. You know the story: The man with children meets woman with children; they marry, their kids meet, love each other, and they never fight or have adjustment issues; they simply and effortlessly live happily ever after. Oh, I forgot the dog. He eats milk biscuits all day. They blended so well we forgot they were a blended family.

In contrast to this made-for-television blended bunch, made 40 years ago, long before the advent of reality TV, many couples in blended families feel the day-to-day challenges of going from strangers to instant family members stack the odds against them.

COUNSELING CAN DRAMATICALLY INCREASE YOUR CHANCES OF SUCCESS

The good news is experts agree the one way to beat the odds is to get educated about step-parenting and blending families. Studies have shown that pre-marital education or counseling of some kind can reduce the divorce rate by up to 30 percent. Couples who seek help also report being more satisfied with their relationships and stay together longer than their counterparts who struggle alone. Ignorance is not bliss, at least not marital bliss. Yet, studies show less than 25 percent seek relationship or educational help before marriage, and less than 50 percent even read a book about re-marriage or step-parenting.

This is unfortunate because there are many resources out there to help you recognize some of the new realities you will encounter the second time around:

1. Your blended family is different from a traditional family in some important ways.

    "It's like playing a game of chess with the rules of checkers! It just won't work," says Jeannette Lofas, founder of The Stepfamily Foundation. Blended families have a different structure, more moving parts and don't share the rich historical bond enjoyed by family members who knew each other and only each other since birth. Blended family members also have a choice to be or not be family. It is a different game, indeed.

    Your new relationship or potentially second marriage will be much more complicated than your first, and the more children and the more partners with children involved, the more complex. In addition, the challenges you two face as a couple can increase dramatically when you add children who have been through a traumatic death of a parent or an acrimonious breakup or divorce, coupled with a potentially bitter ex who inevitably may bring her own set of issues to the mix. You will need to identify and master new skills and unique partnering strategies to meet everyone's needs, peacefully co-exist, and ultimately bond.

2. The role you play as a parental figure or a step-parent is vastly different from the role of a biological parent.

    Emotionally, you may never be viewed the same as the biological parent unless the child is very young, or as the child becomes older and has life experiences of his or her own, and you two have authentically forged a mother-child bond. Legally, you do not have the same rights as a biological parent, other than in the exceptional case of the biological parent who is deceased and you legally adopt the child. While those emotional and legal facts are non-negotiable, it doesn't mean you should be discouraged or can't enjoy a mutually fulfilling and rich relationship with your step-child. It simply means you must respect the biological parent's role and allow yourself to adjust to and embrace a new role that you likely haven't played before — one that doesn't come with a manual.

As Charles Dickens writes in *A Tale of Two Cities*, these may very well be the best of times and the worst of times. Children are hardwired to love their parents, and it may take a while to re-imprint and expand their wiring to include loving you as their parent, too. Even if you have had a positive relationship with a child during the dating process, it is fairly normal for children to go through at least a phase of rejecting the new step-parent once you marry his or her parent. Realizing rejection is simply a part of the bonding process may prevent you from taking it so personally. As equally predictable as the rejection phase is the reality that it will likely pass, too.

3.   Your relationship with your step-child must stand the test of time.

By definition, a relationship with a parent who has a child from a previous relationship means there has been a breakup. Blended families are frequently born out of loss — that is, a parent has either died, divorced, or broken up; and at least one parent's and/or child's dream of their family coming together or remaining together has become their worst nightmare. Yet, the newly minted parents almost always focus on moving forward with their vision of their new relationship and their happily ever after dream, insisting their children catch up with them. Because the children are frequently still mourning the loss of their original family, this expectation is unrealistic for them. The parents may have said, "I do!" while the kids are asking "what shall I do?" as they try to figure out where — or even if — they belong in the new family structure. What if someone in the new family has taken their place? For example, one child may be the eldest or only child in their family of origin, but the middle or youngest child in their new family. Or maybe they have lost their uniqueness as the only boy or girl in the family. The loss of the old and familiar coupled with the unknown of the new family means that creating a well-adjusted blended family will take time.

After the dust settles, events occur over time that spontaneously spur members to form authentic bonds, rituals, and relationships with each other. Time also helps the new family members process their pain, guilt, and confusion around the breakup, or divorce and subsequent remarriage. Consistency and being on the job day in and day out breeds trust and comfort. Most couples that come into my office don't want to wait years, however. Instead, women rush their children and even pressure them to love their new man; even worse, some partners go so far as to push their partner to do something to make their child like them. This practice is almost always counter-productive and will undermine the bonding process more than it ever encourages it. Give your children the time and space to naturally learn, interact with, accept, trust, and value their new parent and new family on their own. Even if they are initially resentful and rebellious, over time they will likely recognize it's in everyone's best interest (and theirs, too) to give your partner or spouse a try. Their independent discovery that they actually like some aspect(s) about their new parental figure or step-father will have far more standing with them than your pushing their new parent on them.

Let it be their choice.

THE PROS CAN DEFINITELY OUTWEIGH THE CONS

Although seldom easy, your new family can survive—if not thrive—once you come to terms with the realities of bringing together your new family members, and you master and employ strategies to help with the blending. Your new family may be well worth the effort and may indeed offer many unforeseen lifelong benefits.

On a personal note, I wouldn't trade my blended family for anything in the world. Mark, Milo, John, Brett, Geno, Ricardo, Bobby, Raymond, Gary, and Sharon—I love my brothers and sisters with all of my heart, as I do my nieces and nephews (too many to name here, and I couldn't fathom slighting any one of them by an omission). I also was blessed with an incredible second mother, Rose, who I grew to love, too. It wouldn't occur to me to insult them or our bond by using words like half, step, adopted, or any other synonym that suggests division. I talk with various members of my blended family several times a week, and we spend holidays together and sometimes vacation with each other a couple of times a year. My family is one of the best gifts ever bestowed upon me. Yes, we fought and disagreed, but what families don't? Because we are family, we worked our way through it.

STUDIES ENCOURAGE BLENDED FAMILIES TO BE MORE PATIENT

- About 75 percent of partners who divorce will remarry, with the majority doing so within two years of their divorce. Blended families have the highest success rate if the couple waits two years or more after a divorce to remarry.

- Psychologists estimate it takes four to eight years for a remarried family to bond and feel like a family.

- The divorce rate for couples who remarry and have children is almost 65 percent. Most of these couples divorce within the first four years, before the family has had time to blend.

These statistics are particularly illuminating for blended families that haven't blended just yet. Blending your family may just take a bit more time than you predicted, so hang in there and trust you married a good partner and are probably doing a lot of things right. As daunting as these statistics sound, the success rates dramatically increase for couples that seek help and stay together.

Note: The purpose of this chapter is to give readers who are in relationships where one or both parents have a child from a previous relationship, and are considering blending their families or have already blended their families, something tangible to think about, and empower them to make proactive versus reactive decisions. It points out many of the avoidable pitfalls that present challenges to the process of merging households. It is in no way meant to be mistaken for psychological advice. This chapter approaches this topic from a general perspective and may not mention numerous factors that impact your blended family. Individuals who need advice for their family should seek the help of a counselor or trusted religious leader.

WHY ARE BLENDED FAMILIES AND SECOND MARRIAGES MORE CHALLENGING?

So you and Mr. Right are in love, and you or he is a parent. Is the next logical step matrimony? After the pain of a possibly devastating breakup or divorce, you've finally found love again. Why shouldn't you be entitled to jump the broom like everyone else? While I agree you should be able to marry the new man of your dreams, I'd be remiss not to mention there is much more to consider than the love you share for each other.

When partners with children are contemplating taking their relationship to the next level, they are best served by proactively thinking their actions through and then taking strategic steps to blend their families. Yet, many partners mistakenly make these decisions reactively and without getting input from children, assuming that because they love their partner, their children will share their enthusiasm, and are shocked when their child rejects their partner and new family structure. If you want to give your blended family a chance to work, then you have to use forethought. Don't allow your actions to be guided by afterthoughts because hindsight isn't 20/20.

It's been my experience, and it is well documented, that few couples are prepared for the unique challenges and frustrations of keeping their romantic life afloat when one or both of you have a child.

Women attempting to date men with children will need to be prepared for:

Romantic Impact

➤ Distrust of your partner's relationship with their child's biological parent. You feel he is spending too much or inappropriate time with his child's mother (or he suspects you are doing the same with your child's father). This is a double-edged sword. Just because you don't like your child's father and couldn't imagine eating dinner with him and your child, doesn't mean he shouldn't be able to enjoy a meal with his ex and their child alone. For their child's sake, this interaction is a good thing and sends the message: "We love and respect each other, and no matter what separates us, we love you and the person most important to you — your other parent." On the other hand, some partners are still sleeping with the ex, and she is responding with hostility toward you because of the hope and feelings their romantic involvement stirs up. Just because you are paranoid doesn't mean they aren't indeed out to get you. That said, if you can't trust him here, just know it isn't going to work anyway.

➤ Parenting and dating are night and day. Losing focus on your relationship with your new partner is a common mistake made by parents in blended families. You must make time for your romantic relationship and guard it religiously. Period! However, many couples don't have a plan for how they are going to keep their relationship alive. They don't even notice they are becoming overwhelmed by the day-to-day activities of a blended family. They start to grow apart and lose that spark. Failing to implement a plan to cultivate you marriage is cultivating a plan for your marriage to fail.

➤ His baby mama's hatefulness is robbing your love of its luster. She is jealous and hostile and manipulates his child, using the legal system to torment you — all of which has taken a toll on your relationship with her child and your man. How dare he reprimand you for being hurt and frustrated, demanding you defer to and respect her because she is the mother of his child? Though her role should always should be respected, that's a lot to ask!

Unrealistic Expectations Around New Family Members Bonding

➤ The challenges associated with trying to bond with a child whose pain seems to be related to your relationship or marriage can be huge. You must accept that the death, divorce, or breakup that made way for your new family has possibly left the child feeling fractured, highly distrustful, and in a dark place because of this unwanted life change. While the partners or spouses had irreconcilable differences with each other, the child loves them both and may have inconsolable pain. They will need to learn to trust again, and it will take time, no matter how wonderful you are. Although it deeply impacts you, it may not be about you.

➤ We live in a microwave age; however, blended families are anything but instant. Partners put unrealistic stress on themselves, each other, and their children to become a happy, well-adjusted blended family overnight.

➤ Difficulty accepting a new parent will take time for some children. If children have spent a long time in a one-parent family, or if children still nurture hopes of their parents reconciling, it may be difficult for them to accept a new parent — at first.

Parenting and Discipline Conflicts

➤ You may find yourself in a lose-lose situation with his child. For example, his child disrespects you and you discipline him; then you are the bad guy who is chastised by his dad. And then there is the biological mother. If you don't discipline the child and let her disrespect you without standing up for yourself, then you are chastised by yourself. The challenge becomes how can you parent and invest in a child with whom you can't win?

➤ The highly emotional issues that cause family feuds involve values that are important to both sides, and they are worth fighting for. Because there is no clear right or wrong answer, it's hard for either side to surrender. These disputes include important topics such as parenting style (e.g., authoritarian versus permissive), what rituals should be honored or disregarded, what constitutes appropriate boundaries, curfews and levels of privacy for a child, what is an appropriate punishment, and who should administer it. Left unresolved, these issue can become a breeding ground for resentment, contempt, and distrust, potentially undermining a couple's ability to communicate or resolve conflicts. Negative feelings can continuously re-emerge and cloud other seemingly unrelated disagreements.

➤ Parental inexperience. You should at least consider whether your mate has been a parent before, and if not, given his disposition and relationship with your child, does he possess the potential to parent your child effectively? Some partners who haven't been a parent before are simply ill-equipped to parent your child (but so are some partners who are parents!). One major added bonus with partners who don't have children of their own is you don't have the added pressure of whether or not your children will reject his children; nor do you have to worry about a difficult biological parent. Yes, it does make dating more difficult and limit an already small pool of men. Nevertheless, it is critical that your new partner is interested and invested in getting to know your children, open to loving and spending time raising them with you, and excited about doing it.

Co-Parenting Conflicts

➢ Feeling used, rejected, disregarded, unappreciated, and unsupported by both your new child and your man can be a bitter pill to swallow. These feelings can be especially painful when you have tried to love his children as if they were your own.

➢ How do you respond to an overly indulgent father who is catering to his children or ex? He may capitulate to his child and ex because he doesn't have custody, was absent from the child's life for a period of time, or finally got custody and is fearful that his custodial status or relationship with his child is fragile. Whether or not he is a good father, accept that men who love their children can frequently find themselves holding the short end of the stick in our legal system. They typically feel the legal system favors women on all custody issues — and it does. Couple that reality with the Black man's natural distrust of the legal system, and you sometimes get a father who is being manipulated by his kids or his ex to gain favor, and maintaining the best relationship he feels he can. While he shouldn't try to buy love, let them run over him, or let his child's mother dictate all matters related to custody, just try to respect that he is authentically trying to do the right thing. He is loving his child as best he can under extremely difficult circumstances.

➤ Confusion and tension created by two households, with different and contrasting standards, rituals, expectations, rules, and parenting styles can be a major challenge when children are treated like friends in one home and children in another.

➤ Understanding and handling the emotional needs of a step-child who is acting out. Perhaps they are responding to feeling like you are showing favoritism toward your biological children, or they don't feel like they fit in the new family structure. Alternatively, they could be feeling loyalty to their biological mother, who may hold deep resentment for your new spouse and family, and openly (albeit, inappropriately) expresses it to her child.

➤ Tension and disruptions can be created when coordinating visitations and custody. Several issues can make visitations particularly challenging: (a) when a child lives in another geographical location, (b) the decision for the blended family to move to your home or your man's home, (c) the impact of custody on school arrangements for all children involved, and (d) you have two girls and he has a son, where will the young man sleep during visitations? Your concerns should be discussed before attempting to move your blended family under one roof and coordinating visitations.

Traditions and Holidays:

➤ Family traditions can wreak havoc. Most families have very different ideas about how annual events such as holidays, birthdays, and family vacations should be spent. Kids may feel resentful if they're forced to go along with someone else's routine, particularly if it leads to them abandoning their own. They will likely blame the new parent or family structure for the change. Try to find some common ground, and look for opportunities to create new traditions for your blended family.

Financial Impact:

➤ Divorce and custody battles puts money in lawyers' pockets, taking money off of families' tables. Your lifestyle and savings could be depleted by the finances associated with a lengthy and expensive legal battle. You won (well, didn't lose), but at great cost. Many men are also required to make child support payments and some may owe back child support payments. In some cases, your man may still be required to make alimony payments to his ex-wife. Failure to pay may result in jail time or other penalties, like revocation of his driver's license.

Either of these scenarios can have a devastating impact on your current lifestyle and threaten your financial future together. It's not your child or ex-wife, yet you're paying for it. In extreme cases, this financial tsunami can result in some harsh choices, such as kids being taken out of private school, absentee parents because they have to get a second job, or having to short-sell your home or file for bankruptcy. However, if you agreed to marry him, you must own your decision and what comes with it—for better or worse.

Any, if not all, of these issues can result in family feuds that do irreparable damage to your romantic relationship and are among some of the top reasons it is so difficult to blend a family successfully.

It is worth noting that the top two reasons for the high rate of divorce in blended families are financial issues and disagreements about raising the children. First, although it may not be possible to fix everything in your financial past immediately, it is impossible to succeed if you two aren't honest and upfront about your financial obligations to your child and your ex-spouse. Failure to disclose is akin to committing financial infidelity, which can be a recipe for financial and marital disaster.

In addition to finances, differences in parenting styles is a major reason for divorce in blended families. People typically think their children should be raised how they were raised, whether or not the biological parent or step-child are in agreement. Herein lies a twofold problem: First, there is no universally agreed upon one-size-fits-all best way to raise a child; even the so-called experts recognize a range of effective parenting styles. Therefore, both of your styles are likely valid in some regard, as divergent as they may seem. Experts do agree, however, that the best measure of a particular parenting style's success is whether or not it is a match for the child's disposition. Some children flounder unless you provide structure and discipline, while others flourish with freedom and autonomy. Because both biological parents may subscribe to different parenting styles, if you haven't developed the trust and relationship to impose a harsher style, you are likely to be thought of as the villain by the child, your partner, and the biological parent; or walked over if your style is considered soft.

Understanding your partner's parenting style and the biological parent's feelings about discipline—in particular her feelings about your administering it to her child—is crucial on several levels. As a partner, you could very well encounter an unimaginably high wall of resistance and pushback from your partner for simply trying to love his child as your own. As a co-parent, you may be in for a rude awakening once his ex gets wind of you disciplining her child. At best, she could become angry if she feels your approach was harsh; and, at worse, she could initiate legal proceedings or challenge unsupervised visitations or custody. For example, I once had a client who filed charges because her ex's new girlfriend took her daughter to the hairdresser. While her trumped-up charges ultimately may be dismissed, she can disrupt your life and make it hell until the lengthy and expensive legal proceedings are finalized, potentially doing irreparable damage to your marriage. You are probably best served playing the good cop and letting the biological parents play the bad cops, especially in the beginning. If the good-cop approach doesn't work, you might consider talking to a professional or accept this may simply be a deal breaker.

Blended families are an emotional, financial, and spiritual investment, and you have to make sure your partner and you are making an informed decision to prepare each other for exactly what you are getting into if you want to avoid becoming another statistical casualty.

HOW CHILDREN ADJUST TO THEIR NEW BLENDED FAMILIES

From day one realize all members are auditioning for a role as a family member. Resist the temptation to try to assert yourself as a parental figure right off the bat. Trust that the child's parental needs and your future parental role will naturally unfold. To get off to a good start, focus on listening, identifying their needs, and asking yourself if you can you meet them. Have fun with each other in the process. Don't resist the need to court each other.

Listed below are some of the ways a child's needs may vary according to personality, stage, age, and gender. Nonetheless, all children have some basic needs that must be met before a strong relationship can be forged.

All children want to feel:

- Positive reinforcement. Always remain positive, employing humor wherever possible. While constructive criticism is sometimes a necessary component of parental love, always start positively by identifying and talking for two to three minutes about some authentic aspect of what they are doing right. If you assume they know what they are doing right, make sure you assume they know what they are doing wrong, too. Children of all ages respond positively to praise and encouragement and have a true need to feel recognized for their contributions. This doesn't mean you should avoid negative feedback. It does mean you should start off positively and never lead with criticism, and make sure it is balanced. And, never ever give criticism in anger.

- Heard. Children don't care how much you know; they do want to know how much you care. Trust they recognize you have more life experiences than they do. Nevertheless, if you want to connect with them emotionally and win their hearts, respect, admiration, and ultimately cooperation, you must demonstrate that you are smart enough to listen to them and consider their perspective. You might be amazed at what they think is important and how their needs are similar to yours.

- Safe and secure. Children want to be able to count on parents and, yes, step-parents, too. Children of divorce have already experienced one or several major losses, feel disappointed and distrustful, and may be understandably reluctant to open up to a new step-parent. Be consistent and stay the course.

- Authentically embraced and loved. This isn't a quick process, and during the frustrating times their trust in you will be most tested. What happens when they disappoint or hurt you? Do you become angry and lash out, or remain loving and patient while firm? Kids know when someone loves them, and that feeling doesn't just occur on trips to Disney.

- Celebrated and not just tolerated. Consider how family decisions impact them, perhaps asking for their input. While you may ultimately make a decision they disagree with, you are probably always best served with getting their ideas if you want to get them onboard. Also, be willing to make sure some aspect of your decision reflects their recommendations, if only in spirit. For example, we are not going to get a big dog because we want to have another child, but you can pick out the small dog and name it.

- Discipline and boundaries. I know I've written in this chapter to let biological parents discipline their child — at first. However, that advice is not meant to be at the cost of your right to parent or to set high standards and rules of engagement for your household. Children need limits and boundaries. It tells them you love them. What you have to recognize early on is to have your parenting experienced in a loving way, you have to build up enough goodwill capital in your account to offset the rejection associated with criticism and harsh discipline.

CHILDREN'S NEEDS WILL VARY BASED ON AGE, STAGE, AND GENDER.

Children of different ages and genders will adjust differently to a blended family, but your goal of establishing a healthy relationship with each child is the same. While the physical and emotional needs of a 6-year-old boy are different than those of a 16-year-old girl, you would be mistaken to assume their fundamental needs to feel important, loved, and secure are different. To be most effective with children of different genders and at various places in their development, you will need to tailor your approach to reflect the unique needs of each child.

<u>Age Differences:</u>

Child's Age	Adjustment Needs

Young children under 10	• May adjust more easily than children at any stage, because a cohesive family unit is their primary source of support. Parents are an integral part of their life and daily activities. • Are most open to a new parent because they are frequently still too young to have developed hardcore and independent opinions. Parental validation is key. • Might feel competitive for their parent's attention, and new parent needs to ensure they have their private time together and continue rituals to avoid potential conflict.
Adolescents aged 10-14	• May have the most difficult time adjusting to a step-family. • Needs more time to bond before accepting a new parent as a parental figure. • May not demonstrate their feelings openly. Can be as sensitive, or more sensitive, as young children when it comes to needing love, support, discipline, and attention.
Teenagers 15 or older	• May have less involvement in day-to-day blended family life. Least likely to view the new parent as their actual parent. • Operates more independently from the family as they have likely formed their own identities and friendships. • Daily activities may be completely separate from family activities, especially once they have a driver's license or their friends do. • While they may appear aloof or indifferent to affection, they value your input and

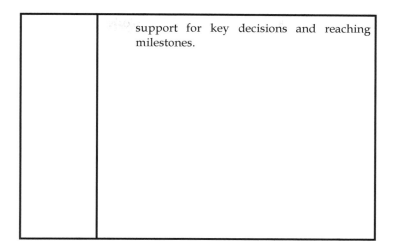

	support for key decisions and reaching milestones.

SEVEN STAGES OF BLENDED-FAMILY DEVELOPMENT

There are seven stages of development that blended families typically go through. Research on blended families suggests some families go through them more quickly than others, while others falter in places and work through their challenges more slowly, while still others fall off. Movement through the stages does not happen precisely, in a timely fashion, or necessarily in a specific or hierarchical order. For example, a family may start out at resistance stage or remain in entanglement stage for an extended period of time. Families that are not progressing frequently are going at it alone and haven't sought out self-help books or the counsel of a professional with the clinical experience and know how to help them work through a particular stage of development, especially in the first few years.

Stage	Features

Utopia	• Both partners have a vision of how this new perfect family will function, reflecting their expectations and dreams of how they will interact with their partner's children and vice-versa to meet the families' collective needs. • Children also have their expectations of how the new family will function to meet their individual needs and what their new life will be like with their new parents and new siblings.
Entanglement	• Often the bubble known as denial is about to burst. The reality of the new blended family begins to set in, and some of the dreams imagined while members were wearing rose-colored glasses become a little shattered. In worst-case scenarios, there are signs their dreams may become a nightmare. Perhaps the parent, parental figure or step-parent, and children have an uneasy feeling that something is going wrong. They begin to secretly ask themselves questions like, "What did we get ourselves into?" and "What happens if we don't like each other and can't get along?" or "This is going to take some work?" • Leaving or disconnecting isn't really an option. Perhaps there is a feeling of being stuck. • Parental figures or step-parents frequently remain an outsider during this stage. • The biological parent's relationship with the child holds considerable influence and may be key in the child buying in to the new family.

Awareness	• Also referred to as the Awakening stage. • Previously held fantasies of the perfect, instant family are long gone. • Step-parents and children are beginning to know the strangers they now call family and are assessing the pros and cons of their new family structure as it relates to them. • Biological parents begin to accept that they are truly the only ones connected to each other and the children.
Resistance	• Also, referred to as the Fight or Flight stage. • Step-parents and children alike begin to express their differences more openly — and defiantly! • This period may witness more tension, confrontations, and the emergence of silos that had been frowned upon in earlier stages. • Parental figures and step-parents become vocal about the need for them to take on more of an active parental role, demand to be included in important decisions related to their step-child, and for adjustments in the new family structure.

Reaction Reformation	• In spite of their differences, all members have begun to settle in and accept their new family as somewhat permanent, which is evidenced by them requesting more influence and input regarding how the family will function and adjudicate conflicts. • They have learned to agree to disagree and develop rules of engagement and boundaries that benefit all. • The family bonds are getting stronger, and enough goodwill, trust, and understanding is emerging to start nipping potential power struggles in the bud. • Note: Trust is a critical component of this stage, and progressing here before being battle tested can present major complications and stress as it is hard to negotiate with members you don't trust.

Integration	• Frequently referred to as the "New Honeymoon" stage, there is less conflict stemming from blended-family issues. Step-children disagreeing isn't viewed as catastrophic, but something that kids do.
	• Roles and rituals are clearly defined, and, when faced with trials, the family unit unites, facing external challenges as a collective.
	• Clearly defined parental figures or step-parent roles are accepted, and unique rituals and traditions begin to emerge.
	• Also, referred to as the "We Are Family" stage.

Fusion	• Your family has stood the test of time and weathered life's ups and downs. All stake holders have skin in the game. The new family has become the new norm. • Members have reliable and solid relationships. • While some children may not ever buy into the new family structure and elect to go their own way or return to the other biological parent's fold, there is clarity about and acceptance of their position. • Your parental figure or step-parent role now brings you and your step-children mutual satisfaction and fulfillment. Members see each other as family, and are prepared to take on generational familial roles, such as uncles and aunts of each other's children. Their family relationships extend beyond their original blended family. • The whole is greater than the sum of the parts. • Congrats! Your family has blended.

Research on blended families suggests some families complete the entire developmental cycle in about four years, while most families take about seven years. Unfortunately, many blended families end in divorce prematurely before the cycle is completed. Couples who successfully blend their families have partners who are more adept at hearing their partner's concerns early instead of dismissing them and minimizing their concerns. In addition, their partner, the step-parent, is able to sympathize with the intense pull that biological parents experience from their own children, and resists the temptation to triangulate their partner—that is, putting their partner in a catch-22, whereby they have to choose between them and their child and the child's mother. Rather, they give them a graceful out. In all, these families seek support and usually have fewer deeply held fantasies and more realistic expectations of what transitioning into a successful blended family will entail.

TIPS FOR KEEPING YOUR ROMANTIC FIRES BURNING WHILE DATING WITH KIDS

Being a new couple with children or newlyweds with children who need to blend into a family is profoundly different from simply being a new couple or newlyweds. New couples and newly remarried couples without children usually spend their first months together enjoying and building their relationship with romantic dinners and gifts, trips, or other courtship-related activities. Couples with children, on the other hand, may not get a honeymoon period, as they are often more consumed with meeting their children's needs than each other's needs. While it is necessary that you focus a lot of your attention, time, and energy on your children making an adjustment into the new family structure and to prune out any dissension before it takes root, it is essential that you keep your focus on cultivating your budding relationship or marriage so that it can blossom, while employing the strengths and skills needed to resolve the marital and blended family conflicts that will surely arise. Without a strong relationship or marriage, you have a weakened, or worse, no, blended family. At the same time, when children witness a strong unified front between their parent and significant other or parents, they will feel more secure and begin to value their new blended family all the more, falling in line as they take comfort in its sense of love, permanence, and stability.

It is critical that you always present a unified front, at least in front of your children. Arguing, making negative comments, or disagreeing in front of them may prove to be your relationship, marriage, or blended family's undoing. At best, children will feel powerless to help their biological parent and become stressed out by this new, negative, and possibly dysfunctional family structure. At worst, this negativity will empower them to come between you two, and otherwise dead end any desire to bond and work through the differences they have with their new siblings and parental figure or step-parent. Why bond with a sibling and parental figure who might not have any connection to or authority over you in a few months should your new family disband? While the two of you love each other and will likely hear each other out, resolve your differences amicably, and move on, your children will likely be left behind to wrestle with the meaning of the fight you two had. They will struggle with why their life has been disrupted, only to find the two of you are infighting, and begin to question the relationship's stability, although you two may no longer recall what the disagreement was about.

THE DOS AND DON'TS OF BLENDING YOUR FAMILY

Dos	Don'ts
Parenting and Discipline	**Parenting and Discipline**
Spend quality time with all children — biological and step. Successful parental figures and step-parents invest time getting to know the new members of the blended family. At the same time, you need to spend quality time with your biological children so they don't feel as though they've lost a parent. Do not let fears of favoritism prevent you from spending time with either child. Do spend quality	**Assume all arguments are the result of a blended family or permanent.** Like all brothers and sisters fall in and out, your children or step-siblings will, too. Over time you all will likely work out your differences or accept them and move on.
	Act in an unloving way, even if you are mad or don't yet like your step-children. Always remain the adult in the room. Instead of feeling guilty because you don't love them as your own, accept the reality that it may take time, or you may never love

time investing in and developing all children.

Make special arrangements to make them feel your house is their home. If some of the kids just visit, make sure they have private space for their personal things and a designated place for them to sleep. Bringing tooth-brushes and other personal items each time they visit will make them feel like a visitor in your house. They won't feel like a member of the new blended family.

Create a list of family rules. Discuss rules with all children and post them in a prominent place. Try to understand the rules and boundaries for the kids in their other residence, and, when possible, be consistent and keep the rules and consequences predictable.

Avoid initially disciplining your step-child. While you should be respected, leave discipline to the biological parent, especially early on. If you must discipline them, try methods other than corporal punishment or hollering.

Avoid getting triangulated. Do not get caught between them as your own—or even like them.

Accept they may not like you, either! In their mind, you may be the intruder who displaced them or their mother. Early on, you don't need to like or love them to play an important role in their lives, although it helps. In spite of these initial feelings, over time you may come to love each other truly and develop a close relationship.

Accept their acting out may not be personal. Because of the pain kids experience during divorce, and may continue to feel with the new relationship or marriage, they may be acting out because they do not have the skills to talk it out and express what's really going on inside. Many couples will come in for counseling and ask me to "fix these kids." Maybe they aren't broken, but your family structure is. Kids are seldom the problem, by themselves.

Forget to court his children. Definitely strive to develop independent relationships with them. No, this doesn't exclude appropriate boundaries or suggest you try to buy them. Demand their respect, but don't be above earning it by spending quality time with them, too. Enjoy them! Recognize they are a package deal. Their vote may be

your man, his child, and the child's biological mom.	critical when you least expect it or most need it.
## Co-Parenting	## Co-Parenting
Recognize that your child needs both parents. Whether your ex was a complete jerk or not, your child will need him to become a healthy, well-developed adult. **Accept that this new woman, or perhaps your old enemy, has an influence on your child and their long-term relationship with their father.** She's likely there during every visitation, perhaps helping with homework and other important life lessons. She may also be picking up pieces your ex would otherwise let drop by the wayside. She may best serve you by making her an ally. **Make peace with the past.** You may have a gazillion legitimate gripes against your ex or his new woman, but the one person who will	**Use your child as a pawn in a high stakes chess match.** Preventing your child from seeing their non-custodial, biological parent is almost always a bad idea. Putting them in the middle of your conflict will stress them out and typically play itself out in some unforeseeable negative fashion. Your past problems shouldn't interfere with your child's current relationship with his other parent. Let that other parent be a parent for your child's sake, or it is your child who will suffer. Granted deadbeat and abusive parents, and parents with active addictions may present an exception to this rule of thumb. **Compete with your counterpart.** Yes, I recognize there are cases where she may seem like or actually have been part of the reason your relationship ended. If so, I recommend you talk to a professional. This is too painful to resolve alone.

most likely be affected if you act on them is your child.

The circumstances surrounding yesterday's breakup shouldn't dictate how your child is raised today. Yes, it hurt or was disappointing, but the pain you can cause your child could be devastating. Don't forgive other people for them, but for your child.

Insist that your kids show respect to their step-parent. It's always sad when I hear a kid who was told "you don't have to listen to him or her." A child is never going to benefit from being told to disrespect adults. You may be setting them up for trouble with authority figures. If you have an issue, it's your job to handle it with the other adults, but make sure your child knows that they are to behave like a child and abide by the parent's rules, unless they run afoul the law, or you legitimately suspect abuse.

Automatically take your child's side against adults, whenever they disagree with their father or their non-biological parent. Your child may be playing both sides against the middle, so make sure you get both sides of the story. Even if you ultimately conclude your child is right, accept the best long-term solution likely involves all parents acting as a team.

Avoid unnecessarily rejecting or taking on his new woman as an enemy. This new woman or wife likely will be a permanent figure who is at every significant event. Like her or not, she deserves to be there in all probability, if only because she is important to your son's father.

Non-Biological Parent	Biological Parent
Defer to the bio-parent. As a parental figure or step-parent, it's important to defer to the bio-parent, even sometimes on issues you know more about, especially at first. Parents are always surprised by that advice, and I realize this advice may seem counter intuitive. But in addition to the step-relationship needing time to develop, it is best served by having the bio-parent on board, if possible. In most cases, when you obtain the support of the bio-parent, the relationship with your step-child has a greater likelihood of success and to flourish quicker. If there's a behavior for which your step-child needs a consequence, let your spouse deal with it and support their decision. Use these experiences as opportunities to hear the child's side and bond with them.	**Don't ever, ever talk badly about your child's biological parent.** Some things are sacred. This is one of them. It will blow up in your face. As enticing as it might be, resist the temptation to let the child know you are being a better mom than your step-child's bio-mom, or a better dad than their bio-dad, even if that parent is clearly flawed or absentee. Rather, it's important to respect their position, consider taking the highroad and upholding them or remain silent. Let the facts speak for themselves. Kids are smart! Even if in denial, they know where their bread is buttered. And if they don't, life is an amazing teacher. **Deny them the opportunity to grieve the death of a parent.** Many children who lose a biological parent because of death or divorce will experience mourning and possible feelings of resistance toward their new step-family. The new relationship or marriage may also further trigger unfinished stages of the grieving process. Give them space and

Get out of the way. Let your boyfriend or spouse have one-on-one time with his or her children—*without you.* This helps reduce the displacement and loss the child might be feeling, and assures him that you value their relationship.	time to deal with their loss on their own terms. **Exclude the child's biological family or extended family from the new family structure.** Successful blended families recognize that these relationships are important to the child and make every effort to strengthen them.
Traditions and Holidays	**Traditions and Holidays**
Establish new traditions. Embrace the uniqueness of your new blended family, and build traditions around them. Always recognize the need to keep past traditions and rituals in place if possible, unless they are diametrically opposed to your beliefs. Even then, try to have a healthy appreciation for the significance they represent to your child and their biological parent. If you must make changes, make them gradually when possible.	**Hastily and callously disregard established routines.** During visitations you should remain consistent with, to the extent possible, or follow the daily routines the child has from the home they live in most of the time. Kids draw stability from routines, and when their routine is not followed, this may lead to increased anxiety and acting out, or unnecessary conflict with the custodial parent.

Expectations	Expectations
Start talking with your children about the possibility of blending your family early. Introduce this concept long before your marriage. Listen and make sure your child feels heard. Set realistic expectations. You likely will invest a lot of time, energy, love, and affection in your new partner's kids that will not be returned immediately. Think of them as gifts to your child and partner that may or may not one day yield a big payoff—a mutually fulfilling and loving relationship.	Expect to fall in love with your partner's children overnight. Getting to know, love, and have affection for them takes time to develop authentically and naturally. Expect your step-children to call you Mom or Dad. Let them decide what they feel most comfortable with here. If they don't naturally settle on a name, meet with them to establish a name that you both are mutually comfortable with.
Bonding requires time and space	**Bonding requires time and space**
Tell the kids that your new man or spouse will not be a replacement for dad. Rather, they are another person to love and support them.	Remarry too soon after the divorce. Recognize the divorce was a drastic family change for them and they may need time to heal and regroup before entering into a new family. In addition to your children, you may also need time to re-evaluate your role in

Let the child set the pace. Every child is different and will show you how slow or fast to get to know them. Shy, introverted, or traumatized children may require you to slow down and give them more time to warm up to you. Given enough time, patience, and interest, most children will eventually give you a chance.

Hold family meetings. Be open to hearing each other out, even when you have differences of opinion. Give all members of the new family a chance to have input into the rules, schedule, and planning of upcoming events. Be open to everyone's ideas.

Find ways to experience real life together. Try to get the kids used to your partner and his or her children in daily life situations. Taking both sets of kids to a theme park every time you get together is a lot of fun, but it isn't reflective of everyday life.

the marriage's demise and give yourself time to heal, so as not to repeat it. Blended families have the highest success rate if the couple waits two years or more after a divorce to remarry.

Assume because you both value family that you have similar parenting styles. Make sure you understand exactly what each other's parenting style entails and how you intend to parent together.

Allow your partner or children to make ultimatums. Your kids or new partner may put you in a situation where you feel you have to choose between them. Remind them they are both an essential part of your life, and neither is going anywhere.

Avoid establishing clear expectations for discipline. Successful blended families establish one set of rules for discipline that apply to all family members.

Love and Money	Love and Money
Combine finances to partner for your whole new family. Successful blended families are willing to cast aside personal agendas and combine your financial resources for the common good of the new family.

Set a discretionary amount the biological parent can spend on children without consulting you. Failure to do so could result in financial infidelity, because he is unlikely to deny his children's basic or educational needs, while funds are being dedicated to remodel your basement.

Set limits on how much you invest in your partner's custody battles, if you don't feel comfortable. Be open, honest and clear with yourself and your partner about your limitations. | **Indulge in gift giving with a tilt toward winning over your children.** Co-parenting is not the time to buy your child; it's a time to teach values and spend quality time with them. While it can be difficult to accept a parent is outspending you to become the cool parent while your humble and fiscal responsibility oriented approach is casting you as the fun police, consider a more balanced approach, like getting high-ticket gifts if they are affordable, and afford opportunities to spend quality time together. For example, get a child with a fascination with marine life a salt water fish tank with a few exotic and colorful fish. In addition to helping them become more responsible by managing their new fish tank, this gift could have a great bonding opportunity if you are passionate about salt water fish. Talk about a double bonus. |
| **Love and Marriage** | **Love and Marriage** |

Communicate often and much. Discuss everything - even the feelings about your feelings, if need be. Avoid keeping emotions bottled up or hold grudges.

Identify areas that make you feel uncomfortable. Successful blended families talk to each other. Your problems won't go away because you ignore them. Know resolving challenges strengthens family bonds. Like the family that prays together, the family that resolves conflicts together also stays together.

Find the support you need to flourish as a couple. Don't do it alone. Locate a step-parenting support organization in your community. Learn how other blended families address their challenges. Recognize blended families that get help or counseling early are 30 percent more likely to avoid divorce.

Focus on your blended family at the expense of your marriage. Raising children is a challenge. Raising other people's children is a special challenge. In a blended family, your marriage has to be special so it can be harder to overcome challenges because you don't have couple time most first marriages enjoy. If you put your marriage on the back burner, you all will likely get burnt, because without a strong marriage there is no blended family. Why go through all the steps to blend your family, only for the two of you to fall asunder?

Forget to court each other and date. Set aside time as a couple by making regular dates, meeting for lunch, coffee or midday trysts. Hire a babysitter and go on dates regularly and weekend getaways quarterly. Always remember to have fun and find ways to grow together, or you will grow apart. Invest in books, magazines, workshops, and marital therapy tune-ups, even if there aren't marital problems. Just like you change your oil every 3,000 miles, get a tune-up!

Although these rules of engagement aren't exhaustive, violating them can be a critical miscalculation when you are dating with children, or married and attempting to blend your family. **Meet Frank and Alexis.** They came into my office after Alexis got into a big fight with Frank because of parenting style differences related to his biological son, Wesley, who is her stepson.

Frank had recently been awarded custody after a lengthy legal battle. During that time, his contact with his son had been inconsistent, consisting primarily of supervised visitations, so he felt somewhat estranged from his son and was very anxious about it. A captain of the basketball team, Wesley wasn't terribly concerned when his report card came back with all Cs and a D. Grades were never really emphasized in his mother's home. However, Alexis was irate and demanded he quit the basketball team immediately and focus on getting his grades up. Frank was upset, too, but he had never told Wesley good grades were a prerequisite of him playing, and he didn't feel changing the rules in the middle of the game was the way to go about disciplining his son. Besides, his mother had recently purchased him two pairs of expensive Jordans to wear for the home and road games, and her entire family regularly attended. Going to the games and everyone meeting up for a meal afterwards was a big family tradition. Alexis, who had never had a child, demanded Frank take action immediately.

Frank felt like he was in a catch-22 and didn't do anything.

Alexis felt extremely disrespected, disregarded, and dismissed when it became clear that Frank wouldn't abide by her demands of pulling Wesley for the season. Frustrated and angered by Frank's inaction, she accused him of catering to his son and ex-wife and lashed out at him in front of Wesley, calling him a wimp and cursing him in an anger-laced rant. Frank was outraged. He began to feel humiliated, disrespected, betrayed, angry, unheard, and alone in the marriage. He was clearly in a no-win situation, and Alexis wasn't letting him off the hook. She couldn't accept that if she made him choose she would eventually lose. By time they came to see me, Frank had shut down sexually, because he felt deeply resentful and contemptuous toward her for pulling his man card in front of his son. He also began to fear she could cost him custody of his son, should they have to go to court again. For the first time in their marriage, he started using the "D" word, and I don't mean Dallas. She thought she was winning her argument, but was in fact losing her man.

They were not speaking to each other when they came into my office, and Frank had begun to withdraw because he felt she was making him choose between his son and his wife. As a divorced parent with a son, Frank stated his biggest mistake in life was choosing a playmate who was 20 years younger than him who had never had children, whereas since gaining custody he needed a soulmate with the maturity and the skill set to step-parent his son, too. To make matters worse, he never introduced Alexis to Wesley during the five years he dated her, so they had not bonded at all prior to getting married. Alexis was asked to go from a stranger to Wesley's mother the first day they met. Wesley and Alexis never embraced each other or bonded. Perhaps had Alexis and Frank implemented the strategies detailed in the dos and don'ts of creating a blended family, they could have saved themselves considerable frustration and pain.

This family feud truly represents what happens when parent and new child just don't mix. Next, we will discuss what happens when you and his baby mama just don't mix.

SEVEN REASONS HIS BABY MAMA(S) MAY BE PREVENTING YOU AND YOUR MAN FROM BEING HAPPY -- AND STRATEGIES FOR DEALING WITH HER

With single-parent households becoming the norm, the chances of finding a single man without a child are rare. No worries! Not all mothers come with drama. In fact, many women out there have moved on with their lives and accepted that their ex has done the same. They are for more concerned with him being a good father. Women like these will always put their children's happiness first.

That said, there are those vicious, acrimonious, unforgiving, and dare I say evil exes who are determined to ruin the child's father's life at all costs. She is the mother of his child and will never disappear.

When an ex takes a scorched-earth approach to co-parenting, the path you travel will be mostly uphill. Yes, he is a wonderful man who loves you, or you wouldn't still be reading. You are deeply attracted to and respect him, and for good reason. However, there's just one obstacle you can't overcome no matter how hard you try. His baby's mama is the nightmare from Elm Street.

And, she's turned your love triangle into the Devil's Triangle.

But why does she behave in such an unreasonable and counterproductive fashion? Does she just not care how all of this dysfunction and tension impacts her child? Does every interaction or decision really have to end in war? And what's up with these late-night calls? Why the tension and angry glares at family functions? You just can't understand why he would date and impregnate or have married such a nut job. It just doesn't make sense. Perhaps she wants him back, is jealous, or can't get over him moving on with his life. You hope she gets a man, so she can get on with life and leave yours alone. But why do you assume your man is an innocent victim? At best, he is guilty of making a poor choice, and then pissing off such a volatile, clearly unstable woman; at worse, he has done some things to hurt her or is still doing some things to fuel the fire.

You need to uncover the truth.

Perhaps you are the victor who won the prize she so desperately covets. Alternatively, the truth may be more unpleasant and complex than you imagined. In either case, you are best served to put on your big girl pants and consider he probably wouldn't have fathered a child with a pure hellion and that he likely played some role in how she feels. In life there are few pure victims. Besides, it's a rare man who lies down with such a woman without any birth control. Even desperate, irresponsible, and stupid men have to respect and enjoy a woman in some real way to risk unprotected sex and getting them pregnant. That he might be an exception to that rule might be something worth looking into before you consider blending your family with him. At the very least, consider he might have done or might be doing a little something to drive her crazy.

There are always at least two sides to a story. And, if you are talking about making a life-long decision about Mr. Right, you need to try and understand both.

One rule of thumb I've found helpful in all of these years of providing therapy is to really listen to people as they tell me their side of the story. If they tell a balanced story, identify their role in the conflict, and take and assign responsibility fairly evenly, I trust they probably are going to be a fair and accountable partner in their next relationship. By contrast, if they tell a story whereby they are always the victim, don't identify their role in the conflict, place blame squarely on the shoulder of their last partner(s), and take only minimal responsibility, I've almost always found that their next relationship ends in a similar fashion. You don't want to find yourself in her position being his other baby mama.

Consider whether or not a few of the reasons below may be why his ex is behaving so inappropriately (and don't be overly distracted by my putting on my cynical hat here):

1. **Could your man still be sleeping with his ex?** I'm not saying all, or even most, men are still involved with their exes. I'm just wondering is it possible that he's still intimate with her, and complaining about you to her like he complains to her about you? If he is, it might be he who has taught her not to respect you and made her feel like you are all that is standing between them having a happy family. I know this sounds cynical, and I'm definitely not trying to

make you paranoid. But, I'd be remiss if I said it doesn't happen.

2. **She knows she can rattle your cage.** So, why not? Hell, you are prancing around with her baby's father in front of the family she's known for years and has shared holidays and significant milestones with related to her child's life and her life, too. Now you are on the scene as the new queen bee. Once she realizes you are so deeply affected by a text, late-night call, or request that he drop everything and come attend to his child ASAP, why not do it for entertainment purposes? She can't control him, so why not control you? (This presumes you trust he isn't sexually involved with her any longer.)

3. **They have always had a dysfunctional relationship.** How did he describe their relationship before the breakup? Why did he leave, or why did she leave him? If he said she was crazy, how did he explain him getting a crazy woman pregnant? Did he indicate any of his behaviors might be making her act crazy? If he is being vague with you about their relationship, have you considered he communicates with her in a vague way, too, which could explain at least a little of her craziness? Ultimately, you have to ask yourself how you would act if your baby's father treated you like he treats her.

4. **She's tired of his sh#+ and is finally fighting back.** Perhaps after years of gently nudging or trying to be tactful, she is pissed off and has flat out rebelled. Could she have gotten fed up, realized she has to go on a rampage to get a response, and now overreacts to set guidelines and get results? This doesn't mean you should be disrespected, but could offer some valuable insights into how she developed her current state of mind. To answer this question, consider how he talks about her and how he conducts his affairs. If you notice things unkempt, lack of follow through, or similar patterns in other friendships (or

a lack of friendships), listen to your Spidey senses and consider he's at least part of the problem.

5. **The drama is a cover-up for how she really feels.** She simply may not be able to deal with her deep feelings for him, the disillusionment of her vision for their family, and the reality that he has gone on with his life. Face it: Of all the people on the planet, they chose to have a child with each other. Yes, she may have accidentally gotten pregnant or even trapped him. While someone clearly got hurt, is angry or disappointed, and their relationship shattered in a major way, the love that exists between two parents cannot be completely broken. Part of her evolution will have to be centered on realizing the love she feels doesn't have to be expressed in anger or retaliation.

6. **The rest of her life is out of her control.** When a woman faces experiences like the loss of a loved one, being stagnant in her career, or otherwise feels like she is on a treadmill in life, she experiences the stress of not being able to control her life. This causes her to hold the reins even more tightly with situations she can control, like her children, your mood, and her ex man.

7. **She put in the hard work, and you are reaping all of the benefits.** Now that he has matured and grown up, she is finally witnessing him becoming the man she always knew he could become, and it hurts and even makes her angry that you are getting all of the rewards when she made all of the sacrifices and investments. Life isn't always fair, and sometimes timing is everything. This is especially true with relationships that take place during the early years after the breakup or divorce. We make mistakes. Unfortunately for your ex, and fortunately for you, those mistakes and growing pains prepare you to be a better partner for your next relationship. It could very well be the case that his child's mother wanted him to be mature enough to love, provide for, and protect her in a way he wasn't capable of

while they were in a relationship. Why couldn't he have loved and respected her like he does you?

Strategies for Dealing With Her

So what do you do when your man's ex cannot let go of the past and get past the pain? You don't want to leave your man and lose out on love, but every interaction with her is so painful it is draining the very joy out of the relationship you are fighting for, and it's hard to see winning anymore. She has declared war and seems to have no interest in peace and doesn't care if her child is a casualty. Other than not wanting to give in to her sinister ways, you no longer can muster up the will to fight the good fight. Nothing you do is working!

Here are a few last chance measures to take once you have realized hell hath no fury like a scorned woman with a child:

1. **Accept she has issues and is *not* going anywhere.** In an imaginary world she would sign over the custody papers and disappear. Alternatively, you might think if she would just grow up, all of these problems would just go away. Yes, that would be a fairytale ending for you and your man, but it would be a nightmare for your child. He needs his mother, no matter how crazy you think she is. If this is to work, you, she, and he (your man) need to find a way to work and mature through this together.

    Some parents are blessed to have a functional relationship with their ex; others not so much. It is important to gain clarity about what type of situation you will be moving into or marrying into. While the situation doesn't have to be ideal, you need to make sure it isn't a deal breaker. If you aren't sure or completely comfortable, perhaps you should postpone taking your relationship to the next level or blending your family until they are able to demonstrate to you that they have worked through some of their differences. You should consider relationship counseling and co-parenting therapy, too. I know this may seem extreme and even risky, however, you could be sparing yourself a divorce or lifelong heartache.

2. **Consider forgiving her and asking for her forgiveness, too.** (Upon re-reading this section, I said to myself, "Did you really write that?" I did!) I know it's hard to imagine, but perhaps you have played a role in your man's ex's rage. I realize this may feel like I am blaming the victim here. I am not. I've just learned in a fight, rarely do any rivals have clean hands. Feuds with exes have usually been intense and lengthy, so no matter how clean your hands may have been in the beginning, it's highly doubtful you've kept them clean.

    I know it may be hard to imagine you need her to forgive you at all, but for the sake of your relationship, blended family, or marriage, please consider the list of dos and don'ts and accept it's fairly unlikely you haven't unintentionally or intentionally hurt her, too. While your friends and even your pastor may agree you are right, it is a rare person who feels her nemesis' side is all wrong and she is all right. I doubt his child's mother is different in this respect. As hard as it is to imagine, there is some version of the events she plays in her head that justifies her actions.

    To begin the healing process you must consider forgiving her and recognize you must ask for forgiveness as well. I am not suggesting you forgive her for her sake, or that you ask forgiveness for her sake, but I am suggesting you do so for the sake of your family. Sometimes in life we have to choose between our pain and what we love, and you may have to let go of your pain to free the love you need to blend your family. Someone has to create the good faith needed to start the healing process on both sides.

    The process of acknowledging each other's pain doesn't require that you agree with each other's version of events. Reaching an agreement on each other's pain or perspective is unlikely and unimportant. Agree to disagree. You always have seen things differently and always will.

3. **Remember, she is still the mother, and at the end of the day she has emotions just like you.** If at all possible, try to talk to her woman to woman. Realize she probably doesn't care about your pain or ending it any time soon, but she might be open to discussing her most important interest — her child. Even crazy folk love their children. She may recognize on a basic level that her child needs his father and is better served with you in the picture than another woman who won't partner with her at all, and may not have her child's best interests at heart.

Put it out there that your first priority is to help him be a great and responsible father. Also, let her know you aren't out to replace her; you acknowledge that there is a bond you cannot break between her, your man, and their child. This might help clear the air a little bit between the two of you. Try to establish that while you're going to set boundaries and rules around your household, you recognize she is the mother who has unchallenged rule over her child. Explain that although you will be playing a big role in her child's life, you are not there to take on her role.

Try to understand where she's coming from.

Recognize he may not have kept it real with her (or she wasn't ready to hear him because of her own denial or anger, and got blindsided). Just try to take a balanced approach instead of assuming she is hell incarnate. Accept that it may not be so personal and she may just need time to move on.

While this approach may seem counter-intuitive, in the long run it will likely get you much further than going toe to toe with a woman who has so much at stake and so many deeply entrenched feelings that no price is too high. Things will only escalate, and your relationship with her child may never recover. Even if you win the war, you may very well lose your man and his child. Believe it or not, she will poison them both against you.

4. **Communicate often.** Catch the snowball at the top of the hill to avoid being crushed and swallowed up by an avalanche at the bottom. Just because you are not the biological parent of his child, it doesn't mean you don't have some say in how his child is treated or raised — or how you are treated. Your feelings are just as important and valid as his, his child's, and his child's mother's. If these feelings aren't expressed early, there will likely be an angry outburst or an all-out rebellion later. After all, healthy relationships entail both stakeholders getting some of their needs met and at least most of them heard so little problems don't become big ones.

5. **Always encourage, support, and let your man be a man and a stand-up dad.** When his child's mother trips or makes your blood boil, let your man know how you feel and let him handle it.

    Make sure your man is a good dad, from spending time with his child, to attending games and making child support payments on time every month. Never let it be said that your man isn't being a father to his child. This will ensure that the child's mother has nothing to complain about, though she may fabricate distortions or magnify small things. His being there for his child should never be in question. And if you have to question the integrity of his fatherhood, consider leaving him and finding a real man.

    Blending family members don't have to like each other, but they do have to respect each other. Respect his child and the child's basic needs, and demand that your basic rights be respected as well.

6. **Time heals all wounds. Things change.** Be the adult in the room. The old adage that fighting fire with fire only results in everyone being burned is true. Hopefully your long-

term water approach to the problem douses her fire over time.

7. **Accept every situation isn't winnable. Sometimes you have to take the "L."** If you aren't happy anymore, aren't getting your needs met, find yourself at odds with him about disagreements related to his child or his ex, find that his child support or alimony payments are robbing you of your financial life blood, and his child refuses to accept you, accept that it's OK to take the "L" sometimes.

Don't let emotions surrounding not wanting to lose to her blind you to the reality that sometimes even when you win, you lose. Ask yourself what you actually are going to win. If it isn't going to bring you happiness, it may not be worth pursuing anymore. Be willing to let go and go on. Blended families aren't for everyone, or possible with everyone.

No, this doesn't mean all your hard work and sacrifice, and attempts to reason with his ex were in vain. Sometimes winning is as simple as getting closure. That is, you can go on knowing you've given it your all, minus the what ifs, and go on with your life. You also have valuable lessons learned and will recognize the telltale signs that some Mr. Rights are Wrong for you. Perhaps you learned to tell the difference earlier on.

8. **Trust in God.** Pray for discernment and guidance. And let that divine inspiration guide your actions and decisions to stay or go, especially because at the end of the day, vulnerable children are involved and their well-being is more important than your feelings.

What Do You Do If Your Kids Just Don't Like Him, or You Just Can't Get Along With His Kids or Baby Mama(s)?

Based on my personal experience as a child raised in a blended family, and my professional experience working with families throughout the years, I have found many of the steps mentioned in this section are among the types of behaviors that could potentially help you successfully blend your new family.

Nevertheless, if you have given it your best efforts, here are some telltale signs it might be time to seek professional help from a therapist if:

- A child directs anger upon a particular family member or openly resents a step-parent or parent.

- A step-parent or parent openly favors one child over another and isn't open to or cannot develop a healthy relationship with any of the other children.

- Members of the family no longer derive pleasure from usually enjoyable activities, such as school, working, playing, or being with friends and family, or there have been significant negative changes in their behavior.

- A child runs away, harms himself, or displays symptoms consistent with depression.

- Legal authorities or child protective services are getting involved.

Accept that these telltale signs may be a red flag that you are no longer simply dealing with simple rebellion or minor adjustment challenges, but your children or family is in crisis and may be on the brink of experiencing some serious complications.

CHAPTER 12

You've Found Mr. Right, Now What?

Date, Move In, Move Out, or Marriage

"It's never too late
to live
happily ever after."

"Three of the most unfortunate myths about
soulmate love are: It always lasts forever;
it doesn't involve struggles; and there is only one."
—Dr. Shane

Rare, precious, and definitely a girl's best friend, soulmates are kind of like diamonds. But they don't necessarily last forever, nor are they always meant to. Only the hands of fate know if a soulmate is for a reason, a season, or a lifetime. Contrary to the myth that there is only one Mr. Right for each of us — and if we blow this divine relationship we will never have another chance at it — the reality is that we all have many potential Mr. Rights.

You will have soul ties with all types of people who come in and out of your life: Some will trigger your awakening, some will nurture your development and help prepare you for a greater purpose, and others will help fulfill your romantic dreams. It may not always be clear which type of role this tie will serve initially.

Even if he is of the romantic variety, and you are "Crazy in Love," as Beyoncé famously sings, when his purpose in your life has been served, it's time to move on, for your own good and maybe his, too. You are best served loving the men with whom you have soul ties with an open fist, understanding that soulmates are best when bound together by choice, not coercion or even contract. Yes, even a soul tie that seems like it will last forever can unravel as quickly as it came together. Instead of growing old together, sometimes couples grow apart. Holding on to a relationship with Mr. Right with a tight fist after his time has passed will only bring you anger, resentment, mental bondage, or destruction; and worse, block you from being able to collect a more valuable gift. Closed fists serve two purposes: (1) clinging to something you are afraid of losing, which is born out of a sense the universe is a place of shortage and fear, or (2) striking out to cause others pain for not meeting your needs. By contrast, an open hand allows you to pluck, plant, and replenish, which is born out of trusting God's universe is a place of surplus and love.

If you've ever had the experience of someone grabbing you with a tight fist, you will recall how much resistance it created. But an open hand can be used to invite you to come closer or be used to let you go, neither of which creates resistance. Learn to love with an open hand and, if need be, release people in a loving way that will set you both free. Letting go isn't giving up; it's realizing just because your desire for his love has a hold on you doesn't mean it is necessarily worth holding on to. If the relationship is meant to stand the test of time, it will only do so because the two of you are holding onto each other with all your might.

If you or he lets go, and you are single again, it does not mean you two didn't share a true soul tie. It simply means it was for a season or a reason, but not a lifetime. It's time to master the lesson he was meant to teach you, move on, and start preparing yourself for your next soulmate.

When thinking of love after a big fight, a breakup, a divorce, or having been widowed, and the subsequent fear of being alone or never finding soulmate love again, I'm reminded of the widely held belief that lightening never strikes the same place twice. Just like you attracted your last Mr. Right, certain laws of nature will serve as a lightning rod to draw your next potential Mr. Right. The ability to cultivate a friendship, share a laugh, compromise in times of emotional conflict, to hear and attend to the needs of your partner and be supportive, and the ability to commit and invest in others (not to mention throw on a cute outfit and wink or smile at a brother from time to time) are traits that serve as a lightning rod for men. If you have had a lover struck by Cupid's arrow before, you undoubtedly possess traits that will draw your next soulmate love.

Have no fear!

You can experience that soulmate connection again or connect for the first time whether: (1) you are struggling with your current man and are trying to reconnect with him again; (2) you have ended a relationship or are divorced and find yourself single again, looking to connect with your next soulmate; or (3) you haven't been in a soulmate relationship before and are wondering how to attract, recognize, or make that connection.

If you are unhappy in your long-term relationship or marriage and the connection you once shared seems long gone, it may be possible to work through your differences and reconnect with him. While studies find most couples come into therapy six years after they should have, talking to a professional can help the two of you learn to turn toward each other when times get tough instead of turning on each other. Therapy can help you start to develop the skills to start hearing, validating and forgiving each other, so you make peace with your painful past and get past the pain. For example, Jill married Jack, but came to feel disappointed when she realized he was a real wallflower at her social events. She fondly thinks of the more dynamic Jim, whose proposal she rejected. Jim is definitely no wallflower; however, his drinking often makes him the life of the party, and occasionally an embarrassment who becomes the subject of the post-party gossip. Finally, Jill fondly reminisces about Jamal, who doesn't drink and is by no means boring; however, he's a workaholic, so if some important deadline has to be met, he is likely to arrive at the party really late or miss it all together. The point isn't every man is fatally flawed, but all relationships have their flaws, and happiness is finding which set of flaws work best for you and working through them together.

Ignoring relationship problems instead of addressing them, and then jumping into a relationship with someone new, will not help you develop the conflict resolution skills needed to fix your problems. That behavior is unlikely to help you find happiness in your next relationship. Happiness is finding which set of flaws work best for you, and committing to work through them together.

Anger, contempt, and resentments stemming from partners feeling their perspective is completely right while their partner's perspective is completely wrong, and their cumulative cynical or hostile attitude toward each other over these distorted perspectives start to pile up. This makes couples feel justified in tossing relationships and marriages aside. And perhaps they jump into a new relationship as if it's a lifeline, only to find problems quickly arise there, too. Instead of changing men, consider looking at the woman in the mirror. If not, you may find you are switching seats on the Titanic.

Whether or not you salvage your relationship, you may benefit from understanding your role in its demise so you don't repeat this pattern in your next relationship. I'm not saying your partner doesn't share some of the responsibility for your problems; both parties share blame in a relationship's demise. I am saying that you have to accept your respective roles and get help, if need be, and determine if you can right the ship. Beyond the pain, resentment, contempt, and feelings of betrayal, you may be surprised to rediscover the Mr. Right you've been longing for is by your side.

As the unmistakable crackling sound of lightening thunders in the background and flashes of bolts zigzag through the sky, much like the tall skyscrapers in Chicago, the lightening rod of your friendship and love has irresistibly drawn lightening to your relationship or marriage again. Although not as rare as lovers or spouses would imagine, when romantic sparks strike the hearts of partners again, it can rekindle the flame in a love left for dead.

Sometimes, though, despite our best efforts to salvage a relationship, lightening's transformational yet elusive power doesn't always reappear. Perhaps you recognized you never had the elements required for soulmate love, or so much damage and neglect has occurred that your lightening rod has lost its seductive powers and there is no getting that spark back. As much as it breaks your heart, especially when young children are involved, some partners and spouses will conclude they are better off apart.

Finally, it may be the case that you have never had soulmate love, and you wonder if that type of connection is in the cards for you. Whether it's helping you re-examine your choices in men or helping you remove the psychological and lifestyle choices that have hampered your ability to find and keep a fulfilling relationship, I encourage you to heed the lessons learned from your past soulmate or soulmate-less relationship(s), and know God has an abundant supply of potential soulmates.

For these reasons, it's never too late to live happily ever after!

29783476R00158

Made in the USA
Middletown, DE
02 March 2016